THE BALAAM TRADITIONS

SOCIETY
OF BIBLICAL
LITERATURE

DISSERTATION SERIES

J. J. M. Roberts, Old Testament Editor
Charles Talbert, New Testament Editor

Number 113

THE BALAAM TRADITIONS
Their Character and Development

by
Michael S. Moore

Michael S. Moore

THE BALAAM TRADITIONS
Their Character and Development

Scholars Press
Atlanta, Georgia

THE BALAAM TRADITIONS

Michael S. Moore

Ph.D., 1988
Drew University

Advisors:
Prof. Herbert B. Huffmon
Prof. Paul Riemann

Library of Congress Cataloging in Publication Data

Moore, Michael S.
The Balaam traditions : their character and development / Michael S. Moore
p. cm. -- (Dissertation series / Society of Biblical Literature ; no. 113)
Bibliography: p.
ISBN: 1-55540-327-1 (alk. paper). -- ISBN 1-55540-328-X (pbk.)
1. Balaam (Biblical figure) 2. Bible. O.T. Numbers XXII-XXIV--Criticism, interpretation, etc. I. Title. II. Series:
Dissertation series (Society of Biblical Literature) : no. 113.
BS580.B3M66 1988
222'.14095--dc19
89-5988
CIP

Printed in the United States of America
on acid-free paper

Contents

Acknowledgments

Many scholars have graciously given of themselves to help me understand these difficult texts better. One of Kathy Sakenfeld's classes on *Numbers* offered an opportunity for initial examination via an oral report. Jim Roberts, Claus Westermann, Antoon Schoors, and Lothar Perlitt each offered valuable comments on various stages of the research as these traditions began to exert more and more of their seductive pull.

Several scholars also shared their unpublished work. Many thanks to Wayne Pitard and Al Wolters for their help, but a special thanks goes to Jo Ann Hackett for sending me a copy of her dissertation/monograph prior to publication, not to mention her numerous letters of kind encouragement. Baruch Levine was a much-appreciated source of intellectual inspiration, good humor, penetrating insight and patriarchal advice. Howard and Reba Marblestone helped to open up this project to the valuable data about Balaam written in Modern Hebrew. Karen Brown consented at the last minute to serve as a reader on my committee. Her thoughtful input, though regrettably hurried, was nevertheless appreciated.

I am especially grateful to my doctoral advisers, Herb Huffmon and Paul Riemann, for their firm direction, collegial approachability, discriminating judgment, and unfailing encouragement.

This book is dedicated to my wife, Caron.

Abbreviations

AB	Anchor Bible
ACh	L'astrologie chaldéenne (Virolleaud)
AfO	Archiv für Orientforschung
AGH	Die akkadische Gebetsserie "Handerhebung" (Ebeling)
AGS	Assyrische Gebete an den Sonnengott (Knudtzon)
AHW	Akkadisches Handwörterbuch
AJ	Josephus, *Antiquities of the Jews*
AJS	American Journal of Sociology
AJT	American Journal of Theology
Akk.	Akkadian
AnBib	Analecta Biblica
ANET	Ancient Near Eastern Texts (Pritchard)
AnOr	Analecta Orientalia
AOAT	Alter Orient und altes Testament
AOATS	Alter Orient und altes Testament Sonderreihe
AP	Aramaic Papyri of the Fifth Century BCE (Cowley)
Arab.	Arabic
Aram.	Aramaic
ARM	Archives royales de Mari (Parrot & Dossin)
ASR	American Sociological Review
AT	Alalaḫ Text (Wiseman)
AUSS	Andrews University Seminary Studies
BA	Biblical Archaeologist
BAR	Biblical Archaeology Review
BASOR	Bulletin of the American Schools of Oriental Research
BBB	Bonner biblische Beiträge
BBR	Beiträge zur Kenntnis der babylonischen Religion (Zimmern)
BETL	Bibliotheca Ephemeridum Theologicarum Lovaniensum
BHS	Biblia Hebraica Stuttgartensia
Bib	Biblica
BibOr	Biblica et Orientalia
bît rimki	*Studies on the Assyrian Ritual and Series bît rimki* (Laessøe)

BJS	British Journal of Sociology
BN	Biblische Notizen
BR	Biblical Research
BWANT	Beiträge zur Wissenschaft vom alten und neuen Testament
BWL	Babylonian Wisdom Literature (Lambert)
BZ	Biblische Zeitschrift
BZAW	Beihefte zur Zeitschrift für die alttestamentliche Wissenschaft
CAD	Chicago Assyrian Dictionary
CAI	Corpus of the Aramaic Incantation Bowls (Isbell)
CBQ	Catholic Biblical Quarterly
CTA	Corpus des tablettes en cunéiformes alphabétiques découvertes à Ras Shamra-Ugarit (Herdner)
CTM	Calwer theologische Monographien
DAT	Deir ʿAllā Texts
DISO	*Dictionnaire des inscriptions sémitiques de l'ouest* (Jean & Hoftijzer)
DMOA	Documenta et Monumenta Orientis Antiqui
Dreambook	*The Interpretation of Dreams in the Ancient Near East, with a Translation of an Assyrian Dreambook* (Oppenheim)
EA	Die El Amarna Tafeln (Knudtzon)
EBib	Etudes Bibliques
EI	Eretz Israel
EJ	Encyclopedia Judaica
Ephem	Ephemeris für semitische Epigraphik (Lidzbarski)
ER	The Encyclopedia of Religion
Erra	The Epic of Erra (Cagni)
EThL	Ephemerides Theologicae Lovanienses
ExpT	Expository Times
EvT	Evangelische Theologie
FRLANT	Forschungen zur Religion und Literatur des alten und neuen Testaments
FS	Festschrift
FTNum	Fragment Targums to Numbers (Klein)
HAW	Handbuch der Altertumswissenschaft
Heb.	Hebrew
Hit.	Hittite
HKAT	Handkommentar zum alten Testament

HSM	Harvard Semitic Monographs
HSM 7494	Harvard Semitic Museum Tablet #7494 (Starr)
HT	Hethitisches Totenrituale (Otten)
HTR	Harvard Theological Review
HUCA	Hebrew Union College Annual
IBoT	Istanbul Arkeoloji Müzelerinde Bulunan Bogazköy Tabletleri
ICC	International Critical Commentary
IDB	Interpreter's Dictionary of the Bible
IDBS	Interpreter's Dictionary of the Bible Supplement
Idr	The Statue of Idri-mi (Smith)
IEJ	Israel Exploration Journal
JAOS	Journal of the American Oriental Society
JBL	Journal of Biblical Literature
JBS	Jerusalem Bible Studies
JCS	Journal of Cuneiform Studies
JNES	Journal of Near Eastern Studies
JPOS	Journal of the Palestine Oriental Society
JSOT	Journal for the Study of the Old Testament
JSOTSup	Journal for the Study of the Old Testament Supplement Series
JSS	Journal of Semitic Studies
JTS	Journal of Theological Studies
KAI	Kanaanäische und aramäische Inschriften (Donner & Röllig)
KAR	Keilschrifttexte aus Assur religiösen Inhalts (Ebeling)
KBo	Keilschrifttexte aus Bogazköy
KTU	Die keilalphabetischen Texte aus Ugarit (Dietrich, Loretz, & Sanmartin)
KUB	Keilschrifturkunden aus Bogazköy
LAB	Ps.-Philo, *Liber Antiquitatum Biblicarum* (Kisch)
LCL	Loeb Classical Library
LS	Liddell & Scott's Greek-English Lexicon
LSS	Leipziger semitische Studien
Maq	*Maqlû* (Meier)
MIO	Mitteilungen des Instituts für Orientforschung (Deutsche Akademie der Wissenschaften zu Berlin)
Neo	Targum Neofiti (Díez Macho)

NJPS	*Tanakh,* New Edition (Jewish Publication Society)
OB	Old Babylonian
OBO	Orbis Biblicus et Orientalis
OG	Old Greek (LXX)
Onk	Targum Onkelos (Sperber)
OLZ	Orientalistische Literaturzeitung
Or	Orientalia
OTL	Old Testament Library
OTS	Oudtestamentische Studien
PEQ	Palestine Exploration Society
Phoen.	Phoenician
PPG	Phönizische-punische Grammatik, 2nd ed. (Friedrich & Röllig)
PsJon	Targum Pseudo-Jonathan (Clarke)
PSSD	Compendious Syriac Dictionary (Payne-Smith)
RA	Revue d'assyriologie et d'archéologie orientale
Racc	Rituels accadiens (Thureau-Dangin)
RB	Revue biblique
RGG	Religion in Geschichte und Gegenwart
RHA	Revue hittite et asianique
RHPR	Revue d'histoire et de philosophie religieuses
RLA	Reallexicon der Assyriologie
RSO	Rivista degli studi orientali
Sam	Samaritan Pentateuch (von Gall)
SANE	Sources from the Ancient Near East
SB	Sources bibliques
SBLDS	Society of Biblical Literature Dissertation Series
SBLMS	Society of Biblical Literature Monograph Series
SBT	Studien zu den Bogazköy Texten
Sem	Semeia
SeT	Studi e Testi
SJLA	Studies in Judaism in Late Antiquity
SO	Sources orientales
SP	Studia Pohl
SPB	Studia Post-Biblica
SPSM	Studia Pohl Series Maior
SS	Studi Semitici
SSI	Syrian Semitic Inscriptions (Gibson)
SSO	Studia Semitica and Orientalia
StANT	Studien zum alten und neuen Testament

Sum.	Sumerian
Šumma ālu	(Nötscher)
Šur	*Šurpu* (Reiner)
Syr.	Syriac
TaanL	Taanach Letter (Albright)
TAPS	Transactions of the American Philosophical Society
TdH	Texte der Hethiter
TDP	Traité akkadien de diagnostics et pronostics médicaux
TDNT	Theological Dictionary of the New Testament
TDOT	Theological Dictionary of the Old Testament
THAT	Theologisches Handwörterbuch zum alten Testament
ThR	Theologisches Rundschau
TSO	Texte und Studien zur Orientalistik
TuL	Tod und Leben (Ebeling)
TZ	Theologische Zeitschrift
UF	Ugarit Forschungen
Ugar.	Ugaritic
UT	Ugaritic Textbook (Gordon)
VC	Vigiliae Christianae
VM	Philo, *Vita Mosis*
VT	Vetus Testamentum
VTSup	Vetus Testamentum Supplements
Vulg	Vulgate
WBC	Word Biblical Commentary
WMANT	Wissenschaftliche Monographien zum alten und neuen Testament
WTJ	Westminster Theological Journal
YOS	Yale Oriental Series
ZA	Zeitschrift für Assyriologie
ZAW	Zeitschrift für die alttestamentliche Wissenschaft
ZDPV	Zeitschrift des deutschen Palästina-Vereins
ZNW	Zeitschrift für die neutestamentliche Wissenschaft

Introduction

The character and development of the Balaam traditions have long been a puzzle. Within the Balaam cycle (Num 22–24), for example, Balaam is portrayed as one of Yahweh's most obedient servants (Num 22:1–21, 31–41; 23:1–24:25), yet this role is juxtaposed alongside a satirical view of him as "blind seer," quite unable to "see" Yahweh's angel standing directly in his path (22:22–30). Mic 6:3–5 preserves a memory which casts him as protagonist against Balak as Israel's antagonist. Other biblical tradents portray him as Israel's defeated enemy, but even within this latter group considerably varied opinions are registered regarding his functional relationship to Yahweh (Josh 24:9–10; Deut 23:4–7; Neh 13:1–2) and Israel (Josh 13:21–22; Num 31:8, 16).

This spectrum of roles is affirmed in the writings of post-biblical Jewish tradents. A small minority continued to portray Balaam as God's "servant" (*servum tuum,* LAB 18:4), in several ways more of a "prophet" than Moses himself (Sifrê Deut 34:10), but the majority continued to denigrate him as "Balaam the Wicked" (*bl'm [h]rš[y]'['],* FTNum 22:30; b. Sanh. 106b; cf. 2 Pet 2:15–16; Jude 11; Rev 2:14). Josephus stands almost alone when he attempts to chart a middle course between these extremes, carefully and deliberately suggesting at the conclusion of his account that readers be allowed to make up their own minds about Balaam (AJ IV:158).

PREVIOUS RESEARCH

At present there is still no scholarly consensus about the character or the development of these dissimilar traditions,[1] and, until very recently, our

[1] J. Wellhausen (*Die Composition des Hexateuchs und der historischen Bücher des Alten Testaments,* 3rd ed. [Berlin: Goschen'sche, 1899] 109–116, 347–352; revisions of two earlier articles) divided the Balaam cycle into parallel literary strands, a hypothesis strongly challenged by A. Kuenen ("Bijdragen tot de Critiek van Pentateuch en Josua. X. Bileam," *Theologisch Tijdschrift* 18 [1884] 497–540). S. Mowinckel's subsequent 2-source solution ("Der Ursprung der Bil'amsage," *ZAW* 48 [1930] 233–271) was thoroughly criticized by W. Rudolph (*Der "Elohist" von Exodus bis Josua* [BZAW 68; Berlin: Töpelmann, 1938] 97–128) and M. Buber (*Kingship of God,* 3rd ed. [London: Allen and Unwin, 1967, first published in 1936] 210–214).

knowledge of Balaam was confined only to biblical and post-biblical sources.[2] Now another witness has dramatically come to light in texts found in 1967 at Tell Deir ʿAllā in the eastern Jordan valley.[3] The plaster fragments found at this site have been paleographically dated to the late 8th or early 7th centuries BCE,[4] and clearly mention Balaam's name.[5] He appears in this tradition as a powerful "seer of the gods" (*ḥzh ʾlhn*) who conveys a message from a divine council to a local populace.[6] We therefore now have clear extra-biblical evidence that a Balaam tradition existed in the Transjordan among peoples who were evidently non-Yahwist and presumably non-Israelite.

Research on the Biblical Tradition

Martin Noth's first attempt to unravel the biblical Balaam tradition was stretched over a bipolar framework inherited from older "2-source" literary

---

W. Gross' newer literary solution (*Bileam. Literar- und formkritische Untersuchung der Prosa in Num 22–24* [StANT 38; Munich: Kösel, 1974]), following closely the literary-critical method of his teacher W. Richter (*Exegese als Literaturwissenschaft* [Göttingen: Vandenhoeck & Ruprecht, 1971]), has not received resounding support (cf. H. Donner, "Balaam Pseudopropheta," in H. Donner, R. Hanhart, & R. Smend, eds., *Beiträge zur alttestamentlichen Theologie: FS W. Zimmerli* [Göttingen: Vandenhoeck & Ruprecht, 1977] 116, nt. 10), nor does Gross really care to elucidate the development of the Balaam traditions in this enormously thorough volume. W. F. Albright's similar disinterest in the character and development of the traditions ("The Oracles of Balaam," *JBL* 63 [1944] 208) is also to some degree perpetuated in the work of D. Vetter (*Seherspruch und Segensschilderung*, CTM 4 [Stuttgart: Calwer, 1974]). Not surprisingly, the newer Pentateuchal hypotheses of R. Rendtorff (*Das überlieferungsgeschichtliche Problem des Pentateuch* [BZAW 147; Berlin: de Gruyter, 1977]) and H. H. Schmid (*Der sogenannte Jahwist* [Zurich: Theologischer, 1976]) conspicuously avoid the Balaam cycle altogether.

[2] Geza Vermes (*Scripture and Tradition in Judaism. Haggadic Studies*, SPB 6 [Leiden: Brill, 1961] 127–177) studied the post-biblical tradition in some detail, but his analysis now needs to be updated because (a) it was published prior to the discovery of DAT, and (b) it followed the older habit of lumping all these traditions into neat bipolar camps: "positive" vs. "negative" (175–177).

[3] The *editio princeps* is the lavish volume by J. Hoftijzer and G. van der Kooij, *Aramaic Texts from Deir ʿAllā*, DMOA 19 (Leiden: Brill, 1976).

[4] Those who identify an Aramaic script here date the text slightly earlier (J. Naveh, "The Date of the Deir ʿAllā Inscription in Aramaic Script," *IEJ* 17 [1967] 256–258: "middle of the eighth century BCE") than those who see it as belonging to the Ammonite series (F. M. Cross, "Notes on the Ammonite Inscription from Tell Siran," *BASOR* 212 [1973] 13–14; "early seventh century").

[5] The name *blʿm* is found in DAT I:3. The patronym *brbʿr* can be read in I:2. The full name *blʿm brbʿr* can be read by combining fragments VIIId and XIIc together. All references follow the improved juxtaposition of the fragments in A. Caquot & A. Lemaire ("Les textes araméennes de Deir ʿAllā," *Syria* 54 [1977] 193–194).

[6] DAT I:1–7.

critics. Noth assumed, with Hugo Gressmann and Sigmund Mowinckel, that Balaam had originally intended to "curse," not "bless" Israel—as if these were the only two possibilities.[7] Thereafter, the tradition developed by stages: God (a) turned the "curse" into a "blessing" (Deut 23:5b–6), then (b) prevented him from pronouncing the "curse" at all "as an element of suspense at the beginning of the Balaam–Balak story,"[8] then (c) caused Balaam to pronounce a "blessing," under divine constraint, instead of a "curse." Working solely from the biblical tradition, Noth thus proposed a simple linear development from "curser" to "blesser" in his initial study.

In his *Numbers* commentary, however, Noth jettisoned this entire developmental schema, preferring instead to assign more credence to the antiquity of "blessing" as a potent phenomenon in its own right, viewing Balaam's "blessings" as primary.[9] Herbert Donner and Alexander Rofé have tentatively agreed in principle that Noth's later solution at least makes more sense than his first one, yet qualify it extensively with differing proposals.[10] Noth's confusing proposals have been rejected by others, however, as a sign of methodological bankruptcy.

Reacting to the narrow restrictions imposed by the "2-source" literary-critical foundation undergirding both of Noth's approaches, Joseph Coppens

[7] H. Gressmann, *Mose und seine Zeit,* FRLANT 1 (Göttingen: Vandenhoeck & Ruprecht, 1913) 322; S. Mowinckel, "Der Ursprung der Bil'amsage," 239; M. Noth, *A History of Pentateuchal Traditions* (Englewood Cliffs, NJ: Prentice-Hall, 1972, first published in 1948) 74–79.

[8] Noth, *A History of Pentateuchal Traditions,* 78.

[9] M. Noth, *Numbers* OTL (Philadelphia: Westminster, 1968, first published in ATD 7, 1966) 175. Hermann Gunkel's influence was probably at least partially responsible for Noth's reversal (H. Gunkel & J. Begrich, *Einleitung in die Psalmen* [Göttingen: Vandenhoeck & Ruprecht, 1933] 293–309), as well as Mowinckel's (*Psalmenstudien V: Segen und Fluch in Israels Kult und Psalmendichtung* [Oslo: Videnskapsselskapets Skrifter II, 1923] 33–57).

[10] Following the later Noth, H. Donner ("Balaam Pseudopropheta," 120–122) prefers to view the "negative" portrayals "als produkte redaktionell-exegetischer Arbeit an Num 22–24" rather than as an old, independent tradition (Noth's earlier position), but only after toying with the possibility that neither of Noth's solutions is correct.

A. Rofé (*Spr Bl'm,* JBS 1 [Jerusalem: Simor, 1979] 31), building on the work of Y. Liver ("The Image of Balaam in Biblical Tradition," *EI* 3 [1954] 97–100), advances several interesting suggestions about the development of these traditions. Rofé believes that the oracles in Num 24 may have belonged to a stratum in which Balaam is revered "like a partner" (*kšwtp,* 31) with Israel in its religion and culture. He would agree with Mowinckel that the oracles in Num 24 preserve the earliest tradition, but deems any attempt to buttress this position with a Wellhausenian literary hypothesis unnecessary and unwarranted. Rofé would argue that the prose of the Balaam cycle takes something away from Balaam's "high prophetic rank" (*drgh nbw'yt 'lywnh,* 45–46), but that it was not until the rise of a Deuteronomic "school" (*'skwlh,* 48) that a concerted effort was made to redefine Balaam's role in Israel. The she-ass story (following M. M. Kalisch, *Bible Studies I: The Prophecies of Balaam* [London: Longmans, Green, 1877]) was inserted much later as a " burlesque" (*bwrlsqh,* 51) designed to blacken Balaam's name completely.

followed his teacher A. van Hoonacker in viewing the fourth biblical oracle (Num 24:15–19) as a redactional addition designed to augment the first three, viewing this material as a unified triad only lately brought under the umbrella of the Israelite "blessing" traditions by means of an appended stock (*brwk//'rwr* formula (cf. Num 24:9 with Gen 27:29).[11]

Departing completely from the older literary assumptions, Dieter Vetter proposed a radically innovative approach, synthesizing the form-critical method of his teacher Claus Westermann with the highly theoretical reconstruction of the oracles offered by W. F. Albright.[12] The resulting synthesis led Vetter to conclude, with Albright, that all four of the biblical oracles in Num 22–24 had come from what Vetter hypothesized to be a lengthy nomadic period prior to the settlement of Canaan, a period characterized by the "soziokulturellen Daseinsbedingungen von Nomadenstämmen."[13]

None of these views has won a consensus. Hoping to resolve the confusion, Ludwig Schmidt recently attempted to resuscitate the Wellhausenian "2-source" hypothesis, employing its familiar postulates as a buttress to Noth's later contention that all other mention about this magico-religious specialist in the Bible must be dependent on the portrayal found in Num 22–24.[14] Yet the chances are negligible that this or any other resuscitative approach will lead a way out of the present impasse. The present montage of dissonant views about Balaam, particularly exampled by Noth's complete reversal of opinion, not only testifies to the sheer complexity of the problem itself, but specifically points out the deeper problem of methodological inadequacy which continues to hamper the best efforts to unravel it.

A few scholars have tried in the past to learn more about the biblical tradition by studying it against the background of other ancient and not so ancient Near Eastern literatures. Intended to introduce an empirical element into the discussion, these attempts consist of rather random comparisons between portions of allegedly relevant extra-biblical material and the Balaam cycle, particularly the biblical oracles in Num 22–24.

Ignaz Goldziher compared the biblical oracles to a species of pre-Islamic

[11] J. Coppens, "Les oracles de Bileam: leur origine littéraire et leur portée prophétique," in *Mélanges E. Tisserant*, SeT 231 (Citta del Vaticano: Biblioteca Apostolica Vaticana, 1964) 71; A. van Hoonacker, "Quelques observations critiques sur les récits concernant Bileam (Nombres XXII–XXIV et XXXI)," *Le Museon* 7 (1888) 61–76. E. Lipínski buttresses this approach by emphasizing the occurrence of the parallel phrases *šlš p'mym* (Num 24:10) and *šlš rglym* (Num 22:28, 32, 33) in the Balaam cycle, translating both "trois fois"; cf. "Trois hébraïsmes oubliés ou méconnus," *RSO* 44 (1969) 93–94.

[12] C. Westermann, "Arten der Erzählung in der Genesis," in *Forschung am Alten Testament* (Munich: Chr. Kaiser, 1964) 9–91; ibid., *Blessing in the Bible and the Life of the Church* (Philadelphia: Fortress, 1978) 49–53; W. F. Albright, "The Oracles of Balaam." Cf. M. Noth, *Numbers*, 175.

[13] D. Vetter, *Seherspruch und Segensschilderung*, 80.

[14] L. Schmidt, "Die alttestamentliche Bileamüberlieferung," *BZ* 23 (1979) 257; cf. Noth, *Numbers*, 173.

"satire/curse" poetry called *hiğâ'*.[15] Since Arabic poets in the Christian era were known to recite *hiğâ'* against their enemies under the influence of daimonic ğinns, Goldziher hypothesized that Balaam ben Beor might have been trying (unsuccessfully) to do the same thing in Num 22–24, even proposing that the oracles of Balaam represent an early exemplar of what later became *hiğâ'* poetry in pre-Islamic Arabic.[16] That Goldziher's hypothesis so quickly fell on sympathetic ears shows how willing scholars were to locate this tradition in some sort of sociohistorical matrix, even though it has now largely fallen out of favor, due in part to the discovery of DAT. Here and there a scholar will still latch onto it as a convenient support,[17] but caution is in order. After all, Goldziher's theory is based on an attempt to harmonize two distinct sets of highly poetic material in two distinct languages from two separate millennia.

Samuel Daiches attempted another comparative analysis once the Mesopotamian ritual and incantation material began coming to light, focusing this time not on the oracles, but on Balaam's praxis in Num 22–24.[18] By comparing Balaam's ritual activity in the Balaam cycle with some of the neo-Assyrian rituals then newly published by H. Zimmern,[19] Daiches concluded that Balaam must have been a Mesopotamian *bārû* priest. In the process of this comparison he

[15] I. Goldziher, *Abhandlungen zur arabischen Philologie. Erster Teil* (Leiden: Brill, 1896) 41–44. T. Fahd associates *hiğâ'* and *riṯa'* poetry with the specialist called *šâ'ir*, who, alongside the *'arrâf* and the *kâhin* magico-religious specialists, "avaient une même source d'inspiration: les djinns" (*La divination arabe* [Leiden: Brill, 1966] 117).

[16] Goldziher, *Abhandlungen*, 42.

[17] Some of those attracted to Goldziher's hypothesis include: S. Mowinckel ("Der Ursprung der Bil'amsage," 243); L. M. von Pákozdy ("Theologische Redaktionsarbeit in der Bileam-Perikope," in J. Hempel & L. Rost, eds. *Von Ugarit nach Qumran: FS O. Eissfeldt* [Berlin: Töpelmann, 1958] 166–168); and A. Rofé, (*Spr Bl'm*, 31). D. Vetter also favorably parallels Balaam with the Arabic *kâhin*, a parallel owing much to the influence of Goldziher's hypothesis (Vetter, *Seherspruch und Segensschilderung*, 72). We should note in passing that all of these "Arabic" parallels are to some degree associated with theories of Israel's "nomadic" origins, theories which are now sharply challenged in some circles. Cf., e.g., N. Gottwald, *The Hebrew Bible: A Socio-Literary Introduction* (Philadelphia: Fortress, 1985) 261–288. Matthias Köckert issues a strong caution against attempts to reconstruct Israel's "nomadic" existence via the pre-Islamic Arabic material; *Vätergott und Väterverheissungen*, FRLANT 142 (Göttingen: Vandenhoeck & Ruprecht, 1988) 312.

[18] S. Daiches, "Balaam: A Babylonian *bārû*," in *Assyrologische und archäologische Studien Hermann von Hilprecht gewidmet* (Leipzig: J. C. Hinrichs'sche, 1909) 60–70.

[19] Daiches worked exclusively from texts published by H. Zimmern, especially his *Beiträge zur Kenntnis der babylonischen Religion* (Leipzig: J. C. Hinrichs'sche, 1899). A major point in Daiches' thesis was based on a fragmentary ritual preserved in a mythological text from Assurbanipal's library (cf. H. Zimmern, "'König Tukulti *bēl nišī*' und die 'kuthäische Schöpfungslegende,'" *ZA* 12 [1897] 320–321, II:1–11); viz., his parallel between an alleged "magical walking" of the *bārû* (*a-la-ki-ja*, II:11) and Balaam's "walk" in Num 23:3 (*'lkh*). Daiches did not have access to HSM 7494, a very important witness to *bārû* ritual as Ivan Starr has shown (*The Rituals of the Diviner* [Malibu: Undena, 1983]).

repeatedly designated this specialist a "sorcerer"[20] but never specified at all what he meant by this term. Daiches did examine the *āšipu* as well as the *bārû Ritualtafeln* and drew some penetrating insights into Balaam's praxis, but ultimately failed to make a clear distinction between the roles enacted by the two specialists, electing instead simply to lock in on the *bārû* as the focal point of his analysis.[21]

Again focusing on the Balaam cycle in Num 22–24, René Largement continued to search in selected portions of "les grandes séries mantiques suméro-akkadiennes" for more parallels to Balaam's oracles and activities in the Bible, hoping by such a study to outline "les phases de l'évolution des elements qui composent le récit biblique."[22] Going beyond Daiches' "sorcerer pure and simple" hypothesis, Largement began to recognize that Balaam enacts a plurality of roles in the biblical tradition,[23] but, like Daiches, most of his insights were simply strung together as random comparisons. Like Daiches, some of Largement's insights are penetrating and provocative, but unfortunately they are not articulated within the parameters of a coherent theoretical frame of thought. Thus the conclusions which he draws from his study seem subjective and are accordingly difficult to evaluate.[24]

Although these embryonic phenomenological studies thus made laudable attempts to begin comparing parts of the biblical material against portions and

[20] "I think there exists evidence which goes to prove that Balaam was a sorcerer pure and simple" (Daiches, "Balaam: a Babylonian *bārû*," 60).

[21] Daiches (ibid., 62) notes the 7 altars and 7 lambs cited in *āšipu* ritual (BBR 49 VI:4–5) only in passing.

[22] R. Largement, "Les oracles de Bile'am et la mantique suméro-akkadienne," in *Memorial du Cinquantenaire, 1914–1964* (Paris: Travaux de l'Institut de Paris, 1964) 39.

[23] Bile'am n'est pas un simple technicien de la divination, mais un extatique" (ibid., 47). Largement explains this pluralism as the adaptation of an essentially urban, upper-class religious function "à la mentalité des populations auxquelles il s'adressait" (ibid., 48). A. Leo Oppenheim strongly emphasizes that Mesopotamian divination itself was not a monolithic phenomenon, but highly pluralistic, particularly in the outlying regions bordering the Sumero-Akkadian sphere of influence (*Ancient Mesopotamia,* 2nd ed. [Chicago: Univ. of Chicago, 1977] 206–227).

[24] Largement hypothesized that the historical Balaam began to understand, during the delivery of his message, that Yahweh was more powerful than his god (Adad), and began to be transformed by Yahweh's word. As stories of the encounter were transmitted to Israelite circles, Balaam and others began to emphasize those elements which they felt would appeal to the Israelites, like ecstasis, while deemphasizing the "unappealing" elements, like technical divination. This philosophy of deliberate adaptation governed the entire history of the tradition's formation ("Les oracles de Bile'am," 48).

The influence of these comparative studies has been considerable. T. H. Gaster, for example, drew heavily and uncritically from the hypotheses of Goldziher, Daiches, and Largement in his phenomenological summary of Balaam as "augur" and "typical soothsayer"; cf. his *Myth, Legend, and Custom in the Old Testament* (New York: Harper & Row, 1969) para. 98.

fragments of other Near Eastern material, most were hamstrung by a lack of published comparative material at the time of publication, coupled with an almost total lack of methodological control. Seldom do these scholars make a distinction, for example, between a given *title* (like *bārû*) and a functional *role* (like "diviner" or "sorcerer"). As will be emphasized below, this was a methodological oversight which served in the long run only to intensify instead of dispel confusion about the character and development of these traditions. In addition, few of these studies made any serious attempt to incorporate the broader spectrum of biblical traditions apart from the Balaam cycle in Num 22–24. Most importantly, none of these studies, by no fault of their own, had access to the Transjordanian Balaam tradition still lying underneath the surface at Deir 'Allā, since all were undertaken prior to the discovery of DAT in 1967.

Research on the Deir 'Allā Tradition

Because the Deir 'Allā texts are so fragmentary and linguistically puzzling, most research to date has been obliged to deal primarily with matters of epigraphy, paleography, and philology. Scholars argue over the inked characters often only dimly preserved on these fragments,[25] over whether DAT is written in an Aramaic or a "national" script like that alleged for the Ammonite inscriptions,[26] and even over the basic question of what to call the language in which the texts are composed.[27]

[25] G. van der Kooij, "A Catalogue of Plaster Fragments Marked with Ink," in the *editio princeps*, 97–170. Cf. the recent discussions in A. Lemaire ("L'inscription de Balaam trouvée à Deir 'Allā: épigraphie," in *Biblical Archaeology Today* [Jerusalem: Israel Exploration Society, 1985] 313–325) and the reponse by E. Puech (ibid., 354–365). A good example of an epigraphical problem with far-reaching interpretative consequences is the third letter in DAT I:2. Hoftijzer (*editio princeps*, 173) reads a *t* (*wbškmt' 'l* "and in these mountainous regions"), Caquot & Lemaire ("Les textes araméennes," 194), read a *l* (*kml[y]' 'l* "selon ces parole[s]"), and E. Puech (*Biblical Archaeology Today*, 356) reads a *ś* (*kmś' 'l* "comme un oracle de El").

[26] J. Naveh ("The Date of the Deir 'Allā Inscription in Aramaic Script") defines the script as Aramaic while F. M. Cross ("Notes on the Ammonite Inscription from Tell Siran") and many of his students hold it to be peculiar enough to be called Ammonite. Jo Ann Hackett offers a paleographic analysis complete with script chart showing strong affinities between DAT's script and those in the Ammonite inscriptions; cf. *The Balaam Text from Deir* 'Allā, HSM 31 (Chico, CA: Scholars, 1984) 9–19, 146–147.

[27] Those who hold the language to be basically *Aramaic* include J. Hoftijzer, *editio princeps*, 300–302; Caquot & Lemaire, "Les textes araméennes," 208; J. A. Fitzmyer, "Review of *editio princeps*," *CBQ* 40 (1978) 94; H.-P. Müller, "Einige alttestamentliche Probleme zur aramäischen Inschrift von Dēr 'Allā," *ZDPV* 94 (1978) 56; S. Kaufman, "Review of *editio princeps*," *BASOR* 239 (1980) 73; P. K. McCarter, "The Balaam Texts from Deir 'Allā," *BASOR* 239 (1980) 50–51; J.-G. Heintz, "Review of *editio princeps*," *RHPR* 60 (1980) 210; M. Delcor, "Le texte de Deir 'Allā et les oracles bibliques de

Nevertheless, at present there does appear to be some basic agreement with regard to the gist of Combination I (particularly lines 1–7, because there is more text to work with here than anywhere else). This tradition shows us a fairly typical divine council, composed of beings called *'lhn* ("gods") who commission a "seer" (*ḥzh*) named Balaam bar Beor to communicate an ominous message to "his people" (*'mh*).

Interpretation of DAT II, however, remains problematic. The text is more fragmentary here than in DAT I:1–7, and Balaam's name cannot be found on Combination II at all. Still, for epigraphical, paleographical, philological, and other reasons which will be elaborated below, few scholars believe that Combination II should be separated from Combination I. The fragmentary condition of DAT II, while problematic, has not prevented the advancement of several intriguing interpretations. Each tentative hypothesis has attempted to piece

Bala'am," *VTSup* 32 (1981) 52; H. Weippert, "Der Beitrag ausserbiblischer Prophetentexte zum Verständnis der Prosareden des Jeremiabuches," in P.-M. Bogaert, *Le Livre de Jérémie,* BETL 54 (Leuven: Univ. Press, 1981) 88; and H. Ringgren, "Balaam and the Deir 'Allā Inscription," in A. Rofé and Y. Zakovitch, *Isac Leo Seeligmann Volume* (Jerusalem: Rubenstein, 1983) III:93.

Those who hold the language to be basically *Canaanite* include: J. Naveh, "Review of *editio princeps,*" *IEJ* 29 (1979) 136; J. C. Greenfield, "Review of *editio princeps,*" *JSS* 25 (1980) 251; M. Dahood, "Review of *editio princeps,*" *Bib* 62 (1981) 127; J. Hackett, *The Balaam Text from Deir 'Allā,* 123–124; and B. A. Levine, "The Balaam Inscription from Deir 'Allā: Historical Aspects," in *Biblical Archaeology Today,* 327–328.

It must be emphasized that most of these opinions remain in a state of flux because our knowledge of Palestinian linguistics is itself in a state of flux. W. Randall Garr (*Dialect Geography of Syria-Palestine, 1000–586 B.C.E.* [Philadelphia: Univ. of Pennsylvania, 1985] 205–235) puts DAT approx. halfway between the Canaanite and Aramaic poles on his "dialectal continuum." E. A. Knauf ("Review of *The Balaam Text from Deir 'Allā,* by J. Hackett, *ZDPV* 101 [1985] 189–191), classifies the language as neither Aramaic nor Canaanite, but as "proto-Aramaic . . . an intermediate stage of the evolution of Aramaic out of second millennium B.C. Central (Syrian) Semitic." Baruch Halpern argues that the DAT dialect "is most economically analyzed as a branch of Canaanite spoken in an accent resembling that of its northern neighbors," adding that, for the near future, "Deir 'Allā should occupy a place in 'Canaanite' studies roughly parallel to the one occupied by Sam'al in Aramaic"; see "Dialect Distribution in Canaan and the Deir Alla Inscriptions," in D. M. Golomb and S. T. Hollis, eds., *Working With No Data: Semitic and Egyptian Studies Presented to Thomas O. Lambdin* (Winona Lake, IN: Eisenbrauns, 1987) 133, 137. Klaus Beyer calls DAT a "hieratic mixture of archaic South Canaanite and spoken Aramaic"; *The Aramaic Language: Its Distribution and Subdivisions,* trans. by J. F. Healey (Göttingen: Vandenhoeck & Ruprecht, 1986) 13, n. 7.

Nascent sociolinguistic observations, sensitive to the distinctions between societal domains within dialects as well as the novel morphological and lexical possibilities characteristic of structured bilingual speech communities, are offered by J. Hoftijzer (*editio princeps,* 301), P. K. McCarter ("The Balaam Texts," 50–51), and E. A. Knauf ("Review of *The Balaam Text,* by Hackett," 190).

together the contours of the Transjordanian Balaam tradition, and must therefore be carefully taken into account in the present study.[28]

Research on the Traditions as a Whole

Current attempts to examine these traditions as a whole have been meager, and those which do attempt such an analysis tend to focus on the influence DAT may have had on the biblical tradition, rather than the influence each may have had on the other, or the question of common influences. Most remain tied to a literary methodology. Alexander Rofé's attempt to explain the connection between DAT and the memory of the Baal Peor incident in Num 31:16 stands as a particularly straightforward example of this tendency.[29] Noting the close parallels in narrative style and content between DAT and the Bible, however, P. Kyle McCarter more cautiously suggests that the author of the narrative in Numbers 22 may have been familiar with some form of the Transjordanian tradition *prior* to the written form of DAT.[30]

[28] Hoftijzer, for example (*editio princeps*, 270–282), interprets Combination II as a series of curses threatening impending doom. P. K. McCarter (cited in J. Hackett, *The Balaam Text*, 80–89) interprets Combination II as a revivification ceremony for the god Adonis. Following a suggestion from F. M. Cross, J. Hackett interprets Combination II as a liturgy for a child-sacrifice ritual, of the sort mentioned in biblical (2 Kgs 3:27) and Punic tradition (KAI 43:11; 162; 163); cf. *The Balaam Text*, 80–89).

B. A. Levine ("The Deir 'Allā Plaster Inscriptions," *JAOS* 101 [1981] 196) views DAT I:1–7 as the communication of an evil omen from the gods which Balaam proceeds to interpret by depicting the disaster which it predicts. Via (unpreserved) "execrations and other forms of magic," Balaam successfully rescues the goddess who was commanded to cover the heavens in DAT I:5–6. For interfering in divine affairs, Balaam incurs the wrath of the gods. In Combination II he is therefore told that his counsel will no longer be heeded (DAT II:9), that he will be consigned to Sheol where his corpse will "moan" (II:12) and that kings will gaze at his corpse there (II:13). Balaam is to be "condemned for what you have said, and banned from pronouncing words of execration" (Levine's translation of DAT II:17). Firmly holding that DAT is an example of "aramäische Prophetien," Hoftijzer reacts strongly to Levine's proposal: "Wenn ihn Levine darüber hinaus als Zeichendeuter und die Götter beschwörenden Zauberer interpretiert, geht er zu weit." Cf. Hoftijzer, "Aramäische Prophetien," in O. Kaiser, ed., *Texte aus der Umwelt des alten Testaments* II/1 (Gütersloh: Gerd Mohn, 1986) 139.

[29] A. Rofé (*Spr Bl'm*, 69–70) hypothesizes that DAT preserves a tradition where Balaam is the founder of a house of prostitution. Aware of this tradition, P then allegedly fashioned his portrayal in Num 31:16.

[30] McCarter ("Balaam Texts," 57) points out two parallels in the narrative structure of each account: (a) both traditions state that God/the gods came to Balaam at night; (b) both state that Balaam "rose in the morning." H.-P. Müller ("Die aramäische Inschrift von Deir 'Allā und die älteren Bileamsprüche," *ZAW* 94 [1982] 238–242) points out several more: (a) similarity in "introduction" between

Following McCarter's lead, Jo Ann Hackett suggests the presence of a "pattern" emerging that

> ties together Balaam, son of Beor; the plains of Moab in the east Jordan Valley; worship of gods with the epithet *šdy;* and various ritual practices.[31]

Hypothesizing Balaam as the leader of a rival cult, Hackett argues that the compiler of the Balaam cycle deliberately set out to entertain his Israelite audience by recasting this hated enemy in the role of Yahweh's "obedient prophet."[32] L. M. von Pákozdy's earlier thesis, while concerned to interpret the biblical tradition as "Redaktionsarbeit," nevertheless tried to show that the main concern of the Israelite tradition was to show the superiority of Yahweh "über jederlei heidnische Mantik, Orakelweisen, Zauberei und Prophetie."[33]

Other scholars have decided to remain with the literary approach. Building on the assumptions (a) that DAT is an "Aramaic" text, and (b) that there was little or no history of tradition lying behind the written formulation of it found at Deir 'Allā, Maurice Delcor has argued for "une source araméenne" underneath the biblical tradition, "connue maintenant par l'inscription de Deir 'Allā."[34] As will become clearer below, we cannot accept either Delcor's assumptions or his methodology.

Hans-Peter Müller has pursued this tack to its logical conclusion, arguing that the Deir 'Allā tradition is a type of literary prism through which both the "positive" and the "negative" strands of the biblical tradition should be viewed.[35] Any doom-oracle against one of Israel's enemies (which he identifies as Ammon) must automatically have been received in Israel as an oracle of salvation. Thus DAT provides the fodder for the essentially "positive" portrayal now found in Num 24. For Müller, the "negative" side of the tradition arose when Israelite

---

DAT I:1 (*spr bl'm br b'r 'š ḥzh 'lhn*) and
Num 24:3 (*n'm bl'm bnw b'r hgbr štm h'yn*);

(b) similarities in names for God: "El" (DAT II:6; Num 24:4, 16) and the root *šdy(n)* (DAT I:6; Num 24:4, 16); (c) common presence of "rods" often associated with fertility/power: *mṭh//ḥṭr* (DAT I:9); *šbṭ* (Num 24:17); (d) common archaic poetic style, one still characterized by a "magisch-bindendes" format.

[31] Hackett, "Some Observations on the Balaam Tradition at Deir 'Allā," *BA* 49 (1986) 220.

[32] Ibid.

[33] von Pákozdy, "Theologische Redaktionsarbeit in der Bileam-Perikope," 164.

[34] Delcor, "Le texte de Deir 'Allā," 65. Hoftijzer (*editio princeps,* 271) and Ringgren ("Balaam and the Deir 'Allā Inscription," 98) both recognize that a rather sizable history of tradition had been built up about Balaam in Transjordan prior to the recording of this tradition on eighth-century plaster.

[35] Müller, "Einige alttestamentliche Probleme," 58–60; "Die aramäische Inschrift von Deir 'Allā und die älteren Bileamsprüche," 214–244.

tradents began to insert Israel's name into the literary slot originally designed for the audience of the DAT "doom-oracle."[36]

Many of these analyses therefore continue to operate within a simple "negative-vs.-positive" bipolar framework first proposed by older literary critics for the biblical Balaam tradition, and thus continue to constrict the entire spectrum of traditions about this magico-religious specialist within an artificial dichotomy. Some of these proposals either ignore the linguistic problems in DAT or gloss over them. Some build interpretations of one or more of these traditions on questionable readings of the available text, while others offer intriguing but often very hypothetical interpretations too dependent on rare terms and/or questionable textual reconstructions. So far we have yet to see a comprehensive, systematic, controlled attempt to examine the character or the development of these traditions against an empirical backdrop of genuinely relevant contemporary material from the ancient Near East.

PROPOSAL OF THIS STUDY

As Noth pointed out in his earlier study, it is manifestly obvious that every Balaam tradition already portrays Balaam as a magico-religious specialist of some repute.[37] The present study will seek to investigate how these variously refracted portrayals compare to the actual roles enacted by selected magico-religious specialists operating during this general period in the ancient Near East, paying particular attention to the relevant material from Anatolia, Mesopotamia, and especially Syria-Palestine.[38] This study will attempt to locate these traditions within their proper sociohistorical matrices.

We will not be lacking for material. A number of secondary studies thoroughly investigate the multiple roles enacted by these specialists as they practiced their crafts within distinct sociohistorical matrices,[39] and a surfeit of

[36] Müller, "Einige alttestamentliche Probleme," 58–59.

[37] Noth, *History of Pentateuchal Traditions*, 76–77.

[38] J. J. M. Roberts points to the "potential value for biblical scholarship" in the ritual texts "that has not yet been fully exploited," "The Ancient Near Eastern Environment," in D. A. Knight & G. M. Tucker, eds., *The Hebrew Bible and Its Modern Interpreters* (Philadelphia: Fortress, 1985) 92. In 1984, J. Balensi suggested that future studies of DAT focus on "une étude comparative des cultures matérielles de la Vallée du Jourdain. Mener à bien une telle étude exige d'être familiarisé avec les archives matérielles des deux rives" ("Discussion," in *Biblical Archaeology Today*, 368).

[39] The following works provide helpful introductions: For Anatolia: A. Goetze, *Kulturgeschichte Kleinasiens*, 2nd ed., HAW 3/2 (Munich: C. H. Beck'sche, 1974) 130–171; Annelies Kammenhuber, *Orakelpraxis, Träume, und Vorzeichenschau bei den Hethitern*, TdH 7 (Heidelberg: C. Winter, 1976); M. Vieyra, "Le sorcier hittite," in *Le monde du sorcier*, SO 7 (Paris: editions du Seuil, 1966) 99–125.

For Mesopotamia: *La divination en mésopotamie ancienne et dans les régions voisines* (Paris: Presses universitaires de France, 1966); J. Nougayrol, "La divination

primary material now enables us to analyze the contours of these matrices in detail.[40]

Thus the basic methodology guiding this study will be phenomenological rather than philological, literary-critical, or traditio-historical. Drawing from the theoretical constructs and categories customarily employed by anthropologists and sociologists of religion, our interest here will focus first on the spectrum of roles enacted by selected magico-religious specialists in the ancient Near East. After this, we will attempt to describe Balaam's roles at Deir 'Allā and in the Bible from the vantage point of this perspective. Then we will compare the roles enacted in the Balaam traditions against this phenomenological *realia.*

It is not unreasonable to assume that the traditional figure of Balaam was originally predicated upon actual practice, even if we choose here not to address the problem of the historical Balaam. Nor is it unreasonable to postulate that divergences in the traditions from the phenomenological *realia* likely indicate varying degrees of development. Congruence between the known Balaam traditions and actual practice will therefore need to be quantified and qualified, and divergence from actual practice in these traditions will need to be examined carefully with a view toward uncovering possible indications of development.

Insights from Role Theory

Examination of the roles enacted by Balaam or any other magico-religious specialist can profit a great deal from the insights and perspectives of contemporary role theory. Though complete unanimity in this or any other area of social scientific theory will never exist,[41] T. R. Sarbin and V. L. Allen have

---

babylonienne," in A. Caquot & M. Leibovici, eds., *La divination* (Paris: Presses universitaires de France, 1968) 25–81; E. Reiner, "La magie babylonienne," in *Le monde du sorcier,* 67–98; O. R. Gurney, "The Babylonians and Hittites," in M. Loewe & C. Blacker, eds., *Oracles and Divination* (Boulder, CO: Shambhala, 1981) 142–173.

For Israel and her neighbors: A. Caquot, "La divination dans l'ancien Israël," in Caquot & Leibovici, *La divination,* 83–113; G. Vajda, "La magie en Israel et le judaïsme," in *Le monde du sorcier,* 127–153; J. R. Porter, "Ancient Israel," in Loewe & Blacker, *Oracles and Divination,* 191–214.

[40] Cf. the primary studies cited above in the "Abbreviations."

[41] Some theorists distinguish between "status" and "role" (R. Linton, *The Study of Man* [New York: Appleton-Century-Crofts, 1936] 113–114), while others talk of "position" and "role" (R. Dahrendorf, "Homo Sociologicus: On the History, Significance, and Limits of the Category of Social Role," in *Essays in the Theory of Society* [London: Routledge and Kegan Paul, 1968] 35–37). W. R. Goodenough criticizes Linton's sharp distinctions between "status" and "role," preferring to use the term "social identity" (W. R. Goodenough, "Rethinking 'Status' and 'Role': Toward a General Model of the Cultural Organization of Social Relationships," in M. Banton, ed., *The Relevance of Models for Social Anthropology* [London: Tavistock, 1965] 3–5). R. Keesing claims greater precision by separating "social identity relationships," "status relationships," and "role relationships"

conveniently summarized several of the more important independent variables which are presently employed by the majority of role theorists to describe the complex phenomenon of *role enactment.*[42] Some of these variables cannot be adapted to an examination like the one proposed here because of the obvious difficulties involved in gathering reliable sociological and especially psychological data from such a vast distance.

Nevertheless, sociological and anthropological insights have already proven themselves to be quite useful for researching the behavior and institutions of ancient societies,[43] and biblical scholars are not unaware that the social scientific paradigm can often generate new approaches to old problems.[44] Contemporary role theory, if responsibly adapted, accordingly offers us an integrated theoretical perspective from which some of the more intransigent problems regarding the Balaam traditions might now be freshly addressed.

The test of any theory is not whether it is "true," but whether it is useful.[45] Role theory is useful because it helps us to describe complex social relationships

---

into separate theoretical categories (R. Keesing, "Toward a Model of Role Analysis," in R. Naroll & R. Cohen, eds., *A Handbook of Method in Cultural Anthropology* [New York: Natural History Press, 1971] 427). These theoretical refinements have not, however, prevented the central metaphor of "role" from effectively guiding researchers into fruitful areas of inquiry.

[42] T. R. Sarbin and V. L. Allen, "Role Theory," in G. Lindzey & E. Aronson, eds., *The Handbook of Social Psychology,* 2nd ed. (Reading, MA: Addison-Wesley, 1968) 489–491. Cf. also the surveys in M. Banton, *Roles: An Introduction to the Study of Social Relations* (New York: Basic, 1965); H. Popitz, *Der Begriff der sozialen Rollen als Element der soziologischen Theorie* (Tübingen: Mohr, 1967); L. Neiman & J. Hughes, "The Problem of the Concept of Role: A Re-Survey of the Literature," *SF* 30 (1951) 141–149.

[43] Cf. the bibliography on ancient Near Eastern social and economic history in N. K. Gottwald, "Israel, Social and Economic Development of," *IDBS,* 467. Cf. also the bibliography in Gottwald, *The Hebrew Bible: A Socio-Literary Introduction,* 615. Baruch Halpern voices dismay at the rise of social scientific methods in biblical studies, but erroneously assumes that such methods are always "generated from data irrelevant to Israel"; *The First Historians: The Hebrew Bible and History* (New York: Harper and Row, 1988) 29. Is the DAT Balaam tradition "irrelevant" to the biblical Balaam tradition?

[44] Cf., for example, M. Weber, *Ancient Judaism* (Glencoe, IL: Free Press, 1952; trans. of 1921 German original); R. P. Carroll, *When Prophecy Failed: Cognitive Dissonance and the Prophetic Traditions of the Old Testament* (London: SCM, 1979); N. K. Gottwald, *The Tribes of Yahweh: A Sociology of the Religion of Liberated Israel, 1250–1050 B.C.E.* (Maryknoll, NY: Orbis, 1979); R. R. Wilson, *Prophecy and Society in Ancient Israel* (Philadelphia: Fortress, 1980); D. L. Petersen, *The Roles of Israel's Prophets,* JSOTSup 17 (Sheffield: JSOT Press, 1981).

[45] Sarbin & Allen, "Role Theory," 489. E. L. Greenstein points to the importance of employing sound theory in biblical studies: "Our conclusions are predicted by our methods. . . . Our methods have been developed in order to serve our theories. . . . One always begins with a theory." Cf. "The Role of Theory in Biblical Criticism," in *Proceedings of the Ninth World Congress of Jewish Studies* (Jerusalem: World Union of Jewish Studies, 1986) 167.

between "actors" and "audiences" more precisely and more accurately. This is its essential value *vis-à-vis* other approaches to the study of human behavior. Since the phrase "playing a role" can be much too vague a construct for describing the complexities and nuances of this social contract, the phrase *role enactment* has been proposed as a conscious attempt to be more precise when describing this phenomenon.[46] Two sub-variables help to hone this precision further. Role theorists focus on: (1) the number of roles enacted by an actor; and (2) the preemption of some roles by others in any given "role set."[47]

Most of the magico-religious specialists examined in this study enact a plurality of roles. Thus, while etymological analyses of the indigenous titles worn by these specialists have a place, they usually offer little help toward analyzing the thicket of ambiguities which tend to blur the dynamics of any given multiple role enactment. When describing social behavior within the theoretical constraints provided by role theory, discussions of *titles* must therefore be kept clearly separate from discussions of *roles*. As R. Dahrendorf puts it,

> positions merely identify places within fields of reference; roles tell us about how people relate to people in other positions in the same field.[48]

Both *bārû* ("diviner") and *šā'ilu* (lit., "inquirer") specialists, for example, could enact roles as "dream-interpreters" in Mesopotamia,[49] but while this role description essentially defines the totality of the *šā'ilu*'s societal function, it describes only one of several roles enacted by the *bārû*. Moreover, both the *SALŠU.GI* ("old woman") and the *LÚMUŠEN.DU* ("ornithomantic") enacted roles as "augur" in Anatolia, but as the Sumerograms indicate, the "augur" role was more central to the *LÚMUŠEN.DU*'s role enactment than it was for the "old woman."[50]

Further, since some roles are more important than others for different audiences at different times, *role preemption* becomes another important factor to consider. There is some evidence, for example, that the "augur" in Anatolia, when working in conjunction with an "old woman," enacted a role as "purification-priest" in certain magical rituals,[51] yet when working alone his more important role ("augur") tends to preempt that of "purification-priest."

Another variable which helps to delimit this study within manageable

[46] Sarbin and Allen, "Role Theory," 489.

[47] Ibid., 491–497. The term "role-set" denotes the total spectrum of complementary roles which can be related in a given audience's mind to a given role. The term was apparently first coined by R. K. Merton, "The Role Set: Problems in Sociological Theory," *BJS* 8 (1957) 106–120.

[48] R. Dahrendorf, "Homo Sociologicus," 36.

[49] Cf. chapter 1 below.

[50] Ibid.

[51] Ibid.

theoretical parameters is that of *role expectations.*[52] This construct describes a set of cognitions held for any given role by both "actor" and "audience," expectations which vary considerably according to actor, audience, locale, and time. The texts examined in this study are a gold mine for researchers interested in the often shifting role expectations which were held by different ancient Near Eastern audiences toward the magico-religious specialists working in their midst at different times and in different places.

Within any given audience, expectations regarding a given role can be homo- or heterogeneous. Some respondents in an audience will interpret a role more generally, some more specifically. Some will hold relatively clear expectations of what a given role should be, while others' conceptions will be unclear, uncertain, or uninformed.[53]

"Role strain" occurs when the role expectations within different segments of an audience or between different audiences are measurably dissonant.[54] As in general "cognitive dissonance" theory,[55] *intrarole conflict* often (but not always) generates behavioral responses aimed at resolving this conflict. These behavioral responses include: (1) the use of actions/rituals in order to modify *external* sources of conflict; and/or (2) the modification of one or more *internal* inputs. These have to do with the habitual behavioral adjustments which take place whenever an audience either ignores one or more of its conflicting role expectations, or actually changes its attitude toward a conflicting role expectation.[56]

"Role strain" and its resultant resolution can be seen in the conflicting role expectations held by Anatolian audiences and their resolution over time with regard to the "old woman," a prominent Anatolian magico-religious specialist. This specialist was expected to purify the king from evil and maintain an aura of magical purity around his person by means of several different types of magical rituals and incantations. Early in the Old Kingdom period, however, rivals within the royal retinue attempted to engage her power in order to challenge the political *status quo* of the "royal couple." Different segments within the same ethnolinguistic audience thus held different, conflicting expectations regarding what roles an "old woman" could or should enact.

In one instance, a king (Hattušili I) attempted to resolve this "role strain" by forbidding a group of ladies at court from speaking to a number of "old

[52] Sarbin & Allen, "Role Theory," 497–506.

[53] Ibid.

[54] W. J. Goode, "A Theory of Role Strain," *ASR* 25 (1960) 483–496, reprinted in Goode, *Explorations in Social Theory* (New York: Oxford, 1973) 97–120.

[55] L. Festinger, H. W. Riecken, and S. Schlachter, *When Prophecy Fails* (Minneapolis: Univ. of Minnesota, 1956). R. P. Carroll has drawn extensively from cognitive dissonance theory in order to analyze the unfulfilled predictions in Hebrew prophecy, concluding that "some of the hermeneutic responses evident in the prophetic traditions are indications of dissonance response, hence the stress on the principle *dissonance gives rise to hermeneutic*" (*When Prophecy Failed,* 124).

[56] Sarbin & Allen, "Role Theory," 541–544.

women" about the future, apparently because their activity, from his perspective, bordered dangerously on "evil" magic.[57] Her role was deemed "inappropriate" from the royal point of view. The *intrarole conflict* of expectations regarding the "old woman's" role at court was thus resolved by a segment of her audience (the king) through *external* means (forbidding her to engage in "evil" magic). Had *internal* modification taken place, the king might have (1) tried to modify his beliefs about her, or (2) accepted her role as "evil" magician, or (3) ignored the intrarole conflict.[58] Repeated successful resolutions of this cognitive dissonance contributed significantly toward the creation of a "traditional" role-set expected of the "old woman," so that by the Empire period there apparently existed a minimum of "role strain" regarding her "proper" place in Anatolian society.

Other examples of "role strain" and the means used to resolve it will be cited below in the course of the study. These examples are given here only as illustrations via introduction. The canons of role theory, and particularly the three variables of *role enactment, role expectations,* and *intrarole conflict* will prove to be very helpful once we begin to unpack the wide range of conflicting role expectations which different audiences brought to the figure of Balaam at different times and in different places.

Roles Enacted by Magico-Religious Specialists

As is customary in most attempts to label the roles enacted in any given society, the classification of the roles enacted by the ancient specialists in this study will be based on the categories worked out by anthropologists of religion.[59]

[57] "Testament" of Hattušili I, cited in Vieyra, "Le sorcier hittite," 104.

[58] Cf. Manasseh's *internal* change of attitude toward Yahwism vs. the Syro-Palestinian magico-religious practices to which he had grown accustomed (2 Chron 33:10–17). Most find it difficult to dismiss this notice about Manasseh as a literary fabrication by the Chronicler; cf. W. Rudolph, *Chronikbücher,* HAT 21 (Tübingen: Mohr, 1955) 315–317; D. L. Petersen, *Late Israelite Prophecy: Studies in Deutero-Prophetic Literature and in Chronicles,* SBLMS 23 (Missoula: Scholars, 1977) 59; J. Blenkinsopp, *A History of Prophecy in Israel* (Philadelphia: Westminster, 1983) 85.

[59] The role labels employed in this study (i.e., "diviner," "exorcist," etc.) have been drawn from categories customarily delineated by anthropologists of religion; cf. A. de Waal Malefijt (*Religion and Culture: An Introduction to Anthropology of Religion* [New York: Macmillan, 1968] 228–245); cf. also M. Banton, ed., *Anthropological Approaches to the Study of Religion* (London: Tavistock, 1978). Working from these anthropological models, the fundamental mandate guiding this study is the desire to reflect all—and only—the roles of these specialists as they are preserved in the ritual/incantation texts.

Appeal is made here to anthropological instead of psychological categories because, as R. Keesing points out, role labelling is a task more readily informed by social anthropology than social psychology ("Toward a Model of Role Analysis," 423–424). Even so, the labeling of roles in any ancient society so far removed from contemporary Western

Also, since it is often difficult to distinguish clearly between "magic" and "religion,"[60] the customary hybrid term "magico-religious" will be used in this study

---

culture must be recognized, in Petersen's words, as a "vexing task" (*Roles of Israel's Prophets,* 35).

This study is therefore oriented to a content-based classification of religious roles (cf. H. Gerth and C. W. Mills, *Character and Social Structure* [New York: Harcourt, Brace, and World, 1953] 22–23, 416–419), rather than, for example, a classification based on "ascribed-achieved" continuums (cf. R. Linton, *The Cultural Background of Personality* [New York: Appleton-Century-Crofts, 1945] 76–78) or a classification based on a "generality-specificity" continuum (cf. J. P. Spiegel, "Interpersonal Influences within the Family," in W. Bennis *et al.*, eds., *Interpersonal Dynamics* [Homewood, IL: Dorsey Press, 1964] 394–409).

Doubtless some will take issue with one or more of the role labels used in this study, but critical hesitation before a particular label should not override the essential need to attempt some sort of taxonomical model pursuant to comparative phenomenological study. In Spiegel's words, "Although I think anyone who tries to do this is bound to fail in certain ways, nevertheless, the attempt is worthwhile" (ibid., 403).

[60] One influential theoretician equated "magic" with "primitive" and "religion" with "civilized"; E. B. Tylor, *Primitive Culture* (New York: Harper Torchbooks, 1958, first published in 1872) vol. I, p. 133. To others, magic was "manipulative" and religion was "supplicative"; J. Frazer, *The Golden Bough* (abridged ed.; New York: Macmillan, 1922) 56–69. To still others, magic was "utilitarian" and religion was "celebratory"; B. Malinowski, *Magic, Science and Religion and Other Essays* (Garden City, NY: Doubleday Anchor, 1954, first published in 1925) 30–38. To a pioneer sociologist, magic was "individual" and religion was "communal"; E. Durkheim, *The Elementary Forms of the Religious Life* (New York: Collier, 1915, trans. from 1912 French ed.) 60. The major problem with all these distinctions lay in the biased presupposition that complex cultures are inherently more *rational* than more primitive cultures. The colonialist prejudices upon which these theories are based have long since rendered them useless to contemporary anthropology.

That many contemporary scholars want to deny *any* distinction between magic and religion, however, is just as problematic. Such a "pendulum-swing" response is probably more of an overreaction to the theorists just mentioned than a dispassionate analysis of the empirical evidence, particularly the ancient Near Eastern evidence. I would certainly agree that any attempt to *dichotomize* between magic and religion as "ideal types" (e.g., in a Weberian sense) *is* antiquated. But one can *distinguish* between magic and religion without *segregating* them into ideal types. The anthropologists A. Malefijt and B. Morris, for example, continue to recognize that there *is* a distinction between magic and religion, yet neither scholar bases this obvious phenomenological distinction on the outdated intellectual theories of Tylor, Frazer, Malinowski, Durkheim, or Weber; see Malefijt, *Religion and Culture,* 12–15; B. Morris, *Anthropological Studies of Religion* (Cambridge: University Press, 1987) 103–106 (critique of Frazer), 30–38 (critique of Malinowski), 106–122 (critique of Durkheim), 86 (critique of Weber).

In short, the schema of *continuum* keeps us on sane theoretical ground. Certainly ancient Mesopotamian culture recognized a distinction between magic and religion, else it would be difficult to explain the culturally-cued distinction between what *bārû*-priests and *āšipu*-priests fundamentally do. Positing a magic-religion *continuum* therefore helps us to conceptualize the ancient Near Eastern data and study it in a methodologically

to designate the ancient Near Eastern specialists examined below.

Each of the roles enacted by these magico-religious specialists stands at a different point on a spatiotemporal continuum between the antithetical poles of "magic" and "religion." The roles enacted by these magico-religious specialists, furthermore, will tend to oscillate back and forth between the poles of this "magic-religion" continuum at different times and at different places for different reasons. With some, this oscillation is greater than with others, often making it difficult to locate these roles on the continuum with accuracy. Due usually to a lack of data, this difficulty cannot always be successfully resolved.

This study will not attempt, however, to analyze the roles of these ancient magico-religious specialists within the parameters of "shaman-priest" continuums like those frequently employed by anthropologists of religion, because for all practical purposes it is impossible to sustain a one-to-one parallel between all the points on each of these continuums.[61] Regardless of the often striking parallels, we simply have no way of ascertaining whether "shamans," particularly those of the Siberian type, ever actually existed in the ancient Near East during the period under investigation in this study.[62]

To the orientation among most anthropologists of religion to focus squarely on the *cultural position* maintained by magico-religious specialists in their broader context,[63] this study will employ these anthropologically-rooted role labels only in order to analyze *societal role*. In other words, a "diviner" is a "diviner" in this study only if he/she enacts the *role* of "diviner," regardless if

---

reproducible way. Such a fluid, dynamic schema is not at all dependent on truly antiquated notions of alleged dichotomies between "primitive" and "complex" societies.

[61] "Shamans" and "priests" are said to be distinct in the following ways: (1) shamans are essentially part-time specialists; priests are full-time specialists; (2) shamanic vocations are usually non-hereditary; priesthoods are usually hereditary; (3) shamans are validated by personal ability; priests are validated primarily by the office itself; (4) shamans become shamans by divine call; priest rarely receive divine calls; (5) shamans aim at control over nature; priests aim at harmonizing humanity's relationship with nature; (6) shamans usually function at times of individual crisis; priests preside at regularly scheduled communal ceremonies; (7) the shamanistic relationship is more of a professional-client type; priestly relationships are more of a shepherd-flock type; (8) shamans are more apolitical; priests are more political (de Waal Malefijt, *Religion and Culture*, 239–240).

[62] B. O. Long allows that the biblical portrait of Elisha "is as close to that of a typical shaman as one finds in the Old Testament"; cf. "The Social Settings for Prophetic Miracle Stories," *Sem* 3 (1975) 49.

[63] Noteworthy among the wholistic analyses of culture and its bewildering variety of configurations is the classic study of Ruth F. Benedict, *Patterns of Culture* (New York: Mentor, 1946, first published in 1934), even though her (stereo)typing of whole cultures into either Apollonian (mild-mannered, conservative) or Dionysian (belligerent, orgiastic) categories often overlooks the subtleties and peculiarities within each. Cf. the justifiable criticisms of Benedict by W. A. Haviland, *Cultural Anthropology* (New York: Holt, Rinehart, and Winston, 1975) 112.

he/she holds the *title* or *position* of "diviner" in any given cultural configuration. The same goes for "exorcist," "seer," "prophet," "sorcerer," or any other *societal role* in ancient Near Eastern society. This theoretical distinction must be maintained in order to account more accurately for socially observable phenomena like overlap between and within the "role sets" enacted by these specialists, role preemption, the often radically different role expectations held by different audiences at different places and times, and the complex of problems attendant to intrarole conflict.

1
The Roles Enacted by Selected Ancient Near Eastern Magico-Religious Specialists

ANATOLIAN MAGICO-RELIGIOUS SPECIALISTS

It is impossible to separate "magic" from "religion" in Anatolian praxis, but it is helpful to distinguish, with A. Goetze, between "magic" and the more or less official "cult."[1] To the latter belong such specialists as the "holy" ^{LÚ}*SANGA*- and *šuppiš*-priests, the ^{LÚ}*GUDU*- priest ("anointed"), the ^{SAL}*AMA.DINGIR.*^{LIM} ("mother of the gods") and the ^{SAL}*ENSI*-priestesses, to name only a few of the better known. These specialists lived next to the temple precincts and took charge of the daily care and feeding of the state gods, the maintenance of temples, and the celebration of calendrical festivals.[2]

At times of crisis, however, such as birth,[3] death,[4] plague,[5] war,[6] royal illness,[7] or other calamity, Anatolians turned to a number of magico-religious

[1] A. Goetze, *Kleinasien.* "Die Magie" is discussed on pp. 151–161, "der Kultus" on pp. 161–169. The interdependence of magic, religion and politics, especially visible in the magical imprecations concluding several state treaties in Anatolia and North Syria, is emphasized by M. Vieyra ("Le sorcier hittite," 104–105) and O. R. Gurney (*The Hittites* [Baltimore: Penguin, 1954] 162). Max Weber defines "cult" as "the relationships of men to supernatural forces which take the forms of prayer, sacrifice, and worship," while "sorcery" is termed "magical coercion"; cf. *Sociology of Religion* (Boston: Beacon, 1963; first published in 1922) 28.

[2] Goetze, *Kleinasien,* 168–169.

[3] G. M. Beckman, *Hittite Birth Rituals,* 2nd ed., SBT 29 (Wiesbaden: Harrassowitz, 1983).

[4] H. Otten, *Hethitische Totenrituale,* Deutsche Akademie der Wissenschaften zu Berlin, Institut für Orientforschung Veroffentlichung Nr. 37 (Berlin: Akademie-Verlag, 1958).

[5] "Plague Prayers of Muršilis," ANET 394–396.

[6] V. Haas and G. Wilhelm, *Hurritische und luwische Riten aus Kizzuwatna,* AOATS 3 (Kevelaer: Butzon and Bercker, 1974) 234–239 (transcription and translation of KUB VII 60). Another transcription of KUB VII 60 is offered by J. Friedrich in his *Hethitisches Elementarbuch,* 2nd ed. (Heidelberg: Carl Winter, 1967) II:42–43.

[7] A. Kammenhuber, *Orakelpraxis, Träume und Vorzeichenschau bei den Hethitern,*

specialists. To avoid calamity altogether (and perhaps also the exorcist's fee!), apotropaic incantations were inscribed on amulets, talismans, and homeopathic figurines and prominently displayed over entranceways or buried in the foundations of houses in order to protect and purify the persons of that house from the threat of portended evil. [8]

The "Old Woman" (ˢᴬᴸŠUGI)

The "old woman" enacted a wide range of roles and was the most prominent magico-religious specialist in Anatolia. Her presence is required at most *rites de passage* and other, unexpected points of crisis. Often it is impossible to distinguish precisely which role or roles she enacts since the boundaries between them are often very fluid, although we can say with a measure of conviction that she does not participate in the technical reading of exta (the function of the ^{LÚ}AZU, and later, the ^{LÚ}HAL). Compounding the factors of time, space, and audience, she sometimes operates in conjunction with other specialists, like the $^{LÚ}MUŠEN.DÙ$ ("augur") and the $^{LÚ}A.ZU$ ("physician"), usually as the director of proceedings. [9]

Many of the personal names of these female specialists are acknowledged to be Hurrian in origin, the language with which she appears to be most comfortable when reciting oracles and incantations (vs. Luwian or Hittite). [10] We also have evidence that these specialists were often organized under the leadership of a GAL $^{SAL.MEŠ}ŠUGI$. [11] Her incantations have been found on numerous

---

16–17 (illness of Kantuzzili, brother of Šuppiluliumas I). A magical purification ritual for the royal couple Tudḫaliya and Nikalmati against the sorcery of Ziplantawi(ya), Tudḫaliya's sister, is studied by G. Szabo (*Ein hethitisches Entsühnungsritual*, TdH 1 [Heidelberg: Carl Winter, 1971]).

[8] "They make a little dog of tallow and place it on the threshold of the house and say 'You are the little dog of the table of the royal pair. Just as by day you do not allow other men into the courtyard, so do not let in the Evil Thing during the night'" (text cited by Gurney, *The Hittites*, 163). See the "Ritual for the Erection of a House" and the "Ritual for the Erection of a Palace" in ANET 356–358.

[9] A. Ünal, "Zum Status der 'Augures' bei den Hethitern," *RHA* 31 (1973) 32; Haas & Wilhelm, *Hurritische und luwische Riten*, 15, nt. 3; V. Haas and H. J. Thiel, *Die Beschwörungsrituale der Allaituraḫ(ḫ)i und verwandte Texte*, AOAT 31 (Kevelaer: Butzon & Bercker, 1978) 22–23. A general discussion of the "old woman" is found in O. R. Gurney, *Some Aspects of Hittite Religion* (Oxford: University Press, 1977) 44–46.

[10] Haas & Thiel, *Allaituraḫ(ḫ)i*, 23, nt. 56; Kammenhuber, *Orakelpraxis*, 123–129. Opinions are divided over whether Silalluḫi (HT 95:14) was the proper name of a ˢᴬᴸŠUGI. Haas & Thiel argue that it was (*Allaituraḫ[ḫ]i*, 23, nt. 56); Otten questions this reading (HT 95, nt. 4).

[11] Haas & Thiel, *Allaituraḫ(ḫ)i*, 22.

protective amulets as well as entire series of tablets, like the series attributed to Allaituraḫ(ḫ)i, an "old woman" from North Syria.[12]

The incantations and rituals of the "old woman" were most often performed by the authority and power of Šaušga, the Hittite-Hurrian equivalent to Inanna (Sum.) and Ištar (Akk.). In some cases the "old woman" identifies herself closely with this goddess while exorcising evil:

> I take away the hex with the help of Šaušga (*DIŠTAR*), through the word, through the command, through the "tongue" I take it away.[13]

Although we need to avoid what some call the Weberian flaw of identifying historical examples with ideal types when describing her diverse roles,[14] it is helpful to present them, for reasons already stated, in anthropologically recognizable categories. The roles most relevant to this study include: "exorcist," "purification-priestess," "incantation-reciter," "diviner," and "sorceress."

Exorcist

As "exorcist," the "old woman" was responsible for freeing and purifying clients from the unseen forces of the Netherworld, before which they lived in constant fear. This was one of her most important roles. In one text a North Syrian "old woman" lists some of these "demons" by name:

> the spell which is called "Paralysis" (*tin-ni-ša-an*) I (take away);
> the "thing which sticks to the mouth" (*dam-me-in-ku-wa-ar*) I take away from you;
> the "eyes" (*IGIḪI.A*) shall she take away for you.[15]

In another, the "eyes" of named divinities are listed:

[12] Ibid., 25. While most extant texts position the stronghold for the "old woman's" activity in Kizzuwatna, Allaituraḫ(ḫ)i was from the region near Alalaḫ. The name Allaituraḫe has also been discovered at Nuzi. Cf. M. P. Maidman, "The Teḫip-tilla Family Revisited," Annual Meeting of the American Schools of Oriental Research, Boston, Mass., Dec. 6, 1987.

[13] Haas & Thiel, *Allaituraḫ(ḫ)i* 134:27′–28′.

[14] Talcott Parsons, "Introduction" to M. Weber, *The Sociology of Religion*, lxiii-lxv. Weber, however, was careful to avoid overgeneralizing from ideal types. He constantly inserted caveats like the following (on the distinction between "priests" and "practitioners of magic"): "Applied to reality, this contrast is fluid, as are all sociological phenomena. Even the theoretical differentiae of these types are not unequivocally determinable" (*Sociology of Religion*, 28).

[15] Haas & Thiel, *Allaituraḫ(ḫ)i* 104:4′–6′. "Exorcism" is defined here as "the driving out of evil powers or spirits by solemn adjuration or the performance of rituals" (G. Parrinder, "Exorcism," *ER* V:225).

the eyes of . . . ^{D}Fate and the ^{D}Kunuštalla-gods I wash away.[16]

In another, similar demonic powers are styled

the "fear before the lion,"

and

the "terror before the snake."[17]

The latter two deities could operate as attendants to the Sun deity, and have been found in offering-lists alongside the much-feared "Seven" (Akk. *Sibitti*).[18] They have also surfaced in tandem with ^{D}Fate and the ^{D}Kunuštalla-gods in other incantations.[19]

Purification-Priestess

As "purification-priestess," the "old woman" was responsible for protecting her client ("the lord of the sacrifice" [Sum. *EN.SISKUR*; Hit. *aniuraš išḫaš;* Akk. *bēl niqê*]) from impurity, whether from known or unknown "sin" (*waštul*) against the gods,[20] from contact between the body/soul/spirit and a material (semen, blood) or immaterial substance (the "evil eye"), or from the deliberate machinations of an evil sorcerer. She purified her clients by "washing" them with water, "anointing" them with salves, and/or "releasing" them from demonic power by burning homeopathic images with fire.[21]

She was especially expert in the use of both animate and inanimate homeopathic substitutes, a fact well illustrated by a Hittite purification ritual for a family in distress.[22] In this ritual, figurines representing the parties in dispute are prepared and placed at their feet. Colored strips of wool are tied around the

[16] Haas & Thiel, *Allaituraḫ(ḫ)i* 106:3′–4′. The ^{D}*Kunuštalla*-goddesses may have been local forms of "mother" deities (*^{D}MAḪ^{MEŠ}*), but this is disputed. Cf. O. Carruba, *Das Beschwörungsritual für den Gottin Wišurijanza*, SBT 2 (Wiesbaden: Harrassowitz, 1966) 30.

[17] Haas & Thiel, *Allaituraḫ(ḫ)i* 146:47–48.

[18] J. Friedrich, "'Angst' und 'Schrecken' als niedere Gottheiten bei Griechen und Hethitern," *AfO* 17 (1954–56) 148. They are mentioned alongside the "Seven" in KBo XIII 245 12′–16′ (cited in Haas and Thiel, *Allaituraḫ[ḫ]i*, 199, nt. 251).

[19] KBo XII 118 15′–17′ (cited in Haas & Thiel, *Allaituraḫ(ḫ)i*, 124–125).

[20] Goetze, *Kleinasien*, 151, nt. 2; 152, nt. 6. Cf. the concept of *hubris* in Greek religion (e.g., Hesiod, *Theogony*, LCL [Cambridge: Harvard, 1970] para. 514–516). Vieyra has called for a comprehensive study of the Hittite notion of *waštul* ("Le sorcier hittite," 120, nt. 1).

[21] Vieyra, "Le sorcier hittite," 105–106.

[22] This is the ritual of Maštikka, a ^{SAL}*ŠU.GI* from Kizzuwatna, treated by L. Rost ("Ein hethitisches Ritual gegen Familienzwist," *MIO* 1 [1953] 345–379), and summarized in Vieyra ("Le sorcier hittite," 110–112). An English translation is found in ANET 350–351. This and related texts are discussed in Gurney, *Some Aspects of Hittite Religion*, 52–58.

necks of the figurines, representing the "impurity" forcing the family to quarrel among themselves. The "old woman" cuts away the colored woolen strips while invoking the name of a particular deity in order to "release" the parties from this impurity.

At the climactic point, a white sheep is brought in. The parties in dispute each spit into the animal's mouth and the "old woman" says, "Thus have you spit out the evil."[23] Having thus transferred the evil to an animate homeopathic substitute, the "old woman" slaughters and buries the sheep in a pit. As the doomed animal is buried from sight, so is the evil which has embroiled the family members in dispute.

Incantation-Reciter

The "old woman" is the "incantation-reciter" *par excellence* among Anatolian magico-religious specialists. Even when working alongside other specialists, she is the specialist who actually invokes the names of the gods and recites the appropriate myths. Often she will deliberately weave the themes of a particular myth into the warp and woof of a purification ritual. This habit makes it quite difficult, at times, to decide whether she speaks of the "release" of a mythical god or hero, like Telepinus or Šaušga (cf. Gilgamesh and Ištar in Mesopotamian myth and ritual) or the "release" of a suffering client.

The "client" (*EN.SISKUR*) can be identified, for example, with Šaušga in her famous "Descent to the Netherworld." To help her client, the "old woman" looks to the treatment for reviving Šaušga as a blueprint. In the Anatolian version of this *myth*, Šaušga is revived by the application of a magical liquid substance. In the *ritual*, the "old woman" rubs a medicinal ointment into the skin of her client while reciting the myth of Šaušga's revival, trusting that, like Šaušga, her client will analogously break free from the Netherworld's hold: "From the beloved brother Šaušga demands, "Take me away; make my body pure."[24]

Another ritual finds the "old woman" chanting an incantation to protect the king and his family against the "Seven" (*ḫadugaeš*, *ᴰIMIN.IMIN.BI-eš*).[25] Elsewhere the "Seven" do not operate on their own but are aligned with other deities in a manner similar to the alignment of these demonic forces with the *Pestgott* Erra in Mesopotamian myth.[26]

[23] Vieyra, "Le sorcier hittite," 111.

[24] Haas & Thiel, *Allaituraḫ(ḫ)i*, 140:24–25. Among other reasons, heroes and gods descend to the Netherworld in order to test the relative strengths of love vs. death. The centrality of this and other basic themes have been noted in "Netherworld Descents" from several different cultures (cf. A.-L. Siikala, "Descent into the Underworld," *ER* IV:303–304).

[25] Cf. the portion of KUB XVII 105 cited by A. Kammenhuber, *Orakelpraxis*, 46.

[26] KBo IV 13 i 13, cited in Kammenhuber, *Orakelpraxis*, 50. Cf. Erra I:23–44 (L. Cagni,

Although many of her incantations are in Hurrian and are therefore very difficult to decipher, enough is known about their content to conclude that the *SALŠU.GI* was one of the primary transmitters of mythic tradition in Anatolian society. Form-critical work has already begun to identify some of the more stereotypical formulae employed in her incantations. Comparisons might also be made to incantations from Mesopotamian and NW Semitic sources.[27]

In the death rituals published by H. Otten, the "old woman" enacts overlapping roles as "purification-priestess" *and* "incantation-reciter." Twice in the series *šalliš waštaiš* ("great passing-away"), for example, she places material on a "scale" (*GIŠNUNUZ*) before the Sun-god and chants incantations which petition the Sun-god's protection for the "soul" of her royal client, now deceased and represented by the "image" of a throne, and later, by a humanoid image made out of fruit.[28]

The first of these "weighings" occurs on the second day of the lament/ritual. After the corpse is burned on the funeral pyre (*ukturi*),[29] the bones are collected and cultically preserved. Then cooks (*LÚ.MEŠMUḪAL.DIM*) and attendants (*LÚmeš GIŠBANŠUR*) set a table for a cultic meal in which the "living" eat together with the "dead," now represented by a human figure "formed" (*GUL-ša*)[30] out of figs, raisins, and olives, and set up in the midst of the extinguished funeral pyre.

At this point the "old woman" places gold, silver, and precious stones on one side of the scale and a clay mortar on the other side, and asks,

L'epopea di Erra, SS 34 [Roma: Istituto di Studi del Vicino Oriente, 1969] 60–62). Seven diseases are subject to Yahweh's will in Deut 28:22.

[27] Haas & Thiel, *Allaituraḫ(ḫ)i,* 43, 48–50. For Mesopotamian form-critical work which borrows heavily from the categories inaugurated by biblical form-criticism, cf. W. Mayer, *Untersuchungen zur Formensprache der babylonischen "Gebetsbeschwörungen",* SPSM 5 (Rome: Biblical Institute Press, 1976). Form-critical parallels between the biblical psalms of thanksgiving and the Baalshamayn oracle from Hamath (KAI 202) have been fruitfully studied by J. C. Greenfield, "The Zakir Inscription and the Danklied," *Proceedings of the Fifth World Congress of Jewish Studies* (Jerusalem: World Union of Jewish Studies, 1969) I:174–191.

[28] Cf. HT 58:3–60:7; 66:1–68:36. Even though *šalliš waštaiš* preserves the ritual used in a royal funeral, Goetze argues that it was very likely representative of Anatolian funerary ritual in general (*Kleinasien,* 170). Cf. Gurney, *Some Aspects of Hittite Religion,* 59–63.

[29] Otten (HT 141) offers several examples in legal and religious literature from Bogazköy in which *ukturi* is the "pyre" used for purification rituals of varied types (cf. Akk. *abru*). One text (KUB XXXIX 11–15) suggests to him that the Sun-goddess of the Earth/Netherworld (who enacts a major role in Anatolian death rituals: HT 22:7; 24:4; 26:1; *passim*) could even be designated as "die Verbrennungsstätte . . . (Scheiterhaufen?)." On the Anatolian custom of distinguishing between a Sun-god of the Heavens and a Sun-goddess of the Netherworld, cf. Goetze, *Kleinasien,* 138.

[30] J. Friedrich defines *GUL-aš* within the following semantic range: "(Schrift, Zeichnung) einritzen; schreiben, zeichnen; markieren; (Weg durch Brei) andeuten; fest einprägen; bestimmen, bezeichnen; beschreiben, aufschreiben" (cited in Otten, HT 142).

> Who brings so-and-so here?

Another "old woman" answers,

> The men of Hatti, the Uruḫḫa-men[31] will bring him here.

The first "old woman" categorically rejects this suggestion:

> They shall not bring him here.

Then the second rather abruptly commands,

> Take the silver and gold!

Apparently, however, this second suggestion is even more unpalatable, for the first "old woman" immediately responds:

> I will not take it (for myself).[32]

Interpretation of this ritual is difficult. It could mean that the first "old woman" participates in this dialogue in order to reaffirm her integrity and competence as the primary magico-religious conduit for ushering the remains of the dead king unto his final resting place, but there may well be other motivations lying beneath the surface at which we can only guess.[33]

The second of these "weighings," reckoned by Otten to have occurred on the eighth day of the ritual,[34] appears after the ritual slaughtering of four animals in a pit: an ox, a sheep, a horse, and a mule. Immediately afterwards, the "old woman" places bread and cheese on the "scale," addresses herself to the Sun-god, and says:

> O Sun-god, look upon these animals we have sacrificed. No one shall tear it away. No one shall legally dispute it.[35]

Several lines later, after a broken section in which the "old woman" does something magical with five *arda*-birds,[36] we get a clearer picture of what the "it" is

[31] Cf. the Hurrian parallel *pi-ra-ti-i-en u-ru-uḫ-ḫa*[*ti*] in the incantation of another *SALŠU.GI* (Haas & Thiel, *Allaituraḫ[ḫ]i*, 148:7), which might be translated "Edelmann im Zustand des Gerechtseins" (ibid., 176).

[32] The *SALŠU.GI* repeats this refusal three times, then breaks the scale and begins to lament (HT 68:33–36).

[33] The dead king's mausoleum (lit., "stone-house," *E.NA*$_4$) came equipped with a specially prepared bed in an inner room, upon which his scorched bones were finally laid, then worshipped as a shrine (HT 68:46–51). Goetze notes the many ash-filled urns discovered in the rocky terrain between Bogazköy and Yazilikaya (*Kleinasien*, 170).

Gurney (*Some Aspects of Hittite Religion*, 60) suggests that the silver and gold refers to the redemptive price offered for the deceased, while G. Szabo (*Ein hethitische Entsühnungsritual*, 101) suggests with regard to a parallel passage that the precious metals might indicate the innocence of the sacrificer.

[34] HT 56–57. Cf. Gurney, *Some Aspects of Hittite Religion*, 61.

[35] HT 58:9–11.

[36] HT 58:15–17 (Gurney, *Some Aspects of Hittite Religion*, 61).

that she is trying to protect for her client. Taking a piece of "sod" (*Ú.SAL*^{LAM}) from a meadow, the "old woman" lays it, too, on the scale, and says:

> Now, O Sun-god, preserve for him this legally-dedicated piece of sod. No one shall tear it away, or legally dispute it. Oxen and sheep, horses and mules shall graze for him on this piece of sod.[37]

The "old woman" thus seeks to insure by ritual means that in the life to come the king will be able to maintain the standard of living to which he has grown accustomed.[38]

Diviner

As "diviner," the "old woman" used a variety of means to determine the future for her clients. A. Goetze provides a good rule of thumb by connecting the ^{LÚ}*ḪAL* (Akk. *bārû*) with the *KUŠ*-oracle (Anatolian version of Mesopotamian extispicy), the ^{LÚ}*IGI.MUŠEN* and ^{LÚ}*MUŠEN.DÙ* with the *MUŠEN*-oracle (Sumerogram for "bird"), and the ^{SAL}*ŠU.GI* with the *KIN*-oracle.[39] Unfortunately, little can be said about the actual mechanics of the *KIN*-oracle, even though it was the most common type of oracle in Anatolia. Some scholars think that it had to do with the drawing of lots (cleromancy) because in it something is "taken" (usually a favorable or unfavorable response) and "given" to the client making the inquiry.[40] It was also often used as a counter-control on *KUŠ* and *MUŠEN* oracles, even as "hair and hem" was sometimes taken in order to confirm or deny the oracles of "prophetic" functionaries at Mari.[41]

The "old woman," however, also appears to be able to interpret a *MUŠEN*

[37] HT 60:1–4.

[38] Gurney, *Some Aspects of Hittite Religion,* 62. Citing parallels in the Rigveda and Homer, Otten argues that "die Aussagen der hethitischen Texte dürfen somit vielleicht als Bestätigung dieser Schau und die hier sich abzeichnende Jenseitsvorstellung dann gleichzeitig als Erbgut der Indogermanen gewertet werden" (HT 140).

[39] Goetze, *Kleinasien,* 149; Kammenhuber (*Orakelpraxis,* 9–13) connects *MUŠEN.ḪURRI* with the *KUŠ*-oracle as well. A basic typology of divination is offered by E. M. Zuesse ("Divination," *ER* IV:376).

[40] In addition to the discussions of Goetze and Kammenhuber, cf. M. Vieyra ("Le sorcier hittite," 108–109). O. R. Gurney, noting parallels between *MUŠEN, MUŠ* ("snake"), and *KIN* oracles, suggests that the *KIN* oracle represented some kind of board game, divided into "favorable" and "unfavorable" halves. The movements of active agents on an enclosed field (birds flying, snakes swimming, "lots" falling) thus seems to determine which response to relay to one's client ("The Babylonians and Hittites," 155–157).

[41] H. B. Huffmon, "Prophecy in the Mari Letters," *BA* 31 (1968) 122; E. Noort, *Untersuchungen zum Gottesbescheid in Mari,* AOAT 202 (Kevelaer: Butzon & Bercker, 1977) 83–86.

oracle or two on occasion,[42] and there is a recorded instance in which a number of *SAL.MEŠŠU.GI*, in conjunction with a cultic priestess named after the goddess Mezzulla, interpreted the movements of a snake swimming in a pool of water.[43] In all likelihood, however, divination of this type was not indigenous to Anatolia.[44]

Sorceress

The "old woman" eventually became the primary practitioner of "good" magic, the specialist expected by Anatolian audiences to confront the charms and spells of sorcerers, the practitioners of "evil" magic. Her basic responsibility here was to "unbind" what others had "bound" or might "bind" upon her client. Since the phenomenology of both types of magic is essentially the same,[45] however, situations arose where she found herself at war with other specialists who, from their perspective, also practiced "good" magic.[46]

At moments like these the "old woman" takes on, for all intents and purposes, the role of "sorceress." Thus we see her petitioning Ištar of Nineveh

[42] Vieyra, "Le sorcier hittite," 109. Uncertainty over the precise nature of the *MUŠEN.ḪURRI*-oracle has little or nothing to do with the functions of either the *SALŠU.GI* or the *LÚMUŠEN.DÙ*, since neither specialist was likely involved with it. Cf. the discussions in A. Kammenhuber (*Orakelpraxis*, 11); Haas & Wilhelm (*Hurritische und luwische Riten*, 50–58). For Mesopotamia, cf. J. Nougayrol ("'Oiseau' ou oiseau?" *RA* 61 [1967] 23–38).

[43] The *MUŠ*-oracle ("snake") is mentioned by Vieyra ("Le sorcier hittite," 109) and Kammenhuber (*Orakelpraxis*, 27–28 [n. 51]). Note also the "snake"-language of the "old woman" Allaituraḫ(ḫ)i in Haas & Thiel (*Allaituraḫ(ḫ)i* 140:21′: *MUŠ ŠA.TÙR*; 146:48: *MUŠ-ia*). The Hittite Code (ANET 195:170) forbids anyone from pronouncing someone's personal name while killing a snake, presumably a prohibition against sorcery.

[44] Cf. the interesting sketch on the history of snake-charming in Mesopotamia/Syria-Palestine by M. C. Astour ("Two Ugaritic Serpent Charms," *JNES* 27 [1968] 16–18). Echoes of this practice are found in TDP 8–10:19–30 and *šumma ālu* 21a, 22a & b. Note also the Neḥushtan, the bronze snake which stood in the Jerusalem temple until Hezekiah's reform (2 Kgs 18:4). Kammenhuber interprets the appearance of the *MUŠ*-oracle in Anatolia as one of the foreign, "exotic" divinatory practices encouraged during the reign of Hattušili III (*Orakelpraxis*, 27).

[45] Pointed out by Vieyra, "Le sorcier hittite," 106.

[46] In line with I. M. Lewis' thesis that the enfranchised classes habitually use witchcraft accusations in order to suppress the disenfranchised (*Ecstatic Religion: An Anthropological Study of Spirit Possession and Shamanism* [Baltimore: Penguin, 1971] 122), it is interesting to note that the *SALŠU.GI*, when cursing a foreign city (KUB VII 60—see below), does not operate as a disenfranchised subordinate, but as a tool of the state. For a parallel, M. Eliade notes that one of the shaman's most important functions is to defend "the psychic integrity of the community" ("Shamanism," *ER* XIII:206). See also his extensive discussion of "evil," "good," and "evil-good" shamans (*Shamanism: Archaic Techniques of Ecstasy* [New York: Pantheon, 1964] 184–189).

to turn her client's enemies into women and strike their wives barren.[47] In another instance, she commands the river gods to turn a sorcerer's spell back upon the sorcerer himself.[48]

One of the most famous of these curses (and most relevant to the present study) is the one launched against an enemy city in KUB VII 60.[49] In this ritual the "old woman" calls on the "gods of the foreign city" (*DINGIR^MEŠ URU^LIM LÚKÚR*) to abandon it: i.e., leave it vulnerable to demonic attack. She provokes their departure by preparing vessels of olive oil, honey, and beer alongside ceremonial fragments of red, white, and blue cloth. She burns incense and recites incantations while holding a tuft of sheep's wool, an eagle's feather, and other symbolic substances in her right hand:

> I have made a path for you out of
> white, red, and blue cloth.
> Now shall you enter into these cloths,
> and, (by) taking these paths,
> You shall turn yourselves to the king's
> welfare.
> Leave your lands . . . .[50]

This invocation is immediately sealed by sacrificing two sheep to the gods and goddesses of the foreign city.

Then the king dons his royal robes, pours out libations to these now-corralled foreign divinities, and calls on the Storm-god to destroy "the city which hates me."[51] The ritual concludes with a curse on anyone who tries to resettle the city, which is consecrated to *Šeri* and *Ḫurri* as eternal pastureland.[52]

The "Augur" (LÚMUŠEN.DÙ)

The Anatolian *LÚḪAL* could be responsible for offering birds (the *MUŠEN.ḪURRI*) to the gods, and the Mesopotamian *LÚḪAL* could "examine" the exterior skin and movements of birds,[53] but divination via the flight and

[47] Goetze, *Kleinasien,* 154, nt. 6.

[48] Vieyra, "Le sorcier hittite," 103–104.

[49] Transliteration and translation in Haas & Wilhelm, *Hurritische und luwische Riten,* 234–239.

[50] Ibid., 236:26–32.

[51] Ibid., 238:12′.

[52] Ibid., 238:23′–26′. *Šeri* and *Ḫurri* are the two steers of the Hattic storm-god.

[53] "Bird extispicy" may have been practiced in Mesopotamia, but the evidence is ambiguous (Nougayrol, "'Oiseau' ou oiseau?," 31–32; Gurney, "Babylonians and Hittites," 151, 153). The burnt offering of birds in Anatolia is treated in detail by Haas & Wilhelm (*Hurritische und luwische Riten,* 50–59, 137–143), who emphasize the appetite of Netherworld deities for "bird-flesh."

sounds of birds was most characteristic of Anatolia.[54] Augurs were regularly consulted over where to house the king for the winter,[55] how to appease departed spirits of the dead,[56] how to appease the wrath of angry gods,[57] how to interpret dreams,[58] how to counteract a sorcerer's curse,[59] how to predict a king's future,[60] how to predict the outcome of a crucial battle,[61] how to stop infection from spreading through an army,[62] and numerous other moments of crisis.

MUŠEN oracles could also function as a check on other types, like the *KIN* and *KUŠ* oracles. With regard to form, the *MUŠEN* omen texts usually preserve the standard protasis-apodosis omen format, but sometimes one finds simple collections of learned reflections on the behavior of birds minus the inquiries which customarily occasion them.[63]

The popularity of augury in Anatolia is further underlined by the fact that ornithomantic activity was conducted by two separate specialists, whereas in Mesopotamia it was subsumed in the work of the *bārû*.[64] One of these magico-religious specialists, the *LÚIGI.MUŠEN* ("the man who observes birds"), apparently enacted only the role of "diviner." The other augur, however (*LÚMUŠEN.DÙ* ["the man who 'makes/operates' birds"]), enacted at least two different roles: "purification-priest" and "diviner," though here again it is difficult to define precisely the parameters of these roles. His title implies that he

[54] A. Ünal, "Zum Status der 'Augures'." On the basis of an OB forerunner to the "bird" tablets of *šumma ālu,* D. Weisberg ("An Old Babylonian Forerunner to *šumma ālu,*" *HUCA* 40 [1969] 87–88) disputes A. L. Oppenheim's thesis that the West was the "*Kulturkreis* of augury" (*Ancient Mesopotamia,* 209), but there is no denying the cumulative evidence that augury was far more popular in the West.

[55] KUB XVIII 12+XXII 15 I 1-14, transliterated and translated by Ünal, "Zum Status der 'Augures,'" 43–44.

[56] Texts cited by Ünal, "Zum Status der 'Augures,'" 29; cf. Kammenhuber, *Orakelpraxis,* 11.

[57] Cf. Haas & Wilhelm, *Hurritische und luwische Riten,* 15, nt. 3.

[58] Texts cited by Ünal ("Zum Status der 'Augures,'" 29). Cf. the Hittite dreams translated by H. G. Güterbock in A. L. Oppenheim, *Dreambook,* 254–55.

[59] The ritual of Puppuwanni, a *LÚMUŠEN.DÙ* from Arzawa, is mentioned by Ünal ("Zum Status der 'Augures,'" 31).

[60] In one case, an *iparwašši*-bird is "set free" and the direction of its flight convinces the augur that rough times lay ahead for his royal client (texts cited by Ünal, "Zum Status der 'Augures,'" 29, 55). This "setting free" may have a parallel in Idr 28.

[61] E.g., whether the Assyrian king can be conquered in battle (Ünal, "Zum Status der 'Augures,'" 30).

[62] The ritual of Maddunani, an augur from Arzawa, begins: "If a plague breaks out in an army, and men, horses, oxen and sheep die . . ." (Ünal, 31).

[63] Ünal calls KUB XVIII 5 a "*Sammeltafel*" and notes that it contains surprisingly few Sumerograms (Ünal, 30).

[64] Cf., e.g., BBR 1-20:8. Cf. also the reference to *iṣṣur ḫurri* "in flocks" in Nougayrol ("'Oiseau' ou oiseau?" 36:9), a datum associated with the *bārû* that O. R. Gurney finds hard to deny to actual augury (*aves alites,* "Babylonians and Hittites," 153–154).

functioned as a "fowler" (Akk. *ušandû*), one who captured and/or bred birds, presumably for divinatory purposes. An extant royal letter exhorts him to scour far-off lands for new, exotic species.[65]

Both specialists operated in associations led by socially recognized leaders, though it is interesting to note that the Sumerograms employed to denote this leadership are different: *UGULA LÚIGI. MUŠEN* ("overseer of the augurs"; cf. the Roman *augur maximus*)[66]; *GAL LÚ.MEŠMUŠEN.DÙ* ("leader of the augurs").[67] Opinions are divided over whether the *LÚMUŠEN.DÙ*-augur was of Luwian or Hurrian origin.[68] Because ornithomantic activity cannot be attested prior to the reign of Muršili II, some even think that this practice, like so much of Anatolian religious culture, was originally imported from elsewhere, perhaps North Syria.[69]

Purification-Priest

As "purification-priest," the *LÚMUŠEN.DÙ*-augur usually performed in coordination with the "old woman" and other specialists.[70] He participates with her in at least one purification ritual involving the use of homeopathic images (clay and silver birds).[71] Another text indicates that his fee for this service was the substantial sum of twenty-five shekels.[72]

[65] KUB XXXI 101 is transliterated and translated in Ünal ("Zum Status der 'Augures,'" 49–51). The king exhorts his augur in lines 30′–35′: "Come, come here! As soon as you have traversed the River Maraššanda, shall [the birds all] be in order on the river. Take [the birds] to the River Azzi and keep a careful watch on all of them. [Do not say], 'Have pity! The river is much too difficult to cross!.'" Cf. further Kammenhuber, *Orakelpraxis,* 130–133.

[66] Ünal, 48.

[67] Ünal, 32.

[68] *Luwian:* Haas & Wilhelm, *Hurritische und luwische Riten,* 15; *Hurrian:* Ünal, "Zum Status der 'Augures,'" 33 (following Kammenhuber).

[69] Kammenhuber, *Orakelpraxis,* 10; Gurney, "Babylonians and Hittites," 155. On the tendency of Anatolian kings, particularly the sickly Tudḫaliya III, to be attracted to foreign magico-religious specialists, see Kammenhuber, *Orakelpraxis,* 138–139. Note also a Cypriot king's request for a *LÚša-i-li našrē* ("eagle-augur," EA 35:26), perhaps a Babylonian specialist "on loan" to Pharaoh.

[70] Ünal, "Zum Status der 'Augures,'" 29–30. The *LÚMUŠEN.DÙ* is seen working with the *SALŠU.GI,* the *LÚ.MEŠSANGA,* the *SALENSI,* and a rather mysterious group of male functionaries called the "men of the staff/rod" (*LÚ.MEŠGIŠ.PA*); cf. Haas & Wilhelm, *Hurritische und luwische Riten,* 15, nt. 3).

[71] KBo IV 2 is the ritual conducted by a *SALŠU.GI* and a *LÚMUŠEN.DÙ* named Ḫuwarlu against a "frightening bird" (*hatugauš; MUŠENḪI.A*); cf. Ünal, 31; Haas & Wilhelm, *Hurritische und luwischen Riten,* 15, nt. 3.

[72] Ünal, 48. Purification rituals were a perquisite of the wealthy as a general rule. Some could involve as many as 1200 birds (AT 126:17–25); cf. Goetze, *Kleinasien,* 160.

Diviner

As "diviner," the ^{LÚ}*MUŠEN.DÙ*-augur excelled in interpreting the future via the flight and sounds of birds, a role which tended to preempt his other role as "purification-priest." Rivers and streams were a popular place for augury, probably because of the ready availability of different species of birds there. A commonly-used barometer for measuring the extent of this activity is the rather extensive technical vocabulary which evolved among the Hittites to chronicle every nuance of bird behavior.[73] Of particular interest for this study are those recorded instances in which birds quarrelled or fought. One augur describes such an instance:

> An *alliya* bird came back up from behind the river flying low; and it settled in a poplar tree. While we watched it, another *alliya* bird attacked it from the vicinity.[74]

Other texts vividly describe how birds of prey "drag off" (Hit. *peda-*) their victims from the battlefield, "win victories" (*tarḫ-*), and "bring (their victims) close" (*uda-*) before the curious eyes of the augurs observing them. Since each activity was felt to correspond in a specific way to the future, the ^{LÚ}*MUŠEN.DÙ* could not afford to misinterpret them. An "inappropriate" interpretation could be fatal.[75]

MESOPOTAMIAN MAGICO-RELIGIOUS SPECIALISTS

There does not seem to be a specific term for "priest" in Akkadian, yet the appearance of so many separate terms for religious offices in OB non-literary texts testifies to the large number of magico-religious specialists operating in Mesopotamia from a very early time.[76] J. Renger has winnowed this number down considerably, to about 32 more or less well attested terms, which he further divides into three basic classes: *Kultpriester, Wahrsager,* and *Beschwörungspriester.*[77] As with the Anatolian specialists, little will be said here about the

[73] Much of this technical lexis is still unclear. Of some twenty-six different species of birds mentioned in the Bogazköy texts, Ünal notes that only the "eagle" (*Á*^{MUŠEN} = Hit. *ḫara[n]*) can be identified with certainty; cf. Ünal, 30, 35–42.

[74] KUB XVIII 5 II 1–4. Transliteration and translation in Ünal, 46–47; English translation in Gurney, "Babylonians and Hittites," 155.

[75] Cf., for example, KUB XXXI 101:24′–25′: "If (you) return without (doing this), you will 'go' to it ('pay for it?') with your heads" (fragment of a king's letter to his augur; cited in Ünal, 50).

[76] J. Renger, "Untersuchungen zum Priestertum in der altbabylonischen Zeit," *ZA* 58 (1967) 110.

[77] Ibid., 112. Some Sumerian exorcistic incantations are treated by A. Falkenstein, *Die Haupttypen der sumerischen Beschwörung,* LSS 1 (Leipzig: J. C. Hinrichs'sche, 1931). The

specifically cultic priests and priestesses, even though some of them, like the *kalû* and *zammāru*, sometimes participate in homeopathic rituals of various types, either alone or in conjunction with others.[78]

The "Exorcist" (āšipu)

While the role-sets of "exorcist" and "diviner/seer" are both enacted by the Anatolian "old woman," they are in principle enacted by separate specialists in Mesopotamia. As a general rule of thumb, "divination" is largely the responsibility of the *bārû*, while "exorcism" is handled by the *āšipu*, apparently with a minimal amount of role overlap, although the two role-sets are complementary.[79] Should a *bārû* learn by divination that a terrible evil was about to occur, the tendency was to call in an *āšipu* specialist to pronounce the appropriate apotropaic incantation (*namburbi*)[80] and/or perform the appropriate purification ritual to protect the client from harm. Although the evidence indicates that magico-religious functions were more highly specialized in Mesopotamia than Anatolia, this datum does not preclude the fact that there was a certain measure of fluidity and overlap between the roles enacted by these Mesopotamian specialists, particularly in areas far removed from the great cultic centers of Mesopotamia proper.[81]

---

earliest hitherto known incantations, those stemming from Fara (Tell Abū Ṣalābīḫ) and Ebla are treated by M. Krebernik, *Die Beschwörungen aus Fara und Ebla*, TSO 2 (Hildesheim/Zurich/New York: Georg Olms, 1984). Sumerian divination is generally introduced by Falkenstein in "'Wahrsagung' in der sumerischen Überlieferung," in *La divination in mésopotamie ancienne*, 45–68. I. Tzvi Abusch deals with the developmental levels of several representative incantations in *Babylonian Witchcraft Literature* (Brown Judaic Studies 132; Atlanta: Scholars Press, 1987).

[78] The *kalû*-priest, e.g., conducts a ritual to bring the Moon (*ᴰSin*) back from the "dead," even to the point of offering the usual *kispu* sacrifice. Cf. the phrase *k*]*i-is-pa ana A-nun-na-ki* in TuL 93:20 and the identical phrase in the ritual conducted by the *āšipu* in BBR 26 IV:43. The *zammāru*-singer conducts a ritual designed to free a "sinner" (*bēl ar-ni*) which shows a familiarity with the paraphernalia and principles of homeopathic magic usually associated with *āšipūtu* (TuL 88–90). Kibri-Dagan's neglect of the *kispu* sacrifice is communicated to him via a *muḫḫum* of Dagan in ARM III 40:16.

[79] Emphasized by E. Reiner ("La magie babylonienne," in *Le monde du sorcier*, 78). Cf. C. J. Gadd, "Some Babylonian Divinatory Methods, and their Inter-relations," in *La divination in mésopotamie ancienne*, 28. Renger documents at least one instance in which *āšipu/bārû* is used together as a composite epithet for the god Nininsina ("Untersuchungen zum Priestertum," 223).

[80] Examples are conveniently gathered in R. I. Caplice, *The Akkadian Namburbi Texts*, SANE 1/1 (Los Angeles: Undena, 1974). Over one hundred of these texts have been found (J. Nougayrol, "La divination babylonienne," in Caquot & Leibovici, *La divination*, 72).

[81] Noted by A. L. Oppenheim, *Ancient Mesopotamia*, 208.

The *āšipu* enacted a plurality of roles complementary to his primary role as "exorcist." Conveniently summed up in a "Manual for the Exorcist,"[82] the roles included at least the following: "exorcist," "purification-priest," "healer," and sometimes "sorcerer."

Exorcist

As "exorcist," the *āšipu* was responsible for the knowledge necessary to free clients from the binding power of a bewildering number of demons. The series *Maqlû,* an incantation series (among many) with which the *āšipu* was supposed to be familiar, lists some of these demons at the end of tablet I:[83]

I raise the torch,
I burn the images of the *útukku,*[84] the *šēdu,*[85]

[82] KAR 44; transliteration and translation in H. Zimmern, "Zu den 'Keilschrifttexten aus Assur religiösen Inhalts,'" *ZA* 30 (1915–1916) 206–213.

[83] Zimmern (n. 82) counts approx. 76 different incipits of incantations and incantation-series in KAR 44, most of them in Sumerian. A candidate for the office of *āšipu* had to learn (memorize?) all of them and probably others for which we have no written record. E. Reiner thus justifiably calls him "un erudit" (*La magie babylonienne,* 71).

On the demons generally, see E. Ebeling, "Dämonen," *RLA* II (1938) 107–113, and E. Unger, "Dämonenbilder," *RLA* II (1938) 113–115.

The following list of demons is from Maq I:136–138.

[84] Sum. loanword (*UDUG*); a demon often associated with the Netherworld, particularly with evil spirits of the dead. Cf. the very similar list in TuL 132:60–62 (VAT # 13657 iii). *Utukku* is the first name in both lists.

[85] *Šēdu* seems to be indigenously Semitic. It is the generic term for "daimon" (good or bad) in Akkadian, Aramaic and Hebrew and seems to be reflected in Syr *šdy* (Pael) and Arab. *sa'd* ("fortune"). For (late) Aram., cf. CAI 3:14; 7:17; 47:2; 48:1. For Heb., cf. Deut 32:17 & Psa 106:37, the only sure occurrences of "daimons" in the Bible. The Akk. word pair ^{D}*Šēdu//ilu* in AGH 40:47, however, finds persistent echo in Heb. *šdy//'lhym* (Job 5:17; 6:4; 8:3; 13:3; 22:17, 26; 27:10; 31:2, 35 *šdy//ryby*), usually in similar contexts of suffering or juridical decision. Note also Meier's translation "*Schutzgott*" for ^{D}*Šēdi* in Maq VIII:91.

F. M. Cross defines Heb *šadday* as "the mountain one" (*Canaanite Myth and Hebrew Epic* [Cambridge: Harvard, 1973] 55), but this etymology is disputed: cf. M. Weippert, "*šdy,*" *THAT* II:873–881; W. Wifall, "El Shaddai or El of the Fields," *ZAW* 92 (1980) 24–32; M. Görg, "Ehrenrettung einer Etymologie," *BN* 18 (1981) 13–15. The Weipperts tentatively rule out a comparison between *šdyn* in DAT I:6 and Akk. *šēdu* primarily on orthographic grounds (M. and H. Weippert, "Die 'Bileam' Inschrift von Tell Dēr 'Allā," 88), but, as W. R. Garr points out, arguments from orthography are precarious when dealing with mixed dialects like Arslan Tash or DAT. Garr holds to the possibility that both *šdyn* (DAT I:6) and *ilyn* (Arsl. Tash I:20) reflect a plural formation **iy(y)in* (*Dialect Geography of Syria-Palestine,* 96).

The Talmud distinguishes between licit and illicit magico-religious activity by calling *licit* activity *m'śh šdym* and *illicit* activity *m'śh kšpym* (cited by G. Vajda, "Israel et le judaïsme," dans *Le monde du sorcier,* 137).

the *rābiṣu*,[86] the *eṭimmu*,[87] the *lamaštu*,[88] the *labāṣu*,[89] the *aḫḫāzu*,[90] the *lilû*, the *lilītu*, the *ardat lilî*.[91]

Some of these demons are habitually present at major *rites de passage*, like those offered at birth and death. Others have names which are indistinguishable from the sicknesses they were supposed to cause. All are exorcized via magical formulae chanted in the name of the client's "protector god" (*ilu amēli*, "god of the man," BBR 26 IV:18) or in the name of the patron gods of exorcism, Ea and his son Asalluḫi.[92]

[86] One of the "Seven" (AHW 935), sometimes associated with Nergal as the "door-watcher" of the Netherworld (ANET 98:52, 60, 67, 74; cf. also Erra IV:17, *ra-bi-ṣu abulli-šu*, "watcher of his gate").

[87] Sum. loanword (*GIDIM*), one of the "Seven" (AHW 263); refers to the spirits of the departed dead in general or to a particular shade, like that of Yaḫdun-Lim (ARM III 40:16). Denizens of the Netherworld, they tremble at the presence of an intruder (ANET 97:21), even when the intruder eventually becomes one of them (ANET 99:152). Homeopathic images were made of them in efforts to release clients from their hold (*ṣalam eṭimmi*, TuL 138:5). The oracle against Egypt in Isa 19:3 also recognizes them (*'ṭym*). Cf. the "houses of the dead" (*É^{MEŠ} ŠA GIDIM$^{ḪI.A}$*) in HT 104:4, 7.

[88] A child-stealing monster in a woman's body, bare-breasted, having a lion's head, the talons of a bird for feet, and suckling a dog and piglet, Lamaštu's winged image has been found on several plaques of bronze and stone (Reiner, *La magie babylonienne*, 80). Cf. further W. Farber, "*lamaštu*," *RLA* VI (1980–1983) 439–446.

Incantations against Lamaštu were voiced very early in Mesopotamia (YOS XI 19, 20, 88, and 89) and at Ugarit; cf. J. Nougayrol, "La Lamaštu à Ugarit," *Ugaritica VI* (Paris: Geuthner, 1969) 393–408. Eventually an entire series was dedicated to her eradication; cf. D. Myhrman, "Die Labartu-Texte," *ZA* 16 (1902) 141–195. Parallels to winged demonic creatures from neighboring cultures are exhaustively cited by T. Gaster, "A Canaanite Magical Text," *Or* 11 (1942) 45–48.

N. B. the striking iconographic similarities between the flying creature at Arslan Tash (Comte du Mesnil du Buisson, "Une tablette magique de la région du Moyen Euphrate," in *Mélanges syriens offerts à M. René Dussaud* [Paris: Geuthner, 1939] I:422) and the flying creature found at Deir 'Allā (J. Hoftijzer and G. van der Kooij, *Aramaic Texts from Deir 'Allā*, pl. #15).

[89] See W. Farber, "*labāṣu*," *RLA* VI (1980–1983) 409–410. This term refers to a demon who apparently attacked the extremities of hands (Šur V/VI:124) and feet (TDP 144:46, reading *ana la-ba-aṣ* with von Soden, AHW 523).

[90] Cf. CAD *A*, 185–186. Besides the close association with *lamaštu* and *labaṣu*, *aḫḫāzu* is associated with the "earth" (Netherworld) in another interesting triad (Šur VII:5/6): waters of the deep (*apsû*) release the *dimītu* disease; the heavens unleash the "oath" (*māmītum*); the "earth" spews *aḫḫāzu* "like a weed." The whole seventh tablet of *Šurpu* describes the extent of this devastation and Marduk's incantations against it.

[91] On these three closely related spirits, most scholars draw a sharp etymological distinction between Semitic words for "night" and the Sum. origins of these demons (cf. G. Scholem, "Lilith," *EJ* 11:245–246; Gibson, SSI III:87), yet E. Porada notes a folk-etymological connection, "*lilû, lilûtu, ardat-lilî*," *RLA* VII/1-2 (1987) 23.

[92] Ea (Maq VIII:89); Asalluḫi (IV:8; *bīt rimki* 39:35); Marduk (Maq I:55); Gilgameš

Purification-Priest

As "purification-priest," the *āšipu* participated in rituals designed to complement these exorcistic incantations with activities saturated in homeopathic magic.[93] Often these rituals used homeopathic images "made" (*epēšu*) out of clay, wax, or loam, and/or "sketched" (*eṣēru*)[94] on plaster or fine flour. Alongside these inanimate images, the *āšipu* also used animate homeopathic substitutes, both animal and human.[95]

One of the most complex of these purification rituals is the series called *bît rimki* ("wash-house"). The ritual tablet for this series is partially preserved in BBR 26.[96] Though late, and attested only for neo-Assyrian kings, the *bît rimki* ritual in BBR 26 well illustrates the breadth of the *āšipu*'s role as "purification-priest" because in it most of the cleansing mechanisms, sacrificial animals, incantatory formulae, and patron deities seen elsewhere in isolation are brought together into one hybrid complex.

The ritual's beginning is partially lost, but from what remains we can ascertain that the *āšipu* priest, while reciting a preliminary incantation over the king's person, begins by "moaning" (*uš-ta-ni-iḫ*, BBR 26 I:11) in a manner not dissimilar to that of the *zammāru*-"singer" at the beginning of a temple renewal

(Maq I:38); cf. also Šamaš (Maq II:123); Gira (Maq II:104); Nusku (Maq II:1); Sin, Nergal, and Ištar (Maq II:193–195).

[93] It is very important to remember, with E. Reiner (*La magie babylonienne,* 78), that apotropaic purification from portended evil (*namburbi*) is just as much an exorcistic phenomenon as the casting out of a demon from a victim that has already been struck. Thus we should regard the charms, talismans, and protective amulets found all over the ancient Near East as exorcism by proxy, a form of "demon insurance." Often they preserve the same stereotypical phrases that we see the *āšipu* recite in the *Maqlû, Šurpu, Lamaštu,* and other incantation series. They were certainly less expensive to use (psychically and economically) than the actual services of an exorcist.

[94] Cf. *GUL-ša* in HT 66:23. *Epēšu* and *eṣēru* are found together in BBR 53. The *āšipu* is responsible for "building images" (*ṣalmē ma-la tēpušu,* 53:7); Nergal's image is "sketched on the wall" (*ṣalam ᴰLugal-gir-ra ša ina igari eṣ-ru,* 53:12); "seven winged images are sketched at the front of the sanctuary" (*VII ṣalmē šu-ut kap-pa ša ina rēš kummi eṣ-ru,* 53:16); these "seven winged images" refer to the Sibitti themselves (54rev:10). The drawing of images on plaster was common in Mesopotamia (E. Reiner, *La magie babylonienne,* 95).

[95] When asked by the gods how to conduct the *āšipu* ritual, a practitioner offers a stereotypical reply by alluding to the stuffing of a sheepskin with aromatic plants, a practice often repeated in Mesopotamian death rituals (TuL 17:18–27; cf. esp. TuL 74–75). Homeopathic substitution of one human being for another is attested only for kings; cf. H. M. Kümmel, *Ersatzrituale für den hethitischen König,* SBT 3 (Wiesbaden: Harrassowitz, 1967) 169–187. As in comparable Anatolian ritual, the "Descent of Ištar/Šaušga" myth-complex is the backdrop against which many of these death rituals are often set (ANET 108; Reiner, *La magie babylonienne,* 90–91).

[96] J. Laessøe, *Studies on the Assyrian Ritual and Series bît rimki* (Copenhagen: Munksgaard, 1955). Cf. reviews of Laessøe by W. G. Lambert, *Bibliotheca Orientalis* 14 (1957) 227–230, and E. Reiner, *JNES* 17 (1958) 204–207.

ritual elsewhere (Racc 44:5, *in-ḫa in-ni-iḫ*). The goal of *bît rimki* is clearly stated on the first tablet: to purify the king (*šarra tu-kap-par,* BBR 26 I:19).

Then we are introduced to the traditional cleansing agents for purifying the temple: the exorcist's "rod" (*ḫultuppû*),[97] "torch" (*gizillû*),[98] "living sheep," "hard copper," "flesh of the great bull," and "barley seed." The exact function of many of these cleansing agents is difficult to ascertain.

Next, seven tables covered with foodstuffs are prepared for consumption by the soon-to-arrive Sibitti. Upon these tables the *āšipu* sets out various kinds of bread, dates, flour, honey, oil, butter, milk, and sweet drinks. Seven incense stands are set up and seven goblets are filled with wine. Column I breaks off here and about 40 lines are missing, but since the material in II:10–17 is likely repetitive, the *āšipu* probably continues his preparations here, setting out seven goblets with strong drink, filling the incense stands with the appropriate aromatic plants, and sprinkling sesam-wine.

Column II picks up after the lacuna with the slaughtering of a he-goat. After repeating the other preparatory activities just mentioned, a ram[99] is also slaughtered. The text describes this purificatory sacrifice in language echoing that found in conventional *bārû* ritual.[100]

The incipit of the first major incantation is in Sumerian and directed to the Sibitti, "O mighty mountain storm, coming from the steppelands . . ." (BBR 26 II:22). A mixture of honey and butter is sprinkled "to the four winds" while the *āšipu* continues chanting.

After completing this invocation, the *āšipu* and his client (the king) leave the temple courtyard to prepare for the *bît rimki* ceremony proper, but not without first magically sealing off the king's "house" (the palace). Exiting through the "door to the outside" (*bābu kamû*),[101] the priest lights "pyres" (*abrū*)[102] on the right and the left of this door, apparently to guard it from

[97] On *ḫultuppû*, cf. CAD Ḫ 231. The "rod" of the *āšipu* is linked in BBR 27 II:12 with *DKUŠ*, the "skin" (cf. the *KUŠ* oracle in Anatolia). The *GIŠlamû* branch is clothed in *KUŠ* in the Akk. death ritual found in TuL 75:20. Cf. the "grapevine" (*GIŠGAPANU*) in HT 32:10–14, clothed in linen cloths and "lowered" onto the "dish of the dead" (*GIŠBANŠUR*). One of the *āšipu*'s titles was "the man with the magic wand" (Reiner, *La magie babylonienne,* 72).

[98] On *gizillû,* cf. CAD *G* 113–115. The "torch" is deified in Šur I:5. The "raising of the torch" is a climactic moment in the burning of homeopathic images (Maq I:135).

[99] Lit., "male sheep (for) the sacrifice" in BBR 26 II:18, 25 (restoring [*IMMER*].*NITA*$_2$ in line 25).

[100] "A right thigh-portion, fatty flesh, cooked flesh" (BBR 26 II:18–19; cf. BBR 1–20:52, 83, 86, passim).

[101] Cf. CAD *K,* 127.

[102] Cf. the *ukturi* in HT 66:1. In a ritual to Sin, an *āšipu* places a lamb, 7 containers of liquid, and 7 loaves of bread on the *abru,* then burns it all as a sacrifice to *DSin* as leader of the Annunaki (AGH 18:14; 20:27). Elsewhere a *kalû* offers a sheep sacrifice to Ea and Marduk on the *abru* (Racc 40:4–5). A bull is sacrificed on the *abru* in Racc 120:6, 13, 16, 22, 25.

possible contamination from the occult events which are about to transpire. Using
a second technique to purify the door, he then kills a ram, smears its blood over
the door, and begs the Sibitti to accept it as a sacrifice: "Accept (it), O
Sibitti . . . accept (it)!" (BBR 26 II:28–29).

The doorway having thus been prophylactically sealed, the *āšipu* begins
constructing the "wash-house" needed to purify the king as well as the "cultic-
huts" (*urigallū*)[103] needed to house the Sibitti when they arrive. Afterwards,
additional preparations are made for sacrifices to Ea, Šamaš, Marduk, and the
king's protective god, Assur (BBR 26 VI:64).

With line 34 of Column IV we take note that all of these preparations occur
at night, because Šamaš' appearance (dawn) is to be the signal for the *āšipu* to
light the censers and usher the king into the *bît rimki*. BBR 26 is corrupt at this
point. According to Laessøe, the so-called "Šamaš cycle" should be inserted
here.[104] In this independent cycle, the king enters a "house" (probably a chamber
within the *bît rimki*) and the *āšipu* recites a prayer (*KI.DUTU.KAM*). The king
responds with an incantation (*šiptu*), washes his hands in a purifying act, and
exits to go into the next chamber of the *bît rimki*. An antiphonal pattern thus
develops in which the *āšipu* and the king proceed through the ritual until the king
has gone through all seven "houses."[105]

Finally, the *āšipu* offers *kispu* to the Annunaki (BBR 26 IV:43). At Mari,
kispu designates the foodstuffs presented during the new moon festival to the
spirits of dead kings (ARM III 40:16–18; IX, pp. 283–286). In later texts,
however, the phrase *kispa kasāpu* comes to denote the offering of food to Netherworld shades in general and the Annunaki in particular (cf. CAD K 426–427).
Parallels to this funerary feast are found in the *šalliš waštaiš* ritual in Anatolia
and the NW Semitic institution of *mrzḥ*[106]

---

[103] BBR 26 III:24; IV:50; BBR 31–37 II:8. Note the important role of the *urigallu* as a
homeopathic image of the Netherworld in TuL 118:20. Two *urigallū* appear again on the
right and left of the *abru* in Racc 120:26. Even as *urigallū* can be sketched (*eṣēru*) on the
walls of sanctuaries in Mesopotamia (BBR 53:14, in connection with the "winged Sibitti"),
the hero Ilḫu instructs Thitmanat to save Kirta's life in the Ugaritic Kirta myth by "constructing a grave (-hut?)" (KTU 1.16 II 25, *qbr tṣr*). This "grave" comes complete with a
"gate" (KTU 1.16 II 27, *ṯġr*), just like the gates on the *urigallu* in Mesopotamia (cf. *š'ry*
š'wl in Isa 38:10). Homeopathic burial may also be alluded to at Pyrgi (KAI 277:8–9, *qbr*
'lm); cf. KTU 1.6 I 17–18, *bḥrt ilm arṣ*. Note also the "lowering" (*niālu*) of images in
āšipūtu ritual (TDP 176:3; TuL 67b:3; 134:15; 149:28; note also BWL 42:69).

[104] Laessøe, *bît rimki*, 83–89.

[105] Ibid., 28–83. Cf. W. Mayer, *Untersuchungen zur Formensprache der babylonischen
"Gebetsbeschwörungen,"* 31–32 (esp. n. 63); R. Borger, "Das dritte 'Haus' der Serie *bît
rimki*," JCS 21 (1967) 1–17.

[106] In *šalliš waštaiš*, food is offered to several chthonic deities as well as the "soul" of
the dead king (cf. HT 28:16–22). Both *šalliš waštaiš* and *mrzḥ* focus on a cultic meal in
which both the "dead" and the "living" participate. Cf. M. Pope, *Song of Songs*, AB 7C
(Garden City, NY: Doubleday, 1977) 225–226. See also O. Eissfeldt, "Etymologische und
archäologische Erklärung alttestamentliche Wörter," in *Kleine Schriften* IV (Tübingen:

Healer

As "healer," the *āšipu* (along with the *asû*- physician)[107] enacted a role which, while comparable to "exorcist," is nevertheless distinguishable. Complementary sub-roles of "diagnostician" and "prognostician" developed over time. As "diagnostician," the *āšipu* manifested an intense curiosity about the diseases and abnormalities afflicting the human body, patiently recording his observations for later generations. While stylistically distinct from those of the *asû*-physician, these diagnoses were eventually collated into at least one standard handbook.[108] In this handbook, consisting of some forty tablets, we see hundreds of traditional diagnoses arranged by sections. One section, for example, is arranged according to the parts of the body; another according to the specific ailments of pregnant women and infants.[109]

As "diagnostician," the *āšipu* first had to decide whether the illness was of natural or supernatural origin. If (after consulting the appropriate handbooks) the diagnosis fell in the latter category, he then had to decide whether it was of divine or purely demonic origin.[110] As "prognostician," the *āšipu* had to face the risky task of predicting his client's fate.[111] Technical terms in these prognoses express the nuances between, say, an illness leading to death, or any number of less serious outcomes.[112] Of the two major outcomes, "life" is predicted 176 times

---

Mohr/Siebeck, 1968) 286–296; and B. Porten, *Archives from Elephantine* (Berkeley: Univ. of California, 1968) 179–186.

On *kispu*, cf. Akio Tsukimoto, *Untersuchungen zur Totenpflege (kispum) im alten Mesopotamien*, AOAT 216 (Kevelaer: Butzon & Bercker, 1985).

[107] *LÚA.ZU*. This specialist can be found as early as the Ur III period in Mesopotamia. He is mentioned at Mari in ARM II 127:9, 12; V 32:8. On one occasion Hattušili III invited Babylonian *LÚ.MEŠA.ZU* and *āšipu*-exorcists to Hattuša for consultation. One of these *LÚ.MEŠA.ZU* was imprisoned and killed for unknown reasons (presumably by Hattušili III; the text is KBo I 10:32′–48′, cited in Kammenhuber, *Orakelpraxis*, 139). Cf. further E. K. Ritter, "Magical Expert (=*āšipu*) and Physician (=*asû*): Notes on Two Complementary Professions in Babylonian Medicine," in *Studies Presented to Benno Landsberger on his 65th Birthday*, AS 16 (Chicago: University of Chicago, 1965) 299–321.

[108] R. Labat, *Traité akkadien de diagnostics et pronostics médicaux* (Leiden: Brill, 1951). The incipit for this series begins "When the exorcist (*āšipu*) goes to the house of a sick person . . ." (TDP 2:1).

[109] Parts of the body: TDP 18–146 (tablets III–XIV); pregnant women and children: TDP 200–230 (tablets XXXV–XL).

[110] See Labat's "Introduction," TDP, xxi.

[111] The Babylonian *LÚA.ZU* mentioned in the letter of Hattušili III (KBo I 10:32′–48′, cited in Kammenhuber, *Orakelpraxis*, 139) may have been executed for offering an "unacceptable" prognosis.

[112] For example, if a baby suffers from inflamed hands and feet accompanied by a vacant stare, or if the tip of a man's nose is hot and cold, or if his upper abdomen is hot and cold, this could be attributed to the "wand" (*ḫaṭṭu*) of a particular god (TDP 224:56;

while "death" appears 423 times.[113] In other words, the sufferer's prognosis was usually gloomy.

Sorcerer

As "sorcerer," the *āšipu* could at times turn the same rituals and curses invoked by the feared practitioners of "evil" magic back onto them, like the "old woman" in Anatolia. Unlike the Anatolian languages, Akkadian has a specific word for "sorcerer/ess": *kaššāpu/kaššaptu.* Several ancient Near Eastern lawcodes legislated harsh penalties against anyone caught engaging in sorcery. According to the Assyrian lawcode, anyone caught engaging in it could be put to death.[114] According to Hammurapi's lawcode, anyone caught even falsely accusing someone of sorcery could be put to death.[115] Unfortunately, there are no extant literary remains of the sorcerers' chants and curses for us to examine, since to collect such material was forbidden. From the exorcistic incantations designed to "undo" their oaths, curses, and hexes, however, a fairly extensive picture of his/her activity can be drawn.

The *kaššāpu* and *kaššaptu* rob young men of their strength and young women of their children (Maq III:8–9). They drive wedges between people and their protective deities, thus leaving them vulnerable to demonic attack (III:16). They invade houses and block a person's path with their curses (III:2, 15). The *kaššāpu/tu* holds "evil words" in his/her heart (III:90). They catch the unsuspecting and ignorant like birds in a snare (III:161). They tie people into knots with their charms and hexes (IV:72). They masquerade as colleagues or comrades, relatives or friends, fellow citizens or foreigners, depending on which roles best serve their malevolent desires (IV:77–79).

As "colleagues," they even disguise themselves as legitimate *āšipu* exorcists, making it difficult to tell one from the other. Some *āšipū* deemed this enough of a problem, in fact, to expend considerable energy differentiating between the two. Each line of Maq IV:117–130, for example, ends with the same phrase:

> So-and-so is a *kaššaptu,* but I am a *pāširu.*

The latter term may indicate, therefore, that a primary function, perhaps even a recognized "title" for the *āšipu* exorcist was "the Unbinder/Releaser."[116]

56:23; 112:29). Cf. the *ḥṭ* of *š'tqt,* El's emissary, which she uses to heal Kirta from his illness (KTU 1.16 VI 8). Perhaps the *ḫultuppû* of the *āšipu* exorcist (BBR 26 I:20) is a parallel. Other terms are listed by Labat (TDP, xxi–xxii).

[113] Ibid., xxviii–xxx.

[114] Assyrian Laws, para. A 47 (ANET 184).

[115] Code of Hammurapi para. 2 (ANET 166). Similar prohibitions are found in Lev 20:27 (against *'wb* and *yd'ny*) and Deut 18:10–11 (against *mkšpym* and *ḥbrym*). For a discussion, see I. Tzvi Abusch, *Babylonian Witchcraft Literature,* 134, n. 99.

[116] Both von Soden (AHW 844–845) and Meier (Maq IV:117–130) translate *pāširu* with

The *āšipu*'s usual purification methods involved the use of homeopathic images, the recitation of the appropriate incantations, the use of various "bathing" rituals, or some combination of these techniques, but like the Anatolian "old woman," the Mesopotamian *āšipu* (and/or his client) also "cursed" enemies directly. The *āšipu* as "sorcerer" can wish aloud, for example, that the Seven Wise Men of Eridu[117] "plan evil" against the *kaššaptu* sorceress (Maq II:124), or that the *šēdu*-demons (*^{D}Šēdê^{MEŠ}*) "seek" after her (II:210). Washing his hands over an image of a sorceress in the second "house" of the *bît rimki,* the king asks Šamaš to turn her "impurity" (*aršu*) back upon her; i.e., to see to it that the evil washed out of his body "drown" her just as the water "drowns" her clay image. The king as client can even wish her dead by means of a bipolar formula similar to that found in Num 24:9/Gen 27:29:

> May she die, and may I live![118]

In sum, even though there are rather well-defined social distinctions between sorcerers and exorcists in Mesopotamia and Anatolia, this does not preclude the fact that magico-religious specialists in both cultures occasionally enact the *role* of "sorcerer" as they attempt by every means at their disposal to defend their clients from harm. In societies (like ancient Anatolia) where the distinction between "evil" and "good" magic is blurred, or where *all* magic is officially relegated to the category of "evil" magic (like Israel), distinguishing between these phenomenologically congruent roles is largely a matter of determining a given audience's role expectations at a given time and place.

The "Diviner/(Seer)" (bārû)

Several Sum. logograms can be translated by the Akk. term *bārû,*[119] a linguistic clue which may indicate this specialist's plurality of roles. In Old Babylonian, *MAŠ.ŠU.GÍD.GÍD* is the primary Sumerogram attested for *bārû,*[120] emphasizing his role as technical extispicist. The designation *^{LÚ}ḪAL* (lit., "the man who decides"), however, came to be the most popular designation for *bārû* in the neo-Assyrian texts.[121]

---

the term "*Löser.*" Both "semasiological dimensions" of *pašāru* are discussed at length by Oppenheim (*Dreambook,* 217–220, 302), who emphasizes that "to tell/interpret a dream" (*pašāru*) is clearly linked to the desire to "release" the dreamer from the dream's evil consequences, by, e.g., transferring its evil to a lump of clay, which is then "dissolved" (*napšuru*) by throwing it into a river.

[117] Sculpted wooden images of the "seven sages" have been found buried in the corners of houses as talismans (Reiner, *La magie babylonienne,* 95–96).

[118] *bît rimki* 39–40:32–47.

[119] CAD *B,* 121; AHW 109; Zimmern, BBR, 86–87; Falkenstein, "Wahrsagung," 45, 51–52; Renger, "Untersuchungen zum Priestertum," 203–204.

[120] Cf. CAD *B,* 121–125.

[121] Zimmern, BBR, 86.

Over the course of time, this uniquely Mesopotamian specialist enacted a wide variety of roles. At least the following are of major import to this study: technical "diviner/seer," the basic role, but also "dream-interpreter," and "reciter of oracles/prayers." In these roles the *bārû* commonly acted as "government adviser."

Diviner

As "diviner," the *bārû*[122] inspected varia as a guide to the future, but by far the most important of these was extispicy. The extispicist could be disqualified by certain blemishes,[123] had to master a technical vocabulary,[124] had to be thoroughly conversant with the appropriate *bārûtu* handbooks, (and therefore have learned scribal skills),[125] and had to be adept at "reading" messages (especially from Šamaš and Adad) in the entrails of animals.[126] Clay liver models, which testify to this activity, have been found as far afield as Mari, Ugarit, Megiddo, Hazor, and Ebla.[127] Even though the *bārû* engaged in other forms of divination, extispicy remained the most "scientific" and was often employed as a check on the others.[128]

This procedure, however, was so expensive that only kings and nobles could afford it. Very early in Mesopotamia other divinatory procedures were employed alongside extispicy, perhaps initially as "poor man" substitutes.[129] Lecanomancy ("oil divination") was primarily a technique of pouring oil or flour into water in order to read its shapes and patterns:

[122] The Akk. noun *bārû* is derived from the verb *bārû* which means "to look upon, to keep an eye on, to watch over, to inspect, to observe" (CAD *B*, 115). This root function helps to define the *bārû*'s essential role-set (cf. Renger, "Untersuchungen zum Priestertum," 204).

[123] "A person with defective eyes, or with a maimed finger shall not draw near to the place for deciding via *bārûtu*" (BBR 1–20:5–6).

[124] Cf. the lists of terms collected by M. I. Hussey ("Anatomical Nomenclature in an Akkadian Omen Text," *JCS* 2 [1948] 21–32), A. Goetze (YOS X, 5–11), and I. Starr (*The Rituals of the Diviner*, 142–145).

[125] *Bārûtu* is a neo-Assyrian collection composed of ten chapters, each containing approx. a dozen 100-omen tablets (no less than 10,000 sentences), arranged in part according to the parts of a sheep's anatomy (esp. the liver). Cf. Nougayrol, "La divination babylonienne," 40–41.

[126] "Šamaš, lord of judgment; Adad, lord of extispicy-rituals (*ik-ri-bi*) and divination (*bi-ri-im*) . . . Invite (*qí-ri*) the gods by means of (cedar) resin . . . In the lamb I am offering place a true verdict (*ki-it-tam*) . . . O Šamaš, you have opened the locks of the gates of heaven (*sí-ik-ku-ri da-la-at ša-me-e*) . . . you judge the case of the great gods (*di-in i-li ra-bu-tim*) (HSM 7494:1–11, cited from I. Starr, *Rituals of the Diviner*, 30, 37).

[127] Gurney, "Babylonians and Hittites," 150.

[128] Nougayrol, "La divination babylonienne," 38.

[129] Gurney, "Babylonians and Hittites," 153.

If the oil divides into two; for a campaign, the two camps will advance against each other; for treating a sick man, he will die.
If the flour, in the east, takes the shape of a lion's face: the man is in the grip of a ghost of one who lies in the open country; the sun will consign it (the ghost) to the wind and he will get well.[130]

Libanomancy ("smoke divination") was the practice of throwing cedar shavings onto a censer in order to observe the patterns and direction of the smoke. For example:

If the smoke bunches toward the east and disperses toward the thighs of the *bārû*, you will prevail over your enemy.
If the smoke moves to the right, not the left, you will prevail over your enemy. If it moves to the left, not the right, your enemy will prevail over you.[131]

The *bārû* also used birds for divination purposes, but the texts are ambiguous regarding specific techniques. The *bārû* could read messages from the gods in the blemishes and unusual colorations of birds' skins (as well as sheep),[132] but there is little hard evidence for actual augury of the Anatolian variety (i.e., by the flight and sound of birds).[133] The *dāgil iṣṣūrī* ("observer of birds"), however, is mentioned in late Assyrian texts[134] as an augur resembling the *LÚMUŠEN.DÙ* type in Anatolia, and the omen series *šumma ālu* gives several examples of genuinely ornithomantic behavior. Like the Anatolian omens, many of these

[130] Ibid., 152. G. Pettinato posits the existence of three different "*Schulen*" of oil-divination, two in the South and one in the North ("Zur Überlieferungsgeschichtliche der aB-Ölomentexte," in *La divination in mésopotamie ancienne,* 105). As lecanomantics, *bārū* had to find out whether an enemy (*nakri*) could be fended off, whether a city could be "seized" (*ṣa-bat*), or whether a "curse" (*arrati*) could be formulated, presumably for pronouncement by an *āšipu* enacting a "sorcerer's" role (BBR 79–82:21–22).

[131] Gurney, "Babylonians and Hittites," 152–153.

[132] "If the head of a bird is entirely dark down to the neck, there will be an eclipse this year . . . . If the back of a bird's skull is pierced, the population of a village will communicate with its enemy . . . . If the head of a bird is uniformly dark, carrying a red spot, the prince's servants will give him evil counsel" (Nougayrol, "'Oiseau' ou oiseau?" 23:7–16).

[133] In the Mosaic code, the poor man who cannot afford a sheep can offer a dove as a burnt offering (Lev 5:7; 12:8; 14:21). In Mesopotamia, the nobleman (*rubû*) can also burn the dove (BBR 60:30–31). See the discussion in Haas & Wilhelm (*Hurritische und luwische Riten,* 139–142). Nougayrol only goes so far as to say that before the neo-Assyrian period it was not deemed necessary to draw any sharp distinctions between the different "observers of birds" in Mesopotamia. All bird activity, divinatory and otherwise, was eventually incorporated into *bārûtu* ("'Oiseau' ou oiseau?" 32).

[134] Nougayrol, "'Oiseau' ou oiseau?" 31–32; AHW 150, *LÚdāgil iṣṣurMEŠ*. Note also an early Akkadian ritual for snaring a raven (*UGAMUŠEN*) in YOS XI 69:7′: "Connect three pegs [. . .] with a thread of wool: it (will be) caught."

also focus on the consequences of "unusual" or "violent" activity, as, for example, when a smaller bird conquers a larger bird:

> If a falcon and a raven struggle with each other, and the raven kills the falcon, the enemy's weapon will prevail over that of the king.[135]

Violent screeching and cawing portended a grim future:

> If a falcon and a raven screech, croak, and caw to each other, the land will be turned into a fortress.[136]

An OB forerunner to *šumma ālu* predicted dire results if fledglings of one species were attacked by predators of another:

> If a falcon removes a captured fledgling from a partridge's nest in the wall of a man's house, . . . his house will be scattered.[137]

Apparently augury was practiced in Mesopotamia by specialists called "bird observers," but it is still rather an open question whether or how much the *bārû* actually participated in it.

Dream-Interpreter

The *šā'ilu* functioned as the primary interpreter of dreams in Mesopotamia.[138] Nevertheless, *bārû* and *šā'ilu* are often mentioned together in lists, and the work of *bārûtu* specifically includes "dream-interpretation" in at least one Assyrian letter:

> *ba-ru-tum ip-pu-šu šu-na-ti i-ta-nam-ma-r*[*u*]
> He performs the *bārûtu*, he experiences dreams.[139]

Šabrû and *maḫḫû* specialists could also receive revelations from the gods by means of dreams.[140] Oppenheim believes that even though the *bārû* participated in this type of divination, specialists in it usually came from a lower social position in the religious hierarchy.[141]

[135] *šumma ālu* 79:36, cited from F. Nötscher, *Or* (old series) 51–54 (1930) 170.

[136] *šumma ālu* 79:34, cited from F. Nötscher, 170.

[137] D. B. Weisberg, "An Old Babylonian Forerunner to *šumma ālu*," *HUCA* 40 (1969) 91.

[138] Oppenheim, *Dreambook*, 221–225; Renger, "Untersuchungen zum Priestertum," 217–218.

[139] The text of this letter from Ninurta-nâdin-šumatiš to Mutakkil-nuska is broken, so it is difficult to tell whether the writer parallels *bārûtu* with *šunātu* or simply lists both alongside other functions, now missing in the lacunae; see E. F. Weidner, "Aus den Tagen eines assyrischen Schattenkönigs," *AfO* 10 (1935–1936) 5:9.

[140] For example, Assurbanipal Cylinder B V:50 (^{LÚ}*šab-ru-u*, cited in AHW 1120); Esarhaddon Inscription 2 ii 12 (*maḫḫu*, cited in CAD *M* I, 90).

[141] Oppenheim, *Dreambook*, 221.

Oracle/Prayer Reciter

In the *bārû* specialist we see the petition-response dynamic very clearly: the priest "petitions" (*ša'ālu*) the deity by means of simple or elaborate prayer-rituals. The deity then "answers" (*apālu*) by writing his answer in the entrails of an animal, the movement of oil on water, the behavior of birds, the movement of smoke, directly through a dream, or by the positions of the heavens.

As "prayer-reciter," the *bārû* followed a conventional liturgical format. J. A. Knudtzon has analyzed some 154 of these prayers, all addressed to Šamaš, and has sketched an "ideal" pattern of six segments, although few prayers actually include all of these elements.[142] They are: (1) an opening prayer of access; (2) a petition for a specific case; (3) prayers petitioning Šamaš to "overlook" (*ízib*) certain impurities affecting the sacrificial animal, the client, or the *bārû* himself; (4) another petition for a specific case; (5) a concluding prayer; and (6) an optional appendix in which the omens (Šamaš' response) are recorded on the tablet.

As "oracle-reciter," the *bārû*, like the *āšipu*, could face the pleasant task of communicating favorable responses, the unpleasant task of relaying unfavorable responses, or he could equivocate and ask for another reading until he received an "appropriate" response.[143] Unlike the "prophet," whom we define here (with Weber) as the primary social functionary responsible for engineering breakthroughs against *status quo* religions,[144] *bārû* specialists normally served as the conservative champions of the *status quo* in Mesopotamia, often even the direct tools of the state for reinforcing it.[145]

Although the problem of intrarole conflict could conceivably arise with the *bārû* as well as with the *āšipu* and *SALŠU.GI* specialists, the likelihood that this could be a problem probably diminished proportionately as the *bārû*'s "extispicist" role gradually preempted all others in his "diviner/(seer)" role-set. While the *bārû* can be found working alongside other specialists when enacting his more subjective roles as "prayer-reciter" and/or "dream-interpreter," the role of "extispicist" generally pointed in a better established direction.[146] Dreams and

[142] J. A. Knudtzon, *Assyrische Gebete an den Sonnengott*, vol. 2 (Leipzig: E. Pfeiffer, 1893) 7–62. See the summary by J. Aro, "Remarks on the Practice of Extispicy in the Time of Esarhaddon and Assurbanipal," in *La divination en mésopotamie*, 109–117.

[143] "My liver oracles (?) are confused, the pronouncement is very difficult, hard to ascertain; investigating the future (*arkâtu*) is far from me" (text cited from CAD *B*, 122). Cf. Nougayrol, "La divination babylonienne," 32. Prayers for forgiveness for "improperly" handling the *tamītu*-word can also include petitions regarding the "frightening nocturnal visions" which sometimes accompany it (AGS 18:7′; 60:7′; 98:3′–4′; 145:4′–5′). The combination "word"+"nocturnal vision" also occurs in Num 22:8–20.

[144] Weber, *Sociology of Religion*, 46–59.

[145] Emphasized by Nougayrol, "La divination babylonienne," 39.

[146] Emphasized by Finet, "La place du devin dans la société de Mari," in *La divination en mésopotamie*, 87.

exta are interpreted on the bases of established scholarly literature. Technical liver readings derive from "empirical" data and therefore are perhaps less open to manipulation than "subjective" personal visions or dreams.[147]

SYRO-PALESTINIAN MAGICO-RELIGIOUS SPECIALISTS

A great abundance of material exists to document the existence, plurality, and complexity of the roles enacted by Anatolian and Mesopotamian magico-religious specialists. The evidence is much more uneven for Syria-Palestine. The sources from Anatolia and Mesopotamia often conserve incantations, oracles, and even the accompanying praxis *in context*. Further, this material was often revered as mysteriously occult over unusually extended periods of time.[148]

Such is usually not the case in Syria-Palestine. Magico-religious specialists cited in the inscriptional evidence are often mentioned simply by title. Seldom is attention paid to phenomenological detail when describing their magico-religious roles, nor can the accompanying ritual-complexes be readily reconstructed. Often just the opposite is the case. Many of the ancient practices mentioned in the Hebrew Bible, for example, have been thoroughly edited and re-edited by tradents quite hostile to magico-religious practices as a matter of religious principle.[149] We do find one clear case of necromantic inquiry in the

[147] Mari and Babylon each had *bārû*-priests enacting overt military roles as the two kingdoms squared off to meet each other in battle (ARM II 22:24–25). Assurnaṣirpal reports the capture of a *LÚḪAL* with the rebels of the land of Suḫi, who trusted in Kassite aid.

[148] The tendency was to preserve the *ipsissima verba* of the incantation's original forms and language (like Sumerian and Hurrian), even when these incantations were no longer completely understood, in order to unlock occult power via precise magical formulae. Noting this tendency, F. M. Cross and R. J. Saley marvel at the "fantastic conservatism of magical themes" at Arslan Tash; cf. "Phoenician Incantations on a Plaque of the Seventh Century B.C. from Arslan Tash in Upper Syria," *BASOR* 197 (1970) 47.

Note, for example, the phrase "the house I enter, you shall not enter" in YOS XI, 92:28–29 and Arslan Tash I:5–6. Since magico-religious praxes and formulae change little over extended periods of time, diachronic analyses are thus of limited value when studying the roles enacted by these magico-religious specialists. For general discussions, see J. G. Frazer, *The Golden Bough* (New York: MacMillan, 1963, abridged edition) 56–69, and H. Koester, *Introduction to the New Testament, vol. I: History, Culture, and Religion of the Hellenistic Age* (Philadelphia: Fortress, 1982) 379–381.

Greek and Jewish incantations from the Christian era preserve epithets as old as the third millennium; cf. Hans Dieter Betz, ed., *The Greek Magical Papyri in Translation, Including the Demotic Spells*, vol. I (Chicago: Univ. of Chicago, 1986); K. Preisendanz, *Papyri Graecae Magicae: Die Griechischen Zauberpapyri*, 2nd ed. (Stuttgart: Teubner, 1973–74); C. D. Isbell, *Corpus of the Aramaic Incantation Bowls*, SBLDS 17 (Missoula: Scholars, 1975).

[149] A. Caquot, "La divination dans l'ancien Israël," in Caquot & Leibovici, *La divination*, 83.

Bible (1 Sam 28:6–19), whereas the practice of extispicy, the queen of the divinatory "sciences" in Mesopotamia, is virtually ignored, almost as if it never existed (but cf. Ezek 21:26).

On the other hand, we do have several descriptive terms for magico-religious specialization from the Syro-Palestinian inscriptional material as well as the historical, legal, prophetic, and apocalyptic sections of the Hebrew Bible, even if mainly from lists of prohibited practices. Broadly common institutional denominators also link Syria-Palestine with its Near Eastern neighbors. The social institution of the funerary feast, for example, is well-documented for Mesopotamia, Anatolia, Syria, Ugarit, Phoenicia, Israel, Elephantine, and Nabatea.[150] The Hittite king Muršili II and Saul, the Israelite king even seem to recognize basically the same means of divine inquiry at moments of crisis: *dreams, oracles* and *prophets.*[151]

On the basis of the biblical and Syro-Palestinian evidence, therefore, we can learn much by studying these practices, licit and illicit, within theoretical parameters congruent to contemporary research in the social sciences.

"Diviners"

Divination was geographically widespread and technically diverse in Syria-Palestine. Of direct relevance to the present study are the practices of ornithomantics, cleromantics, oneiromantics, lecanomantics, rhabdomantics, and necromantics.

Ornithomantics

Perhaps as a result of Hurrian influence,[152] ornithomantic activity is attested as early as the beginning of the 15th century on the Idri-mi Stele.[153] This stele records the story of Idri-mi, a resident of North Syria, who fled Aleppo to take refuge among a group of *ḫăpiru* in Canaan, later returning to conquer Alalaḫ. While in Canaan, Idrimi says that he "looked into lambs" (*puḫădē abrima*) and "released birds" (*iṣṣūrē u-za-ki*) in order to divine the will of Adad (Idr 28), a

[150] On the Semitic variations of the funerary feast, see Pope, *Song of Songs,* 210–226; Eissfeldt, *Kleine Schriften* IV, 286–296; Porten, *Archives from Elephantine,* 179–186.

[151] 1 Sam 28:6; ANET 396, with reference as well to priestly incubation. See also Goetze, *Kleinasien,* 147–148.

[152] Cf. Haas & Thiel's attempt to distinguish the Sumerian, Akkadian, Canaanite/North Syrian, and Luwian components of the incantation rituals of Allaiturah(ḫ)i, the "old woman" from Alalaḫ (*Allaituraḫ(ḫ)i,* 46–51). The general religious syncretism of this area is emphasized by R. T. O'Callaghan, *Aram Naharaim,* AnOr 26 (Rome: Pontifical Biblical Institute, 1948) 117–118.

[153] S. Smith, *The Statue of Idri-mi* (London: British Institute of Archaeology, 1949); ANET 557–558.

deity we know to be the "lord of extispicy-rituals and divination" in Mesopotamian *bārûtu* ritual.[154] Idrimi thus enacts in Canaan two of the major roles associated with the "diviner/seer" role-set in Mesopotamia. The likelihood is strong that the verb used to describe the ornithomantic part of this activity refers specifically to divination by means of observing the flight of birds since it appears elsewhere in OB bird-omens of this type.[155]

We also have a letter in the Amarna correspondence (EA 35:26) in which a king of Alašia (probably Cyprus) asks Pharaoh to send him "a man who inquires (via) eagles" (*LÚša-i-li našrē*), but it is difficult to specify from this one reference more precisely what kind of ornithomancy this king might have had in mind.[156]

One of the many lists in the Alalaḫ texts indicates a distribution of rations (AT 281). The second entry in this list states that one *PA* of emmer was to be set aside as birdseed for the *IGI.E* bird in the custody of the *LÚMUŠEN.DÙ* (Akk. *us/šandû*). This specialist appears to be a counterpart or at least a near-cousin to the *LÚMUŠEN.DÙ* of Anatolia. If so, the Anatolian rituals in which he participates as "diviner" and "purification-priest" might help to illuminate a similar function at Alalaḫ[157]

Cleromantics

Evidence for early cleromantic activity in Syria-Palestine may have surfaced in the 12th–10th century arrowheads found in Lebanon and points south, and inscribed in Phoenician.[158] Should these bronze arrowheads have been used for cleromantic purposes, this would indicate a very early provenance for cleromancy in Syria-Palestine, antedating the neo-Babylonian practice cited in Ezek 21:26 by several centuries.[159] In support of this, Arab cleromancy is attested by the *'istiqsâm* in pre-Islamic Mecca, an oracle which consisted of bringing forth a marked arrow from a packet.[160] Something akin to this occurred in the ancient

[154] See I. Starr, *Rituals of the Diviner*, 30, 37 (*DIM be-el ik-ri-bi ù bi-ri-im*).

[155] Weisberg, "An Old Babylonian Forerunner to *šumma ālu*," 89 ii 3. See CAD *Z*, 29.

[156] H. L. Ginsberg ("A Ugaritic Parallel to 2 Sam 1:21," *JBL* 57 [1938] 209–210) justifiably denies that actual ornithomantic praxis lay behind sections of the Aqhat myth in KTU 1.19 I 32–35 (bird flight) and KTU 1.19 II 56–III 45 (bird "extispicy").

[157] Gurney suggests that ornithomancy in Anatolia was imported from Syria ("Babylonians and Hittites," 155).

[158] SSI III:6.

[159] Opinions diverge. J. T. Milik compares the names on these arrowheads with census lists of Ugaritic bowmen and interprets them as weapons ("An Unpublished Arrowhead with Phoenician Inscription of the 11th–10th Century B.C.," *BASOR* 143 [1956] 3–6). S. Iwry feels they were used mainly for divination ("New Evidence for Belomancy in Ancient Palestine and Phoenicia," *JAOS* 81 [1961] 27–34). F. M. Cross would not exclude either possibility ("The Origin and Early Development of the Alphabet," *EI* 8 [1967] 8–24).

[160] T. Fahd, "Une pratique cléromantique à la Ka'abah préislamique," *Semitica* 8 (1958)

Israelite institution of *'ûrîm* and *tummîm,* lots which were also, according to Priestly sources, stored in a sacred "packet" (the ephod).[161]

The *kōhēn* ("priest") is the primary specialist responsible for early Israelite cleromancy, according to biblical historians,[162] but we also find the *qōsēm* ("diviner") included in lists of officers (Isa 3:2) and associated with the *nābî'* ("prophet"), the *ḥōzeh* ("visionary"), and others (Mic 3:7; Jer 27:9; 29:8; Ezek 13:9; 21:34; 22:28; cf. Zech 10:2). Because the title given this specialist corresponds etymologically to Arab. *qsm* ("assign [by lot]"), most surmise this *qōsēm* originally to have been a cleromantic, but this represents an etymological fallacy which says little about the range of roles which might have been enacted.[163] *Qōsēm* magico-religious specialists are also cited for Philistia, Ammon, Edom, Moab, and Phoenicia by biblical tradents.[164] Further, we know of a "house of divination" (*bt qsm'*)[165] and the practice of *qsm*-divination within a *mrzḥ* at Palmyra,[166] as well as the presence of *mqsmh* at Dûmah.[167]

Qōsēm specialists are cited among the leaders of Judah-Jerusalem alongside other magico-religious specialists (Isa 3:2–3). Within some wisdom-circles, even the king himself was associated with *qesem,* though presumably in a broad sense (Prov 16:10). Judean *qōsĕmîm* delivered "answers" from God (Mic 3:7), had

---

55–79; *La divination arabe,* 180. E. W. Lane cites classical Arabic sources for interpreting *qsm* X (*'istaqsâm*) in a divinatory sense, as in the phrase "he sought to know what was allotted"; cf. *Arabic-English Lexicon* (Beirut: Librairie du Liban, 1968) 2998. H. Wehr and M. Cowan put more emphasis on explicit cleromancy by translating *'istaqsâm* "to seek an oracle from the deity, cast lots"; cf. *Dictionary of Modern Written Arabic* (Ithaca: Cornell, 1966) 763.

[161] Exod 28:30; Lev 8:8. Cf. Caquot, "La divination dans l'ancien Israël," 87; H. B. Huffmon, "Priestly Divination in Israel," in C. L. Meyers and M. O'Connor, eds., *The Word of the Lord Shall Go Forth: Essays in Honor of D. N. Freedman* (Winona Lake, IN: Eisenbrauns, 1983), pp. 355–359.

[162] 1 Sam 14:19; 23:9; cf. Judg 17:5.

[163] "Das alte Wort für das Losorakel ist bei Arabern und Hebräern *qsm;* die abgeleiteten Bedeutungen haben sich bei den Arabern anders und reicher entwickelt," Wellhausen, *Reste arabischen Heidentums,* 2nd ed. (Berlin: de Gruyter, 1927) 143. Fahd sees the Hebrew *qōsēm* only as one element within the larger institution of *kōhēn,* and that the *qōsēm*'s function gradually shifted away from cleromantic praxis over time (*La divination arabe,* 95). A role theorist would label Fahd's view an example of "role strain" resolution.

[164] Philistia (1 Sam 6:2); Ammon (Ezek 21:34; Jer 27:3, 9); Edom, Moab, Tyre, and Sidon (Jer 27:3, 9).

[165] J. Cantineau, "Tadmorea," *Syria* 17 (1936) 349:3.

[166] H. Ingholt, "Un nouveau thiase à Palmyre," *Syria* 7 (1926) 129:3–4. J. T. Milik denies any explicit divinatory connotation to *qsm* at Palmyra (*Dédicaces faites par des dieux et des thiases sémitiques à l'époque romaine* [Paris: Institut français d'archéologie de Beyrouth, 1972] 110).

[167] According to the Islamic historian Ibn al Kalbî, *mqsmh* was once consulted in deciding whether to attack a lunar sanctuary in Dûmah (cited in R. Savignac & J. Starcky, "Une inscription nabatéenne provenant du Djôf," *RB* 64 [1957] 211); cf. Fahd, *La divination arabe,* 184, n. 2.

"visions" (Zech 10:2), dreamed dreams (Jer 29:8), and probably charged fees for their labor (Mic 3:11), thus apparently enacting a wide range of divinatory roles. In the North *qsm* praxis apparently did not have official approval (1 Sam 28:8-9; Deut 18:10, 14).

Oneiromantics

Kings, prophets, and others dreamed dreams in Syria-Palestine. At Ugarit, Kirta learned he would have a son by means of a dream (KTU 1.15 III 46-51). In Israel, Solomon learned by a dream how best to govern his nation (1 Kgs 3:4-5; 9:2). A *nābî'* could also receive a "vision" (*mar'â*) or a "dream" (*ḥălôm*, Num 12:6), but this phenomenon in and of itself was judged, in some circles at least, to be an inadequate basis for distinguishing between competing claims for prophetic authority (Jer 23:25-28).

Oppenheim divides oneiromancy into three planes: (a) revelations of the deity, which may or may not require interpretation; (b) reflections of the dreamer's state of mind, emotionally or otherwise; and (c) mantic dreams in which forthcoming events are foretold.[168] Combinations of categories (a) and (c) often meant that "laymen" needed help from "specialists" in order to interpret dreams. In Mesopotamia, this special role was enacted by the *šā'ilu*, and, on occasion, the *bārû*.

In the Joseph story, the dream interpreter is called a *pōtēr*. Joseph is designated by this term (in pre-Elohistic material)[169] because of his prowess as an oneiromantic (Gen 40:8; 41:13). A possible Aramaic cognate (*mĕpaššar*) is applied to Daniel as an interpreter of dreams (Dan 5:12). As was noted above, Akk. *pašāru* is a two-tiered term for describing the "interpretation" of dreams (*Dreambook* 339:19), and the stative participle *pāširāk* may even have been a specific epithet for "(I am) the Unbinder" in an *āšipūtu* ritual (Maq IV:117).

Aram. *ptwr*, moreover, appears on a funerary inscription from Heǧira,[170] a dedicatory inscription for a sanctuary in Djôf,[171] on fragments from Hatra,[172] and in AP 83:21. Because this evidence is so fragmentary, Savignac and Starcky gingerly translated *ptwr* on the Heǧira and Djôf inscriptions with the rather

[168] *Dreambook*, 188-190.

[169] A Jenks, *The Elohist and North Israelite Traditions*, SBLMS 22 (Missoula: Scholars, 1977) 72, nt. 51. Corporations of oneiromantics, under strict supervision, were evidently tolerated by the rabbis in the Tannaitic period (Caquot, "La divination dans l'ancien Israël," 94-96). D. B. Redford contends that the dreams in the Joseph-novella are rooted in antiquity and are therefore indispensable to the structure of the narrative, although some of them (like Gen 41:5-7) might well be secondary expansions on the basic dream motif; cf. *A Study of the Biblical Story of Joseph*, *VTSup* 20 (1970) 69-70.

[170] Savignac & Starcky, "Une inscription nabatéenne provenant du Djôf," 210.

[171] Ibid., 215.

[172] Ibid., 210, nt. 2.

generic term "*devin*," supporting this translation via the religious contexts in which the term is found, and the fact that similar personal names (*mlk, mlkywn*) precede *ptwr'* on each inscription. *Ptwr* on the Hatra fragments and the Harrow papyrus is customarily translated "table" (of "release"?), based on an Akkadian term for "table" (*paššūru*).[173]

In light of the twofold meaning of the Akk. term *pašāru*, the possibility therefore exists that *ptwr* also had a twofold meaning. If so, this would imply that the roles enacted by persons bearing this title in Syria-Palestine were not limited to the "interpretation" of dreams. As corroborating evidence, witness the interesting fact that one of the events Daniel is summoned to "interpret" (*pšr*) is *not* a dream (Dan 5:16). Moreover, in a parallel description, the term *šābar* is also used once to designate the "breaking/interpreting" of a dream (Judg 7:15), perhaps a demonstration that this semantic phenomenon was not limited to the root *ptr* in Syria-Palestine.[174]

Lecanomantics

While lecanomancy is well-attested in Mesopotamia, we know relatively little about it for Syria-Palestine. The *bārû* could be designated an "expert in oil" (*apkal šamni*, BBR 1–20:120; 24:23; CAD *A* II, 173), but *apkallu* is a term more often used to designate sages and "the wise" among the gods.[175] At Palmyra we find *'pkl* employed to designate a magico-religious specialist attached to the cult of Azîzû (*'pkl' dy 'zyzw*).[176] At Hatra, groups of *'pkl*-specialists evidently had designated leaders(*'pk[l]' rb' d'lh'*), and received good "omens" (*nḥš*).[177] We have no way of knowing, however, whether actual lecanomantic activity was ever practiced at Palmyra or at Hatra by these specialists. The term *'pkl* could have been used there in a "religious" sense only secondarily.[178]

[173] *Paššūrū* tables were an essential part of *bārûtu* ritual, denoting either the altar upon which foods were laid out or the dishes themselves in which the gods' food was placed (cf. Zimmern, BBR, 94).

[174] In Judg 7:15, M. Fishbane reads *šibrô* as a *shaphel* of *br*, "thus comparable to *šubru>barû*"; *Biblical Interpretation in Ancient Israel* (Oxford: Clarendon, 1985) 457.

[175] Several divinities are called *apkallu:* e.g., Ea (Maq IV:74); Gira (Maq IV:75); Nabu (AGH 108:37); and Marduk (AGH 80:88). See CAD *A* II 171–172.

[176] Ephem I:203. It is instructive to note that the Palmyrenian deities 'Azîzû and 'Arṣû are twin hypostases of the Venus-star deity, viz. as morning and evening star; cf. J. Henninger, "Zum Problem der Venussterngottheit bei den Semiten," *Anthropos* 71 (1976) 135. Thus the *'pkl dy 'zyzw* was possibly associated in some way with the Ištar complex of traditions.

[177] Hatra 67; cf. A. Caquot, "Nouvelles inscriptions araméennes de Hatra," *Syria* 32 (1955) 261–272.

[178] Other terms for religious functionaries have root meanings which are only secondarily connected to a religious function. The term *ummânu*, which means simply "artisan, specialist, expert," appears in TaanL 1:20 and is translated "wizard" by W. F. Albright

The patriarch Joseph "practices divination" (*nḥš ynḥš*, Gen 44:5) by means of a "silver cup" (*gby' hksp*, 44:2) in an apparent reference to lecanomancy.[179] In sum, the evidence does not allow us to draw precise conclusions about the roles enacted by lecanomantics in Syria-Palestine.

Rhabdomantics

In the Kirta myth from Ugarit, reference is made to a rhabdomantic action which probably reflects actual Canaanite praxis. After seeking in vain for an "exorcist/healer" among the gods to heal Kirta of his illness,[180] El himself decides to exorcise the king's illness by magical means (*iḥtrš*, KTU 1.16 V 26).[181] El fashions an image from clay, infuses it with life, and sends it flying to Kirta on his sickbed.[182] Upon arriving, this image, whom El has named *š'tqt*, revives Kirta by tapping him on the head with a magic "wand" (*ẖṭ*, KTU 1.16 VI 8). Similar "wands" serve analogous functions in Mesopotamian (TuL 74:4) and Anatolian (HT 32:9–14) ritual.

The "rod of God" carried by Moses (*maṭṭēh hā'ĕlōhîm*, Exod 4:2–4, 20) has Mesopotamian parallels in the "cedar rod" employed by the *bārû* specialist (an instrument expressly called "the darling of the great gods" *n[a-ra]m ilāni rabûti*,

solely on the basis of its religious context. The term *ḥrṭmyn*, usually translated "magician" in Dan 2:27, may come from a root meaning "to sculpt" since the noun *ḥrṭyt* probably means "sculptures" at Carthage (Ephem I:24).

Gzr, from the verb *gzr*, "to cut" (cf. KAI 222A:40), is preserved in Dan 2:27 to describe "magical craftsmen" (*gzryn*), and may even be a description of Daniel himself in the Prayer of Nabonidus (*gazir*, IQPrNab I:4); see further, A. Dupont-Sommer, *The Essene Writings from Qumran* (Gloucester, Mass.: Peter Smith, 1973, originally published in 1961), 322, n. 3. The close relationship between craftmanship and the crafting of homeopathic images is vividly illustrated in Isa 44:9–17. H. Koester sums up the relationship well: "The magician is not a priest or theologian . . . he is a craftsman" (*Introduction to the New Testament* I:379).

[179] Caquot, "La divination dans l'ancien Israël," 104. Caquot cites several who attempt to dissociate Joseph from *nḥš* activity. From the perspective of this study, the important datum to note is that Joseph enacted multiple divinational roles: he was a lecanomantic *as well as* an oneiromantic.

[180] Cf. the role of "Asalluḫi, exorcist (*MAŠ.MAŠ*) among the great gods, through whose charm the dead lives, the sick gets up" (Šur IV:99).

[181] I.e., El enacts here the *role* of "sorcerer," but in actuality he is practicing "good" magic by "engraving" this clay image to "release" Kirta, not "bind" him (KTU 1.16 V:26). The term *ḥrš* is another term, like *ḥrṭm*, *gzr*, and Akk. *ummânu*, which is closely associated with the manufacture of homeopathic images, but which, apart from the world of magic, can be used neutrally to describe any sort of "engraving" (cf. perhaps *aḫ-r[i-šu]* in EA 226:11, as tentatively suggested by Hoftijzer in DISO 97). Persons "skilled in (magical) engraving" (*ḥkm ḥršym*) operated in the Jerusalem cult in Isaiah's time (Isa 3:3).

[182] An analogous phenomenon occurs when Ea makes an image (called Aṣûšunamir) to deceive Ereškigal into handing over the leather flask containing the water of life to revive Ištar from the dead. See ANET 108.

BBR 24:9) and the *ḫultuppû* of the *āšipu* (BBR 26 I:20). In Israelite priestly tradition, the *maṭṭēh*-"rod" is closely associated with the evolution of *kōhēn* specialists into an authoritative priesthood, particularly in the legend of Aaron's budding rod (Num 17:23). In the prophetic literature, Hosea inveighs against Israel for allowing "its rod" (*maqlô*) to "speak" (Hos 4:12), evidently a blanket condemnation of an oracular form of rhabdomancy.[183]

Necromantics

As in Mesopotamia and Anatolia, where spirits of the departed dead are honored by food offerings at the appropriate feasts, or expelled by incantations in the presence of their images (see above), the spirits of the Syro-Palestinian dead must also be treated with extreme caution. Magico-religious specialists who try to communicate with them thus face a very dangerous task (cf. 1 Sam 28:12).[184] Funerary feasts originally designed to appease them gradually evolved over time into elaborate social exercises for distancing the living community from their capricious terror. By this means, the fear of the Netherworld was at least partially neutralized by enveloping it within the folds of cathartic ritual.

Special funerary associations, called *mrzḥ* in both Canaanite and Aramaic,[185]

[183] R. Press sees rhabdomantic praxis underlying God's intention to make Israel "pass under the rod" (*šebeṭ*) in Ezek 20:37; cf. "Das Ordal im alten Testament," *ZAW* 51 (1933) 129.

[184] Saul's medium (*ba'alat 'ôb*, 1 Sam 28:7) sees *'ĕlōhîm* coming up from the Netherworld (*hā'āreṣ*, 28:13; cf. KTU 1.4 VIII 8–9; 1.15 III 3), but the text is silent regarding what praxis she may have used. Caquot suggests that a censor deliberately cut both praxis and incantation out of the story for theological reasons ("La divination dans l'ancien Israël," 100). Because the necromantic specialists *'ōbôt* and *yid'ōnîm* ("chirp and mutter," Isa 8:19), many rabbis followed the OG of Lev 20:27 (*eggastrimuthos*) and designated them "ventriloquists." The Mishnah (Sanh VII:7) asserted that the *ba'al 'ôb* divined by throwing his voice from his *šěhî*—a term usually rendered "armpit," but translated "pubis" by R. Gordis (cited in A. Caquot, "La divination dans l'ancien Israël," 101). Later rabbis believed that Balaam divined "via his male member" (*bě'amātô*, b. Sanh 105a). Cf. further H. Hoffner, "*'ôb*, " *TDOT* I:130–134.

Since the *'ôb* may have been an aperture to the Netherworld among ancient Near Eastern peoples, cf. the "smoke hole" of the Altaic Turks and the opening at the foot of the "cosmic tree" among some Siberians (A.-L. Siikala, "Descent into the Underworld," *ER* IV:300). Caquot ("La divination," 101) suggests that *'ôb* represents a ritual instrument played by a necromantic; cf. *'ōbôt*, Job 32:19; cf. also the Inanna-musical-instrument (^{GIŠ} ^{D}*INANNA*) played in Anatolian death-rituals (HT 66:20; 72 II:5).

[185] Possible etymologies are discussed by O. Eissfeldt, "Etymologische und archäologische Erklärung," 286–296. A close relationship to the licentious Mayumas festival, a Mediterranean celebration featuring wife-swapping, appears in midrashic commentaries on the biblical *marzēaḥ* (Lev Rabbah 5:3; Num Rabbah 10:3). The mosaic map on the floor of the 6th-century church at Madeba calls the Transjordanian area where the Baal Peor

evolved to incorporate and regulate these necromantic rituals. We see these associations attacked by Amos ("cult-association of revelers" [*mirzaḥ sĕrûḥîm*] Amos 6:7) and Jeremiah ("the *marzēaḥ*-house" [*bêt marzēaḥ*] Jer 16:5) because of the idleness and licentiousness associated with them. Yet because the institution was so deeply rooted in Canaanite culture,[186] it continued for a long time, in spite of the Hebrew prophets' denunciations. Eventually, we see the domesticated shells of these originally vibrant social organisms preserved in *mrzḥ* associations in Phoenicia,[187] Egypt,[188] Transjordan,[189] and Syria.[190] In the latter

---

apostasy occurred *Bētomarsea hē k(ai) Maioumas*, "the house of *marzēaḥ*, which is Mayumas"; cf. H. Gressmann, "*Hē koinōnia tōn daimoniōn*," ZNW 20 (1921) 228, n. 4. The biblical traditions about Baal Peor note that licentious sexual conduct occurred (Num 25:1–5) in the context of eating sacrifices for or with the dead (Psa 106:28; MT reads simply *wayy'ōkĕlû zibḥê mētîm;* OG reads *nekrōn*, a plural genitive). S. Dean McBride has suggested that *bêt mĕ'ahăbāy* ("the house of my friends") in Zech 13:6, appearing in the anti-*nābî'* polemic of Zech 13:2–6, may be referring to the *marzēaḥ* (cited in D. L. Petersen, *Late Israelite Prophecy*, 51).

In spite of this cumulative evidence from Mesopotamian, Anatolian, Ugaritic, Israelite, Jewish, and Christian sources, some still deny that the *marzēaḥ* was at root a funerary feast. See, for example, C. E. L'Heureux, *Rank Among the Canaanite Gods: El, Ba'al, and the Repha'im*, HSM 21 (Missoula: Scholars, 1979) 206–212. A good summary of views on the *marzēaḥ* is found in M. Pope, "The Cult of the Dead at Ugarit," in G. D. Young, ed., *Ugarit in Retrospect: Fifty Years of Ugarit and Ugaritic* (Winona Lake, In.: Eisenbrauns, 1981), pp. 159–179.

[186] Akk. tablets from Ugarit and Amarna refer to it (AHW 617; CAD *M* I 321). Cf. *É LÚ.MEŠmar-za/i-i* ("house of the *marzēaḥ*-men") at Ugarit, referring to funerary associations at two different towns. El drinks himself into a stupor while sitting in his *marzēaḥ* house (KTU 1.114 15). Both M. Pope (*Song of Songs*, 219) and C. Gordon (UT 19:2313) read *m(?)rz'y* in the "Rephaim" texts as a variant of *mrzḥ*, interpreting these texts in the context of a feast to which the "spirits of the dead" (*ilnym*) have been invited by Daniilu (KTU 1.20 I 2; 1.21 II 1, 5). N. B. the rare verb *ṣmd* ("to yoke") appears in KTU 1.20 II 3; Num 25:3; and Psa 106:28. Cf. O. Eissfeldt, "Kultvereine in Ugarit, in *Ugaritica* VI, 187–195.

P. Matthiae proposes that some of the rooms found in palace Q in the Western lower city at Ebla were used for the funerary cult; i.e., as sanctuaries for worshipping *rpum;* "Princely Cemetery and Ancestors Cult at Ebla During Middle Bronze II," *UF* 11 (1979) 563–569.

[187] KAI 60:1 (Piraeus inscription); 69:11–16 (Marseilles tariff). The Marseilles tariff mentions a *ḥzt*-offering as a regular part of the "gods' funerary feast" (*mrzḥ 'lm*, KAI 69:11, 16). Isa 28:15 seems to preserve a distant parallel, where "cutting a covenant with Mot" is paralleled by "making *ḥzh* with Sheol" (*'im šĕ'ôl 'āśînû ḥōzeh*). *Ḥzh/t* seems to have implicit funerary associations in both KAI 69:11 and Isa 28:15. Cf. also the incantation in KTU 1.82 5–6, specifically the plea to Baal: "you are pledging your covenant to death; [over] (its) repudiation I would rejoice," *tģrm. lmt. brt*k. [l]ḫp. an. arnn;* J. C. deMoor and K. Spronk, "More on Demons in Ugarit (KTU 1.82)," *UF* 16 (1984) 240.

[188] Aramaic ostracon from Elephantine (Ephem III, 120:3).

[189] Ephem III, 278.

[190] *Zbyd'* inscription (Ephem II, 281–282); *Šlm'* inscription (Ephem II, 303–305); *Yrḥy*

stages of its development, the *mrzḥ* association apparently evolved from a magico-religious funerary cult shrouded in mystery and secrecy into a respectable priestly guild,[191] led by non-magical leaders preoccupied with rather mundane administrative tasks, like collecting dues[192] and convening meetings.[193]

"Seers"

Magico-religious specialists enacting roles as "ecstatics" and "prophets" tend to stand on peripheral socioreligious planes in Anatolia and Mesopotamia, at least in the "official" publications which constitute the bulk of our evidence.[194] "Prophets" and "seers" may stand closer to the center of things in Syria-Palestine, but remain marginal. Scholars have only recently begun to analyze the relevant terminology and socio-religious functions of these specialists within theoretical parameters congruent to contemporary social science.[195] In this study we will

---

inscription (Ingholt, "Un nouveau thiase," 129); *'glbwl* inscription (Ephem I, 343:2); *Haddudan* inscription (J. Cantineau, "Textes palmyréniennes provenant de la fouille du temple de Bel," *Syria* 12 [1931] 117–119). The tesserae are treated by J. T. Milik, *Dédicaces faites par des dieux.*

[191] Note the "priests of Bel" (*kmry bl*) which comprise at least two separate *marzēaḥ* associations at Palmyra (Ephem II, 281:4; Ingholt, "Un nouveau thiase," 129:5). Both "priests" and "laymen" could preside over the *marzēaḥ* at Palmyra (pointed out by Eissfeldt, *Kleine Schriften* IV:289).

[192] "To Haggai: I spoke to Ashian about the money for the *mrzḥ*" (Elephantine ostracon, Ephem III, 120:1–3).

[193] The phrase "when he assumed the leadership of the *marzēaḥ* (*brbnwt mrzḥwt*) is repeatedly found on dedicatory inscriptions from Palmyra (Ephem II, 281:4; 304:1; Ingholt, "Un nouveau thiase," 129:2). A Greek translation of this Palmyrenian phrase appears on a bilingual inscription (*sumposiarchos*, Ephem II, 304:4).

[194] Of the specialists with descriptive titles, cf. Hit. *šiunianza* (translated "prophet" in ANET 396a:11; Goetze, *Kleinasien,* 147); Akk. *mu/aḫḫû/muḫḫûtu* ("ecstatic," cf. Huffmon, "Prophecy in the Ancient Near East," *IDBS* 698; Noort, *Untersuchungen zum Gottesbescheid in Mari,* 71); *āp(i)lu/āpiltu* ("answerer," Huffmon, "Prophecy," 698; Noort, *Untersuchungen,* 69–70); and *assinu* ("cult-functionary," Huffmon, "Prophecy," 698; Noort, *Untersuchungen,* 70). There are other terms. The rarity of direct revelation in the ancient Near East is stressed by O. R. Gurney ("Babylonians and Hittites," 143). The secondary socio-religious status of these specialists is pointed out by Huffmon ("Prophecy in the Mari Letters," 121), while G. Dossin stresses the incompleteness of our knowledge about these specialists generally ("Sur le prophétisme à Mari," *La divination en mésopotamie ancienne,* 86).

[195] Of recent studies, R. R. Wilson (*Prophecy and Society in Ancient Israel,* 135–295) draws heavily from the theories of I. M. Lewis (*Ecstatic Religion,* 1971) regarding the roles enacted by specialists in "central" and "peripheral" cults in Africa. Wilson's approach is welcomed by some, but sharply criticized by others for the same reasons that Ruth Benedict's theories have been criticized. Even as Benedict's division of all cultures into Apollonian and Dionysian categories fails to take full account of the subtleties and complexities within each individual culture, so Wilson's "central" and "peripheral" categories have been

focus only on the primary roles enacted by the Syro-Palestinian "seers": "sacrificial-priest," "diviner," "oracle-reciter," and "government adviser."

Sacrificial-Priest

As "sacrificial-priest," Samuel, described as a *rō'eh*-seer, was expected to bless the sacrifice on a "high place" (*bāmāh,* 1 Sam 9:12–14), in a ceremony where a fixed number of "invited" (*haqqĕrû'îm*) persons ate a cultic meal (9:13, 22, cf. 24). This closed ceremony could not begin until the *rō'eh* "blessed" (*yĕbārēk*) the sacrifice (9:13). A "butcher" (*ṭabbāḥ,* 9:23)[196] worked closely with Samuel in preparing portions of the sacrifice (9:23–24), and some of these portions evidently had more status than did others (9:24).[197]

On at least one occasion, therefore, a *rō'eh*-seer (Samuel) enacted a role as "sacrificial-priest" over a cultic association in which another functionary played a subordinate role to his lead.[198] We are not told the *raison d'être* for this cultic association, nor are we made privy to the precise contours of the *rō'eh*-seer's praxis. The seven-fold repetition of "eating" (*'kl*) in 1 Sam 9:5–24 may be intended, however, to emphasize an important dimension of this occasion. In one famous confrontation between specialists, a northern *kōhēn* intimates a (cultic?) linkage between "prophesying" and "eating," citing this linkage as a characteristic of *ḥzh*-"seeing" in the South (Amos 7:12, *'kl//nb'*).

Eventually sacrifices on high places were outlawed in Israel (2 Kgs 23:8–9). The editors responsible for codifying the socio-religious equation in 1 Sam 9:9 (*rō'eh > nābî'*), may have intended this to neutralize the "unacceptable" elements of the *rō'eh*-seer's praxis (perhaps another example of "role strain" resolution).[199]

---

criticized for failing to take the subtleties and complexities of Hebrew prophecy fully into account; cf. G. Mendenhall, "Review of *Prophecy and Society,* by R. R. Wilson," *BA* 44 (1981) 189–190. For a discussion of the distinctions between Mary Douglas' and I. M. Lewis' schemata, see B. Morris, *Anthropological Studies in Religion: An Introductory Text* (Cambridge: University Press, 1987) 231–233.

As noted above, D. L. Petersen (*The Roles of Israel's Prophets*) examines the roles enacted by the Heb. prophets via the theoretical constructs of contemporary role theory. Also helpful is J. Lindblom's work (*Prophecy in Ancient Israel* [Oxford: Blackwell, 1957]), even though its hybridization of "role" and "title" limits applicability to this study.

[196] Cf. the attendant roles enacted by the *LÚ.MEŠMUḪAL-DIM* ("cooks") in the Anatolian version of the funerary feast (HT 66:15).

[197] Cf. the stereotypical formula for the shoulder and thigh portions of the slaughtered animal in BBR 1–20:52 and the *bît rimki* ritual (BBR 26 IV:39–40): "right thigh portion, *ḫinṣâ*-flesh, *šumê*-flesh, *silqu*-flesh."

[198] Among the several functionaries operating in the *mrzḥ* headed by *Yrḥy, Zby* served as the one in charge of *bt dwd',* "the place of the cauldron" (H. Ingholt, "Un nouveau thiase à Palmyre," 129:8). *Dûd* refers to a cultic cauldron/pot also in Hebrew tradition (1 Sam 2:14; Jer 24:1).

[199] See the discussion in Lindblom (*Prophecy,* 83–104), Wilson (*Prophecy and Society,*

Slightly conflicting role expectations may also have been subtly resolved by the Chronicler when he introduces us to the same individual twice via different titles ("Hanani the *rō'eh,*" 2 Chr 16:7; "Jehu, son of Hanani the *ḥzh,*" 2 Chr 19:2). At any rate, southern tradents continued to portray the *rō'eh*-seer favorably, if no longer explicitly as "sacrificial-priest" (Isa 30:10; 2 Chr 16:7–10).

Diviner

As "diviners," seers may have operated in Syria-Palestine very early. Some think the Ugar. root *ḥdy* is an ancient forerunner to the Heb./Aram. word *ḥzh,* interpreting the latter term derivatively.[200] Others question this equation, preferring instead to view *ḥzh* as Aram. in origin, downplaying the Ugar. evidence.[201] Heb. *ḥzh* could relate to Ugar. *ḥdy* (i.e., **ḥdy*) or it could relate to Old Aram./Biblical Aram. *ḥzy* and Arab. *ḥazā* (i.e., **ḥzy*). Etymological possibilities aside, one finds little appreciable difference in meaning between these cognates.

Nevertheless, Ugar. *ḥdy* is repeatedly used in the formula "I/he opened/cut open its/their liver(s) and peered in" (*ibq' kbd*[*t*]*h/hm waḥd,* KTU 1.19 III 3–4, 32–33; *ybq' kbd*[*t*]*h/hm wyḥd,* KTU 1.19 III 10, 24, 38), and this peculiarity cannot be ignored. Daniilu performs this act three times on birds as he "looks" for the remains of Aqhat. Certainly this is not extispicy of the Mesopotamian type, because Daniilu makes no attempt to read a message from the gods in the entrails of these birds. He is only trying to find the remains of his son in order to give him a proper burial.[202] The narrator of this myth, however, seems to be making deliberate use of known ornithomantic *language* in order to tell Daniilu's story. Secondary support for this conclusion comes to light in the person of the Arab. *ḥzy,* who, in addition to his other divinatory roles, was an ornithomantic familiar with both *aves alites* (divination by flight of birds) and *aves oscines* (divination by sound of birds).[203]

---

139), and Petersen, (*Roles of Israel's Prophets,* 38–40). Mowinckel earlier proposed that the Israelite *nĕbî'îm* gradually absorbed the divinatory roles of the *rō'îm* over time (*Psalmenstudien III: Kultprophetie und prophetische Psalmen* [Oslo: Jacob Dybwad, 1923], 18)—another probable example of "role strain" resolution. The redactional and phenomenological solutions do not seem to be mutually exclusive.

[200] H. L. Ginsberg, "Lexicographical Notes," *VTSup* 16 (1967) 72; M. Dahood, "Ugaritic-Hebrew Lexicography II," *Bib* 45 (1964) 407–408.

[201] E.g., M. Wagner, *Die lexicalischen und grammatikalischen Aramäismen im alttestamentlichen Hebräisch,* BZAW 96 (Berlin: deGruyter, 1966) para. 93–98. A. Jepsen downplays ("*ḥzh,*" TDOT IV:281) and T. Fahd (*La divination arabe,* 112–113) ignores the Ugaritic evidence.

[202] Noted by Ginsberg ("An Ugaritic Parallel to 2 Sam 1:21," 209–210) against Ch. Virolleaud and R. Dussaud. For a discussion, see provisionally A. Haldar, *Associations of Cult Prophets Among The Ancient Semites* (Uppsala: Almqvist & Wiksells, 1945) 80.

[203] "When a crow croaks in front of a man, and he desires to obtain some object of want, he says, 'It is good,' and goes forth: when it croaks behind his back, he says, 'This

Ḥzyn evidently enacted divinatory roles at Hamath in the 9th century, but we do not know what kind, how many, or for how long.[204] We can only note a few characteristic elements in the Zakkur inscription which overlap those found elsewhere, notably the common tendency for desperate kings to summon "diviners/seers" whenever war seemed imminent, as well as the common role of "oracle-reciter" which they enact once they arrive. We also know that Anatolian and Mesopotamian kings customarily employed "diviners" to guide (or, better, legitimate) their decisions at moments of military crisis exactly like the one facing Zakkur.[205] But because of the frustrating lacunae, we cannot discover whether the Hamath *ḥzyn* practiced ornithomantic, cleromantic, lecanomantic, or some other kind of Syro-Palestinian divination on Zakkur's behalf, or even whether they employed technical means of divination at all.

We also find *ḥzh* "diviners/seers" in ancient Israel, especially in Jerusalem circles. That these magico-religious specialists enacted the role of "diviner" is usually surmised from the repeated association of *ḥzh* with *qsm* in Judean sources (Mic 3:7; cf. Ezek 13:9; 22:28), though too much should not be made of this association. Like the Mesopotamian *bārû*,[206] furthermore, Judean seers were expected to give "answers" (*'nh*, Mic 3:7) from the deity to divinatory requests.[207] If Eliphaz' description is at all typical (Job 4:12–16), the *ḥōzeh*-seer received his visions (*ḥezyōnôt*) at night while in a deep sleep (*tardēmāh*). He felt a "hand" on him, then "saw" the dim outline of a "form" (*tĕmûnāh*, cf. Num 12:8). Often the seer received a nocturnal audition as well.

Enacting roles as "diviners/seers," *nābî'*-prophets sometimes "see" visions called *maśśā'* (Nah 1:1; Hab 1:1; cf. Lam 2:14).[208] Judgment oracles against

---

is evil,' and does not go forth. When a thing passes by him from the direction of his right hand, he augurs (*yḥzy*) good from it; but if from the direction of his left hand, he augurs evil from it" (Lane, *Arabic-English Lexicon*, 563, citing from the 13th-century work *Tāğ al-'Arūš* by az-Zabîdî). The mechanics of this Arabic oracle are amazingly similar to the Hittite *KIN* and *MUŠEN* oracles practiced by Anatolian diviners over two millennia earlier.

Ḥdyn is listed as a personal name by F. Gröndahl (*Die Personnamen der Texte aus Ugarit*, SP 1 [Rome: Pontifical Biblical Institute, 1967] 134). Whether it was related to a socio-religious specialty, like the Hebrew names Oded (2 Chron 15:1, 8; 28:9) and Iddo (2 Chron 12:15, both from *'dd*), cannot be determined.

[204] Emphasized by J. F. Ross, "Prophecy in Hamath, Israel, and Mari," *HTR* 63 (1970) 2.

[205] Cf. the "old woman's" curse against an enemy city (KUB VII 60), and a *bārû*'s divination on behalf of Zimri-Lim's army (ARM II 22:24–25).

[206] Cf. AGS 1:13′–24′ (one of Šamaš' "answers").

[207] Close parallels between Ugar. *'dd* and Akk. *āpilu* are suggested by A. Malamat, "Prophetic Revelations in New Documents from Mari and the Bible," *VTSup* 15 (1966) 211–214. According to a Phoenician inscription from Cyprus, *ḥzym* may even have been organized into associations under the leadership of a "chief-seer" (*rb ḥz[y]*); cf. T. Nöldeke, "Phönicische Inschrift," *ZA* 9 (1894) 401:4.

[208] On *maśśā'*, see M. Saebø, *Sacharja 9–14*, WMANT 34 (Neukirchen-Vluyn:

foreign nations are often labeled by means of *maśśā'* (Isa 13:1; 14:28; 15:1; 17:1), but Lam 2:14 clearly shows that it could also be used to describe oracles "seen" on Judah's behalf. A polemic against false prophets in Jer 23:33–40 is structured around a clever pun on *mś'*, evidence that the technical meaning for the term *mś'* was well known, at least in the South.

Oracle-Reciter

Syro-Palestinian seers enacted the role of "oracle-reciter" alongside other specialists, like the *nby'* and the *'yš 'lhym*, specialists customarily subsumed under the role-label "prophet."[209] *Ḥzyn*-seers are also associated with specialists called *'ddn* at Hamath in the famous oracle from Zakkur's god Baalshamayn (KAI 202:12–14). Judging from the limited Ugaritic evidence, this *'dd* may also have been a magico-religious specialist charged with returning "answers" (KTU 1.4 III 11 *//twb*?; cf. Herdner, CTA 4 III 10, *y[t]b;* Gordon, UT 51 III 10, *y*[ ]). Baal uses a mediator, for example, in his sensitive negotiations with Mot, calling this specialist both *'dd* and *dll* (KTU 1.4 VII 45–48). Arab. cognates help to define the latter term's semantic range (*dalīl*, "guide," "pilot"; *dallāl*, "middleman," "broker").[210] In Syria-Palestine, David's *ḥōzeh* Gad (called *nābî'* in 2 Sam 24:11, but not in 1 Chron 21:9), enacts a similar mediatorial role, "returning" (*šûb*, 2 Sam 24:13) oracular messages from Yahweh to David, and presumably also inquiries from David to Yahweh.[211]

Government Adviser

Enacting roles as "prophets" (in the socio-religious sense), both *rō'îm* and *ḥōzîm* recited oracles which directly challenged the religious *status quo* (Isa

---

Neukirchener, 1969) 137–140; P. A. H. de Boer, "An Inquiry into the Meaning of the term *maśśā'*," *OTS* 5 (1948) 212–213.

[209] See Wilson, *Prophecy and Society*, 135–141. D. L. Petersen (*Roles of Israel's Prophets*, 43–50, 70–88), argues for a sharp geographical separation between *ḥōzeh* in the south and *nābî'* in the North, but this distinction is not readily accepted by everyone. G. Fohrer holds simply that "die Propheten in stärkerem Masse spontan und häufig in ekstatischem Zustand handelten, während die Priester sich in stärkerem Masse technischer Mittel bedienten (z. B. Losorakel)"; *Studien zu alttestamentlichen Texten und Themen (1966–1972)* (BZAW 155; Berlin: deGruyter, 1981) 159.

[210] W. F. Albright, "The North Canaanite Poems of Aleyan Baal and the 'Gracious Gods,'" *JPOS* 14 (1934) 130; Wehr & Cowan, *Dictionary of Arabic*, 289.

[211] H. Haag finds in Gad a Jebusite magico-religious specialist assimilating to Yahwistic traditions; cf. "Gad und Nathan," *Archäologie und altes Testament: FS K. Galling* (Tübingen: Mohr/Siebeck, 1970) 141–42. Using I. M. Lewis' categories, R. Wilson designates Gad a "central intermediary using prophecy to maintain the society" (*Prophecy and Society*, 264), but downplays any "mediatorial" role (ibid., 263).

30:10), confronting kings personally for their lack of faith (2 Chron 16:7–10; 2 Sam 24:11–14), and warning the nation repeatedly about the consequences of its immoral behavior (2 Kgs 17:13). The roles enacted by these Syro-Palestinian magico-religious specialists, however, covered a relatively wide span of both the "politics-religion" and "magic-religion" continuums. In contrast to their roles as "prophets," they also enacted religio-political roles as tools of the state, like their *bārû* counterparts in Mesopotamia.

In later biblical texts this latter supportive role seems to be the more frequent typology. Thus we find seers described as directing musical liturgies (1 Chron 25:5; 2 Chron 29:30),[212] advising kings (1 Chron 21:9; cf. KAI 202:12–14), recording history (1 Chron 29:29), and performing the administrative tasks necessary to conserve and enhance the central religious and political structures of the Judean state (1 Chron 9:22; 26:28).

Syro-Palestinian seers, therefore, enacted a relatively wide spectrum of roles, roles which oscillated most noticeably on the magic-religion continuum because of the pressures brought to bear by the variables of time and audience expectation. Sometimes they function as "sacrificial priests" and "prophets," but at other times enact rather domesticated roles as "liturgists" and "government advisers." The changing sociohistorical and political postures of the audiences before whom they performed are to a large degree responsible for these rather significant oscillations.

"Exorcists"

Compared to the breadth and depth of exorcistic activity in Mesopotamia and Anatolia, or even to the prevalence of Syro-Palestinian divination in all its forms, evidence for Syro-Palestinian exorcism is shallow and sketchy, but not absent. It is in this geographical and phenomenological area of magico-religious specialization that our evidence is unfortunately most uneven, partially for religious reasons (cf. 2 Kgs 23:4–25), but also probably because of the vicissitudes of archaeological chance. The present dearth of information about Syro-Palestinian exorcism clearly underlines one of the primary reasons why the Deir ʿAllā texts are such an important find.

In Israel, most of the primary roles enacted by the *āšipu* specialist in Mesopotamia and the "old woman" in Anatolia, viz., "exorcist," "healer," "purification priest," "incantation-reciter," and "sorcerer," are wholly redefined and subsumed, either to Israel's mainstream religious specialists[213] or to the

[212] Cf. the Akk. *zammāru*-singer (BBR 60–70). Huffmon suggests, from analyses of the cognate evidence at Mari and Nineveh, a certain antiquity for the musical specialists cited in Chronicles ("The Origins of Prophecy," 180), but D. L. Petersen questions this antiquity on redactional grounds (*Late Israelite Prophecy*, 57; *Roles of Israel's Prophets*, 112–113).

[213] I. Mendelsohn, "Exorcism," *IDB* II:199. The relative uniqueness of the Israelite *kōhēn* is a matter of sharp dispute. Cf. the differing points of view in Fahd (*La divination*

sovereign person of Israel's deity (see, e.g., Psa 91:3–6). Thus, while it remains problematic to point to a particular human specialist as an Israelite "exorcist," these primal roles continued to be enacted, yet drastically remolded to fit the constraints imposed by Israel's Yahwistic parameters.[214]

We know that all Syro-Palestinians, including Israelites, feared a number of domestic and imported demons.[215] We also see magico-religious specialists whose roles overlap considerably with those of the "old woman" of Anatolia and the *āšipu*-exorcist of Mesopotamia. At Ugarit, an incantation specialist called *mlḫš* excelled in "charming" snakes by magical means,[216] while El himself engages in a homeopathic healing activity almost certainly reflective of Canaanite exorcistic praxis (see above).[217] Biblical tradents warned Israel repeatedly against a number of exorcistic specialists,[218] taking pains to draw sharp distinctions, for example, between faith in Yahweh and reliance on homeopathic images.[219]

---

arabe, 92–97) and R. Abba, ("Priest and Levites," *IDB* III:876–889). Cf. also J. Renger ("Untersuchungen zum Priestertum," 112, nt. 5).

[214] G. von Rad and W. Eichrodt both overgeneralize from a lack of explicit demonic language in the Bible to a corresponding absence of demonic activity in Israel (von Rad, *Old Testament Theology* [New York: Harper and Row, 1962] I:278; Eichrodt, *Theology of the Old Testament* [Philadelphia: Westminster, 1967] II:180).

[215] G. Vajda, "Israel et la judaïsme," *Le monde du sorcier*, 129–133. T. H. Gaster discusses terms like *'l/'lhym, šdym*, and *š'rym* ("Demon," *IDB* I:817–820). B. Levine argues persuasively that "in the ancient Israelite mentality, the reality of anti-God forces was present, and was inculcated by stringent ritual codes, administered by the priesthood, but affecting the Israelite community at large," *In the Presence of the Lord: A Study of Cult and Some Cultic Terms in Ancient Israel*, SJLA 5 (Leiden: Brill, 1974) 91. G. Fohrer derives the Israelite view of illness ultimately from demonic sources (*Studien zu alttestamentlichen Texten und Themen*, 172–187).

[216] *Ugaritica* V, 7:5 (passim), cited in M. C. Astour ("Two Ugaritic Serpent Charms," 13–15).

[217] This is the section of the Kirta myth where El heals Kirta via the demoness *š'tqt* (see above). J. Nougayrol has noted the lack of explicit evidence for Canaanite magico-religious activity in general: "en Ugarit comme ailleurs, il avait dû exister de tout temps des pratiques magiques et des procédés divinatoires, probablement moins élaborés, et, comme les autres techniques, transmis par apprentissage ou enseignement verbal, c'est-à-dire sans laisser de traces" ("La Lamaštu à Ugarit," in *Ugaritica* VI, 407).

[218] Magico-religious specialists in this category include: *mĕkaššĕpîm* ("sorcerers," Deut 18:10; 2 Chron 33:6; cf. Akk. ^{LÚ}*kaššāpu*), *ḥăbārîm* ("enchanters," lit. "binders," Psa 58:6; Deut 18:11; cf. Isa 47:9, 12), *mĕlaḥăšîm* (Psa 58:6; Isa 3:3; Jer 8:17; cf. *mlḫš*, Ugaritica V, 7:5; cf. *laḫāšu*, CAD *L*, 40–41; *lḫšt*, Arslan Tash I:1; II:1), *mĕnaḥăšîm* (Deut 18:10; cf. Ezek 16:36), *mĕ'ônnîm* (Deut 18:10; Lev 19:26) *ḥăkam ḥărāšîm* (Isa 3:3; cf. Syr. *symwn ḥrš'*, "Simon the Sorcerer," PSSD 159), *gāzĕrîn*, (lit. "cutters," Dan 2:27; 5:11; cf. KAI 222A:40; *gazir*, 1QPrNab I:4), *ḥarṭumîm/n* (lit., "engravers," Dan 1:20; 2:2; 2:27; 5:11), and *'aššāpîm* (Dan 1:20, cf. Akk. *āšipu*).

[219] "Idols" (*gillûlîm*, lit. "rolled things") were made (1 Kgs 15:12; Ezek 22:4) of wood, stone, silver, and gold (Deut 29:16). They could also be sketched on walls (Ezek 8:10). They could be humanoid in form (Lev 26:30; Ezek 6:5), were often associated with lewdness

Moreover, since the phenomenology of exorcism can pertain either to *immanent* or to *portended* evil,[220] other examples of "exorcism" ("the driving out of evil powers or spirits")[221] can be adduced: e.g., a divine *namburbi* ritual at Ugarit,[222] and the apotropaic incantations found on gypsum portal plaques at Arslan Tash.[223]

In an Ugaritic myth designed to account for the snake charmer's power, Ḥoran, a Netherworld deity, participates in a ritual which has rather precise parallels with *namburbi* rituals in Mesopotamia.[224] Whereas a living homeopathic image, Aṣûšunamir, is created in the "descent of Ištar" to bring Ištar "back to life" (ANET 108), Ḥoran here engages in a *namburbi*-type ritual in order to recapture the ability to "bring to life" (i.e., procreate).[225] Only after his virility is restored can he proceed to the "house of incantation" (*bt mnt*) and contract marriage with the "mother of the stallion" (*um pḥl*). This myth could not have been understood by an audience unfamiliar with the exorcistic praxis of *namburbi.*

Several demons appear by name on the portal plaques from Arslan Tash: "flyers" (*'pt'*, I 1),[226] "stranglers" (*ḥnqt*, I 4),[227] "night demons" (*llyn*, I 20),[228]

(Ezek 6:9; 23:49), and accepted children as sacrificial offerings (Ezek 16:36; 23:37). Illicit construction of an *'ēl* is directly countered in Isa 43:10 (*lĕpānay lō' nôṣar 'ēl*, "before me no god/daimon was formed"); cf. Isa 54:17 (*kol kĕlî yûṣar 'ālayik lō' yiṣlaḥ*, "no vessel/ weapon that is formed against you will succeed"—a promise from Israel's God for protection).

220 E. Reiner, "La magie babylonienne," 78.

221 G. Parrinder, "Exorcism," *ER* V:225.

222 *Ugaritica* V, 7:64–67.

223 SSI III:78–92.

224 The major parallels between the Ugar. and Akk. rituals involve (a) the use of the same "medicinal" plants in basically the same order, and (b) the "uprooting" of a tamarisk in both texts as a magical symbol of the evil which is homeopathically "uprooted." Akk. examples are collected in R. Caplice, "Namburbi Texts in the British Museum," *Or* 34 (1965) 116–120 (Caplice's text 6), 125–129 (text 10). Cf. also Oppenheim (*Dreambook*, 302), and Astour ("Ugaritic Serpent Charms," 23–26).

Ḥoran also appears at Arslan Tash (I:16), and T. H. Gaster thinks he enacts a role similar to that of Nergal ("A Canaanite Magical Text," 62). Cf. further M. Hutter, *Altorientalische Vorstellungen von der Unterwelt: Literar- und religionsgeschichtliche Überlegungen zu "Nergal und Ereškigal,"* OBO 63 (Göttingen: Vandenhoeck und Ruprecht, 1985) 70–73.

225 The *maštakal* plant was widely used in virility charms (Astour, "Ugaritic Serpent Charms," 25, nt. 75).

226 The term *l'pt'* appears on the torso of the winged sphinx, so a *p* is usually restored in *l'[p]t'*, the incipit of the main incantation. Some, however, keep only *'t'*, and read it as the second element of the Aramean goddess *'tr't'* (Atargatis), who is often portrayed as a winged sphinx (e.g., SSI III:84). Gaster reads *'pt'* in the singular, then tries to tie this demoness directly to Lamaštu ("A Canaanite Magical Text," 45–49). H. Torczyner claims to find flying *'pt'*-demons in Job 10:22, "A Hebrew Incantation Against Night-Demons," *JNES* 6 (1947) 20.

the "splatterer" (*mzh*, II 1),[229] the "evil eye" (cited via several synonymous *'n*-epithets, II 2, 4, 8, 11, 12),[230] and a being named *Ssm* (I 2, 27).[231] Note also the "crushers" (*phṣt*, I 21)[232] and "the spoiler daimon" (*'l šyy*, II 3).[233] Counterparts to these demonic beings are described elsewhere by similarly colorful epithets, some of which have been preserved on the silver images of demon-chasing dogs in Mesopotamia, talismans inscribed with names like "he-does-not-hesitate-to-bite," "expeller-of-evil-things," "he-chases-the-demon-Asakku," and "murderer-of-his-adversaries."[234]

Other plaster plaques, inscribed with the images of Ea and Marduk (the patron gods of exorcism), the Sibitti, and Nergal were hung over doors (BBR 54:38) and hearths (54:15) in Mesopotamia as well as Anatolia.[235] In addition to

[227] First connected in the Arslan Tash *editio princeps* to the Arabic night-demon *Qarinat*, also called the *ḥnq 'lḥml*, "lamb-strangler" (du Mesnil du Buisson, "Une tablette magique de la région du Moyen Euphrate," I:421–34). J. C. L. Gibson (SSI III:85) points out a parallel with the Ugaritic goddesses *iltm ḫnqtm* "the two strangling goddesses" (cf. UT 19:982).

[228] On the basis of newer photographs, Cross and Saley ("Phoenician Incantations," 46) claim to see a clear *n* in *llyn*, which if valid would preclude Gaster's earlier reading of *lly*[*t*], "Lilith."

[229] Following Cross ("Leaves from an Epigraphist's Notebook," *CBQ* 36 [1974] 488, nt. 17) and parsing as a causative ptc. of *nzh*, "to sprinkle." *Mzh* is associated with the splattering of blood in the Bible (Lev 4:6, 17).

[230] The "Big-Eye" (*rb 'n*, II:2), "Bug-Eye" (*gl*[*y*] *'n*, II:4; cf. Num 24:4), and "Consumer of Eyes" (*mgmr 'nt*, II:9–10 [Cross]) are epithets aptly illustrated by the sketch on the tablet of a large-eyed demon swallowing a human being. Cf. the "raging eye" in the Anatolian incantations of the "old woman" (Haas & Thiel, *Allaituraḫ(ḫ)i* 104:6').

[231] *Ssm* appears to be a Canaanite deity, found in the proper name *'bdssm* at Ugarit (UT 73 rev:6) and Cyprus (KAI 35:1; 40:3; 49:11). He is identified here as a "son of *pdršš'*." *Pdr* (UT 23:5) and *Pdry* (KTU 1.4 I 16) are deities at Ugarit, and the name ^{D}*pi-id-di-r*[*i-ya*] in Mesopotamia is believed by some to be associated with Ištar (A. Deimel, *Pantheon Babylonicum*, text no. 2998, cited by Donner and Röllig, KAI II, 44; see also Gaster, "A Canaanite Magical Text," 52–58).

[232] Written on the she-wolf (Arslan Tash I 21), reading with W. F. Albright, "An Aramean Magical Text in Hebrew from the Seventh Century B. C.," *BASOR* 76 (1939) 9; and Cross & Saley, "Phoenician Incantations," 46. Gibson (SSI III, 87–88, n. 21) reads *lḥṣt*, "(to the) outside"; du Mesnil (cited in SSI III, 87, n. 21) and Röllig (KAI 27:21) read *mḥṣt*, ("smiter!").

[233] Arslan Tash II 3, 5–6, reading with Cross, "Leaves from an Epigraphist's Notebook," 488, n. 20. Gibson (SSI III, 90, n. 3), however, is inclined to read *'l šyy* as an epithet for Baal.

[234] Reiner, "Le magie babylonienne," 95–96.

[235] Goetze, *Kleinasien*, 153. On a tour through the British Museum, E. Reiner noted an incantation written on black stone with a hole in the top, just like the portal plaque from Arslan Tash. Investigating further, she found that the incantation on this amulet corresponded to Erra III iv 3–15; "Plague Amulets and House Blessings," *JNES* 19 (1960) 148–155. Note also that the Ugaritic incantation in KTU 1.82 20–30 is designed to prevent demons from entering houses.

this apotropaic practice, we noted above how other portal-protection techniques included the shedding of blood on doorposts (BBR 26 III:20–21; cf. Exod 12:7) and the burning of "pyres" (*abrū*) before doorways (BBR 26 III:25; Racc 120:25–27). Like his "erudite" (Reiner) counterparts in Mesopotamia and Anatolia, furthermore, the "exorcist" who wrote the *namburbi*-like incantation on Arslan Tash II also showed familiarity with a learned literary tradition: he explicitly states that he copied his incantation from a series called *mglt m'nn*, the "Scroll of the Enchanter" (II 12–13).[236]

Specific demons listed in the Bible include the Lilith demoness (*lîlît*, Isa 34:14), *rešep* (Deut 32:24; Ps 76:4; 78:48; Cant 8:6; Hab 3:5), *deber* (Ps 91:5–6; Hab 3:5), *qeṭeb* (Deut 32:24; Ps 91:6; Hos 13:14), the "vampire" (*'ălûqâ*, Prov 30:15), the "arrows of Shadday" (*ḥiṣê šaday*, Job 6:4; cf. Job 34:6; Ps 91:5), the "king of terrors" (*melek balāhôt*, Job 18:14), the "seven" (*šeba'*, Deut 28:7, 25; N.B. the seven diseases named in 28:22), the "terror of the night" (*paḥad lāyĕlâ*, Ps 91:5; Cant 3:8), and Azazel (Lev 16:8, 10, 26).[237]

Traces of exorcistic praxis are thus probably retained in the wearing of alarm bells on the high priest's robe (Exod 28:35), the fumigation ceremony on *yôm kippur* (Lev 16:12–13),[238] the wearing of blue tassels (Num 15:38), and the binding of *mĕzûzôt* on head, hands, door, and gate (Deut 6:8; 11:19), not to mention the purely magical elements still preserved in some of the prophetic legends (e.g., 2 Kgs 13:21).[239] Worthy of further note in this regard is Neḥushtan, a bronze serpent whose origin is traced back to Mosaic times (Num 21:9), and who was honored in the Jerusalem temple for generations before its destruction by Yahwistic reformers (2 Kgs 18:4).[240]

In other words, we may not yet be able to elucidate the roles enacted by Syro-Palestinian exorcists with the same degree of precision as we can with Anatolian and Mesopotamian exorcists, but there does seem to be enough clear evidence available to reject categorically Eichrodt's view that "ancient Israel knew nothing of a world of evil spirits."[241]

[236] Cross, "Leaves from an Epigraphist's Notebook," 489. Whether this *mglh* was "canonical," or even indigenously Syro-Palestinian, should remain an open question.

[237] Gaster, "Demon," 818–821. The Talmud (*b. Pes* 110a) mentions a certain *'šmd'y* as "king of the demons" (*mlk' dšydym*).

[238] H. Zimmern saw a close relationship between the Akk. and Heb. cognates of D *kpr*, but refused to postulate identical ritual praxes. He preferred instead to view the Hebrew term as an Akk. loanword borrowed very early, but developing its own identity in Heb. (BBR, 92). For more recent discussions of *kpr*, cf. Levine, *In the Presence of the Lord*, 123–127, and N. Kiuchi, *The Purification Offering in the Priestly Literature*, JSOTSup 56 (Sheffield: JSOT Press, 1987), chapter 4, "The *KIPPER* Problem," pp. 87–109.

[239] Vajda, "Israel et la judaïsme," 132.

[240] Ibid. Cf. K. R. Joines, "Serpent in the Old Testament," *ZAW* 80 (1968) 107.

[241] Eichrodt, *Theology of the Old Testament*, II, 180. A thoroughgoing critique of the Hegelian presuppositions underlying Eichrodt's and von Rad's sharp dichotomy between Canaanite "magic" and Israelite "religion" is offered by Gary A. Anderson, *Sacrifices and*

Summary

To summarize our results to this point:

(1) Magico-religious specialists in the ancient Near East enact a variety of roles, roles which stand in tension between opposite poles of a spatio-temporal magic-religion continuum. Roles closer to the "religion" pole on this continuum are primarily enacted within the parameters of a "diviner/seer" role-set. Roles closer to the "magic" pole are enacted within the parameters of an "exorcist" role-set.

(2) Magico-religious specialists in Mesopotamia enact complementary role-sets as "diviners/seers" and "exorcists." Role overlap, conflict, and preemption are minimal since separate specialists are usually employed for each role-set.

(3) Anatolian and Syro-Palestinian magico-religious specialists, however, are not as neatly separated into distinct societal categories. A single specialist (e.g., the "old woman") often enacts roles on both ends of the magic-religion continuum.

(4) The Syro-Palestinian "seer" looks to be a volatile position somewhere between the poles of "magic" and "religion" on the magic-religion spatio-temporal continuum, and may even reflect a "middle ground" between the role-sets of "diviner" and "exorcist." The frustrating lack of evidence, however, prohibits our fluid speculations from crystallizing into firm conclusions.

Offerings in Ancient Israel: Studies in their Social and Political Importance, HSM 41 (Atlanta: Scholars, 1987).

2
The Roles Enacted by Balaam Bar Beor at Deir ʿAllā

BALAAM AS "DIVINER/SEER"

Prior to the discovery of the Deir ʿAllā texts, we had no way of gauging the following characterization with any degree of precision:[1]

> Now there was at that time living in Mesopotamia a man famous for divination who had been initiated[2] into divination in all its forms,[3] but among them (i.e., the various forms of divination) he inspired awe by means of his great proficiency[4] in augury.[5]

[1] Philo, VM I 264.

[2] *ememuēto.* The verb *mueō* is often found in the passive to denote initiation ceremonies attendant to the mysteries. In 3 Macc 2:30, for example, Ptolemy IV Philopator proclaims a pardon for any Jew willing to join "those who have been initiated into the mysteries" (*tois kata tas teletas memuēmenois*). The OG of Num 25:5 uses the term *teleō* in the perfect passive (singular!) to translate *niṣmādîm,* the *nipʿal* participle of the verb *ṣmd,* a term for initiatory union attested in the "Rephaim" texts (KTU 1.20 II 3) and other texts associated with the institution of *marzeaḥ* (cf. Psa 106:28). Symmachus preserves the plural in Num 25:5, translating *tous muēthentas.* Whether Philo was aware of Symmachus' translation is a tantalizing question.

[3] Philo mentions in the previous paragraph (VM I 263) that Balak desired to fight the Israelites via divination (*manteias*) and augury (*oiōnous*). He also says that the Moabite king was familiar with *arais,* the usual term in Homer for "imprecation, curse" and personified as a goddess of destruction in Sophocles (LS, s.v. *ara*). Balak's decision to hire Balaam thus implies that this religious specialist, in Philo's view, could enact complementary roles as both "sorcerer" and "diviner."

Other Jewish tradents agree with this pluralistic assessment of Balaam's abilities. Ps.-Philo (LAB 18:2), the Fragment Targums (FTNum 22:5), and Philo (VM I 268) know him as a "dream-interpreter." Philo elsewhere emphasizes his role as "seer" (VM I 289), and Ps.-Philo (LAB 18:7) refers to his role as a "sacrificial-priest"; i.e., one who reconciles men to God via "whole burnt offerings" (*holocaustomata*).

[4] *Sugkekrotēkōs* denotes the discipline necessary to perform difficult tasks by "welding together" one's resources into an efficient whole. Often used of the military, it serves here as an apt description for the training required of professional diviners and exorcists.

[5] *Oiōnoskopia* (lit., "the seeing of birds"). The OG of Num 23:23 translates Heb. *naḥaš* with *oiōnismos,* perhaps an oblique reference to Balaam's proficiency in augury.

Philo's description of Balaam son of Beor as a magico-religious specialist familiar with several types of divination, yet specializing in ornithomancy, is remarkably supported by the characterization now found in the Deir 'Allā texts.

Unfortunately, DAT I is pockmarked with lacunae. Lines 7–9 speak clearly of birds and "rods," but the remainder of this reconstructed plaster text is very difficult to decipher, a situation which continues to provoke scholarly disagreement.[6] Since this section continues to focus on what has been "seen" (*wkl ḥzw*, I:14), however, there seems little warrant for transferring it *en masse* to a genre far removed from that which is "seen" in lines 1–9. Still, any serious analysis of Balaam's roles from lines 10–16 would be difficult to articulate and even more difficult to defend.[7] For the purposes of this study, there is fortunately no need to go beyond the relatively legible material in DAT I:1–9 to obtain information about the major divinatory roles enacted by this specialist in the DAT tradition.

Structurally, DAT I:7–9 appears analogous to the "answering" section of the Assyrian prayers collected by Knudtzon; i.e., the optional *omens* section.[8] Even as the *bārû* sometimes leaves a final section on the tablet in order to write down Šamaš' "answers" (which are "seen" in the exta, the oil, or the stars), we find listed here several different types of divine "answers," all of them unusual to the point of becoming bizarre. As was noted above, this "answering" function was repeatedly enacted by diviners of all stripes in Anatolia, Mesopotamia and Syria-Palestine.[9]

Like the ornithomantic *Sammeltafel* KUB XVIII 5,[10] though, none of the "petitions" which elicited these particular "answers" have been preserved in DAT I:7–16. A number of uniformly unfavorable "answers" are simply set forth in list

[6] The term *qb'n* in DAT I:10 can be read either as a verb ("to aggrieve," Hoftijzer) or as a noun ("hyenas," Caquot & Lemaire, McCarter). *Ḥmr* in the same line can be read either "wine" (Caquot & Lemaire), "wrath" (Hoftijzer) or "ass" (Levine). *'nyh* in I:11 can be translated either "poor woman" (Caquot & Lemaire, McCarter) or "female (answering) oracle" (Hoftijzer, Levine). Many more examples could be cited. As a general rule, the closer one gets to the bottom of the tablet, the greater the number of suggested readings.

[7] This has been repeatedly pointed out in the reviews of the *editio princeps* by J. Fitzmyer (*CBQ* 40 [1978] 94), J. Naveh (*IEJ* 29 [1979] 135), S. Kaufman (*BASOR* 239 [1980] 73), J. Greenfield (*JSS* 25 [1980] 251), and M. Dahood (*Bib* 62 [1981] 125). H. & M. Weippert note that in matters of substantive detail there will always be questions ("Die 'Bileam' Inschrift," *ZDPV* 98 [1982] 78), but E. A. Knauf's radical pessimism is unjustified ("Review of Hackett, *The Balaam Text from Deir 'Allā*," *ZDPV* 101 [1985] 191).

[8] *Assyrische Gebete an den Sonnengott*, 50–57.

[9] Knudtzon (ibid., 51) was inclined to restrict the mode of divine "answering" in the Šamaš prayers solely to haruspicy (e.g., AGS 29:20'; 33:10'), even though he was aware of astrological "answers" in contemporary prayer-texts. To these modes of answering we should also add lecanomancy (BBR 79–82 III:16–25) and perhaps even cleromancy, should the Assyrian *SU.BIR* (BBR 75–78:21; Zimmern, "Ledertasche") have served the same storage function for the sacred lot as the ephod in Israel and the Arabic cultic *bayt* (cf. Fahd, *La divination arabe*, 138–141).

[10] A. Ünal, "Zum Status der 'Augures' bei den Hethitern," 30.

form. Lacking more evidence, it is difficult to know whether a (standardized?) *Sammeltafel,* along the lines of KUB XVIII 5, lay underneath this text. Not to be excluded is the possibility that the quasi-narrative format in DAT I:7-16 might also indicate a measure of oral and/or literary development.[11] Neither possibility seems to be mutually exclusive.

Since different types of divination were often employed as counterchecking measures in the ancient Near East, we must also reckon with the possibility that these omens are the result of counterchecking petitions, in response to the oneiromantic oracle "seen" and reported in lines 1-7.[12] We have already seen that this is especially to be suspected in instances where an oracle was for some reason deemed "inappropriate."[13] That we now find the intimation of several different *types* of oracles listed in DAT I may thus imply that the diviner's client, though stunned by the first oracle, kept trying to elicit a different "answer," launching several more inquiries through complementary divinatory channels.[14]

[11] This caveat will be raised here, with Hoftijzer (*editio princeps,* 271), in order to avoid assuming, *a priori,* that this inscription lacked a history of oral and/or literary tradition. It is also important to remember that prior to the Deir 'Allā discovery Balaam ben Beor had already been linked by Jewish tradents to Moab (Num 22-24), Ammon (Num 22:5, mss Sam, Syr, Vulg), Midian (Josephus, AJ IV:104, 123, 126), and even Amalek (Esther Rabbah 7:13), linkages which indicate several evident but unknown histories of tradition. Four decades prior to the Deir 'Allā discoveries, Mowinckel already felt that there must have been "viele mehr oder weniger mirakulöse und märchenhafte Geschichten und Anekdoten im Umlauf," since even the earliest biblical traditions already introduce him as a "bekannte Grösse" ("Der Ursprung der Bil'amsage," 237).

[12] H. Ringgren, "Balaam and the Deir 'Allā Inscription," 95-96: "the birds are auguries portending calamity." B. Levine calls the material in DAT I:7-9 an "omen," emphasizing that the section on birds is a "projection of what is to come, not a report on what had already occurred, or is occurring" ("The Deir 'Allā Plaster Inscriptions," 199).

[13] This "inappropriateness" could be explained as ambiguity in the liver itself (CAD *B,* 122), but note the fate of the Babylonian *LÚA.ZU* hired by Hattušili III, who died because of an "inappropriate" response to an oracle (i.e., one that offended the king; see Kammenhuber, *Orakelpraxis,* 139, re KBo I 10:32'-41').

[14] In Anatolia, *MUŠEN* oracles were used as counterchecks on *KIN* and *KUŠ* oracles (Kammenhuber, *Orakelpraxis,* 10). In Mari, "hair and hem" was taken as a countercheck on the words of various types of oracle givers; cf. Huffmon, "Prophecy in the Mari Letters," 121-122; Noort, *Untersuchungen,* 83-86). Neither Saul nor Muršili were slow to consult prophets, oneiromantics, cleromantics, nor in Saul's case, even necromantics. *Āšipu* exorcists were known to repeat the same incantations over and over (three was a common number) in order to secure a favorable response from the gods (AGH 40:51; TuL 146:7-10; BBR 26 III:35-IV:12). It is therefore not all all unusual to see here an oracle followed by a series of other oracles, nor to see this series begin with *MUŠEN.*

While it is customary, furthermore, for kings to employ separate specialists to confirm or deny oracles, the evidence for this phenomenon is rather limited to large urban areas where magico-religious specialists were plentiful (cf. Mari; Noort, *Untersuchungen,* 83-85). Such a practice may have represented the ideal, but may also have been economic-

Balaam as Ornithomantic

Apparently the first three of these are ornithomantic, each likely obtained through differing types of augury. From the data preserved, we have no real reason to imagine that the DAT Balaam engaged in bird extispicy (assuming that such ever existed in Syria-Palestine)[15] or in ornithomantic burnt offerings of the Anatolian variety.[16] Should Balaam have been a specialist charged with counter-checking his own dream-vision, he as "augur" may simply have observed events that had a direct bearing on the immediate future of his client.[17] As with the Anatolian *LÚMUŠEN.DÙ*-augur, this role might even have been preemptive within the DAT Balaam's greater "diviner/seer" role-set.[18]

The particular events "seen" by this specialist were not so much "unnatural" as "unusual"; i.e., difficult to read, much less interpret.[19] Professional Near Eastern augurs presumably were supposed to be familiar with the "canonical" handbooks on augury, which were at least partly standardized compilations of noteworthy ornithomantic incidents. Alongside those incidents known from Arzawa,[20] Kummani,[21] Aleppo,[22] and Canaan[23] perhaps we should now view these ornithomantic omens in Transjordan.

---

ally and culturally impractical in areas far removed from these urban centers (cf. A. L. Oppenheim, *Ancient Mesopotamia,* 208).

[15] I.e., assuming that Daniilu's practice of "peering" into the exta of birds was at least shaped by incantatory language characteristic of Canaanite ornithomantic praxis (KTU 1.19 II 56–III 45).

[16] Haas & Wilhelm, *Hurritische und luwische riten,* 50–58. Note the possible parallel to *MUŠENḪURRI* in the *'ṣr dbḥ* ("sacrificial bird") offered by Kirta on the roof of his house to El (KTU 1.14 II 17–18; III 59). It is unclear whether the shooting, plucking, and burning of a heavenly bird, related in the story of El's seduction of two young women (KTU 1.23 38–39), is rooted in ornithomancy or even in ornithomantic language.

[17] The problematic term *'ḥr'h* in DAT I:2, if based on a root *'ḥr* meaning "after" (Caquot & Lemaire, "Les textes araméennes," 194–195; McCarter, "The Balaam Texts," 52; Levine, "Plaster Inscriptions," 196; and Hackett, *The Balaam Text,* 35) would find parallels in *bĕ'aḥărît hayāmîm* (Num 24:14) and *'aḥărê dĕnāh* (Dan 2:29). In the Šamaš prayers, note also *šumma libbi . . . kalūmi ša-lim arkīti,* "when the heart . . . of the lamb answers . . . hereafter" (AGS 29:20'; 33:10'). While still inclined to read *'ḥr'h* from *ḥr'* ("to burn"), Hoftijzer now lists *'ḥr* as another possibility ("Aramäische Prophetien," 140, n. 2c).

[18] Huffmon suggests the intriguing possibility that these bird terms might be "code-words," like those used for the reading of livers in Mesopotamia (private communication).

[19] Cf. McCarter, "The Balaam Texts from Deir 'Allā," 58–59.

[20] See Ünal, "Zum Status der 'Augures,'" 31, citing KUB VII 54 i 1ff, which records a ritual performed by a *LÚIGI.MUŠEN* named Maddudani against pestilence in an army.

[21] See Ünal, 32, citing KBo XI 1 9ff, a prayer of Muwattili to Tešub of Kummani in which he mentions an "evil bird" and a *LÚMUŠEN.DÙ.*

[22] See Ünal, 32, citing KUB XXVII 13 iv 22, a cultic text for Hadad of Aleppo.

[23] "For seven years I lived among the Ḫāpiru-people. (Then) I released birds (to observe their flight) and looked into (the entrails of) lambs (and found) that after seven years Adad had become favorable to me" (Idr 27–28, cited in ANET, 557).

All professional augurs were trained by formal schooling and practical experience to interpret omens. As in any profession, however, some were better at it than others. The most resourceful augurs "inspired awe," in Philo's words, because they had the knowledge, insight, and experience to interpret the most difficult, "unusual" omens. These specialists were truly the magico-religious celebrities of their day. often summoned from vast distances to work for anyone willing to pay the fee.[24] The survival of Balaam traditions on both sides of the Jordan is likely indicative of this particular augur's superior talents.

The omens of DAT I:7–9 seem to reflect violent behavior between different species of birds.[25] The first focuses on *aves oscines* ("bird sounds"). The few omens of this kind preserved in Mesopotamia are predominantly concerned with the "crying out" of birds, particularly eagles, falcons and ravens.[26] One section of *šumma ālu,* for example, systematically aligns several omens about falcons and ravens into a pattern which has deliberately been structured as a primitive behavioral continuum.[27] This behavior begins innocuously enough: both species eat together and play together without engaging in hostilities. Gradually, though, their behavior turns more and more violent. They "cry out" (*šasû*) at each other, then attack, then eventually kill each other.

The more violent the birds' behavior becomes in *šumma ālu,* the more ominous become the interpretations. Augurs witnessing this deteriorating behavior uniformly interpreted it as portending a disastrous future. When reading for a king, the sound of birds screeching and cawing at each other could be read as a sign from the gods of imminent international tension.[28] Preparations for war would thus be in order on the basis of such omens. If a falcon killed a raven, this meant that the king would conquer his enemy.[29] If a raven killed a falcon, this meant that his enemy would conquer him.[30] If a bird preyed on the

[24] Note the Cypriot king's request for a *LÚša-i-li našrê* in EA 35:26, whom O. Weber (EA, p. 1102) felt was probably a Babylonian specialist "on loan" to Pharaoh. Every administrative district surrounding Mari had its own *bārû,* according to one letter (ARM II 15:25–29). Some *bārū,* like Ilšu-nâṣir, commanded armies (ARM II 22:23) and managed palaces (ARM IX 153). Other magico-religious specialists, like Pariamaḫū the Egyptian, were extensively employed by foreign courts (Kammenhuber, *Orakelpraxis,* 140).

[25] Note the verbs *ḥrpt* ("to reproach"), *ṣrh* ("to claw at"; cf. Syr. *ṣr',* PSSD 483–484), and *nšrt* ("to lacerate"); see McCarter, "The Balaam Texts," 54–55.

[26] Symbolic meaning was drawn from the sounds uttered by these birds while flying over cities (*šumma ālu* 66:8), perched in houses (66:16; 67:5), perched behind kings (79:24), or perched in palaces (79:28).

[27] *šumma ālu* 79:31–38.

[28] "If a falcon and a raven screech, croak, and caw to each other, the land will be turned into a fortress" (*šumma ālu* 79:34).

[29] *šumma ālu* 79:35.

[30] *šumma ālu* 79:36. The twist at Deir 'Allā is that, in addition to the prey "reproaching" (*ḥrpt*) the predator, even normally non-violent birds like the swallow and the dove "lacerate" (*nšrt*) each other. Assuming this interpretation of Combination I is correct, perhaps this is an omen presaging continued domestic strife of the sort which always

fledglings of another species, this also signified future disaster.[31]

While the DAT omens thus appear to stand within the ornithomantic mainstream in DAT I:7–9, details remain sketchy. We have little evidence, for example, for ascertaining whether these ornithomantic omens were read in the context of an international crisis, like those in *šumma ālu,* or in one of the other diverse contexts already cited above from Anatolian sources: birth, death, marriage, family life, war, sickness, demon possession, or sorcery—to name only a few of the life crises for which we have documentation.[32] Since an (oracular?) "inquiry of the king" (*š'lt mlk*)[33] appears in DAT II:15, however, the possibility that this specialist worked in the employ of a royal client should probably be accorded high priority.

Balaam as Rhabdomantic

Syro-Palestinian rhabdomancy is closely associated with the mysterious power of *regeneration.* When El wanted to regenerate Kirta from mortal illness, for example, his emissary *š'tqt* revived the king by means of a magic "wand" (*ḫṭ*).[34] The characteristic that set Aaron's "rod" (*maṭṭēh*) apart from all others was its regenerative power (Num 17:23). Hosea inveighed against Israelites who "inquired" (*šā'al*) of a "rod" (*maqqēl*) via a "spirit of harlotry" (*rûaḥ zĕnûnîm*), alluding apparently to a rhabdomantic practice whereby oracles were divined at traditional sites in his day (Hos 4:12).[35]

---

accompanies economic depression. Another possibility is that this is a case of deliberate hyperbole of the sort found in *šumma izbu.*

[31] "If a falcon removes a captured fledgling from a partridge's nest in the wall of a man's house (i.e., to eat it [IV:1–7]) . . . his house will be scattered" (D. Weisberg, "An OB Forerunner to *šumma ālu,*" III:25–29). Other omens drawn from violence between species read: "If an eagle seizes a dove in the window of a man, evil will overtake that house" (ibid., II:22–26); KUB XVIII 5 ii 3: "While we watched, another *alliya*-bird came up and attacked" (cited from Ünal, "Zum Status der 'Augures,'" 46).

[32] Ünal, "Zum Status der 'Augures,'" 29–30.

[33] *Š'lt* is paralleled by *š'ltk* in II:16 and has been read as a noun in both instances; cf. Caquot & Lemaire ("Les textes araméennes," 207; Hackett, *Balaam Text,* 134; Hoftijzer, "Aramäische Prophetien," 147). It is, of course, impossible to be dogmatic.

[34] KTU 1.16 VI 8.

[35] N.B. the "oak of divination" near Shechem (*'ēlôn mĕ'ônnîm,* Judg 9:37). H. Gressmann (*"koinōnia tōn daimoniōn,"* 15) did not take the "spirit of harlotry" (*rûaḥ zĕnûnîm*) metaphorically in Hos 4:12, but literally, translating "Hürdämon." He further read *šēdîm* with Hitzig for MT *šĕwārîm* in Hos 12:12 (a suggestion preserved by K. Elliger in the BHS apparatus). OG apparently read *śārîm,* translating *archontes* ("leaders"). Should Hos 12:12 have preserved a memory of "sacrifices for *šēdîm*" at Gilgal (cf. Psa 106:28, 37), the ambiguities surrounding the events cryptically connoted by Micah's admonition to "remember what Balaam ben Beor answered (*'ānāh*) . . . from Shittim to Gilgal" in Mic 6:5 could now be more decipherable. Shittim, of course, was where ancient Israel whored after the Moabite women and ate sacrifices to their gods (Num 25:1).

According to a segment of the biblical tradition, Balaam carried a *maqqēl* with him to Moab. When he unmercifully beats his she-ass with it, we are doubtless supposed to conclude that this specialist is not only "blind" but also incompetent: he does not know how to use his *maqqēl* properly (Num 22:27).[36] By way of reminder, *bārû* specialists in Mesopotamia used cedar "rods" in their cultic ceremonies, even giving them a special name, "darling of the great gods,"[37] and *āšipu* specialists often used "rods" in healing and purification rituals.[38]

One cannot discuss this regenerative power in Syria-Palestine, however, without discussing sexual procreation. In fact, Canaanite sources rarely address this subject in any other context. Ḥoran is ready to marry, for example, only after performing the appropriate apotropaic ritual for regaining his sexual virility.[39] After this, his *ḥt*[40] becomes strong "like a torrent, streaming like a stream." Very similar language is found in the Šaḥru/Šalimu cycle (KTU 1.23). When El gets into the mood to spawn offspring, his penis (euphemistically called a "hand," *yd*) expands "like the sea . . . like the flood" (KTU 1.23 33–35). Significantly, El's "hand" is also described as a "rod" (*ẖṭ*) and a "staff" (*mṭ*) in this same cycle (KTU 1.23 37), a word-pair now essentially reduplicated in DAT I:9 (*mṭh//ḥṭr*).[41] The decision whether to locate El's consorts in the category "wife" or "daughter" is further decided via a cledomantic omen set in the context of their reaction to El's manipulation of this "rod" (KTU 1.23 39–46).[42] The phallic imagery in these

[36] A. Rofé strongly emphasizes the satirical elements of the she-ass story, not as ancient folkloristic remnants, but as one of the main compositional themes in this "burlesque" (*Spr Bl'm*, 55). W. Rudolph, on the other hand, argued that J incorporated an already-formulated saga, in spite of its unfavorable portrayal of Balaam, because it so dramatically portrayed Yahweh's superiority over this "feindlichen heidnischen Seher" (*Der "Elohist" von Exodus bis Josua*, 111).

[37] BBR 24:9. See Zimmern's discussion on p. 89.

[38] Reiner, "La magie babylonienne," 72. The *lammu* and *ẖaṭṭu* are mentioned in TuL 74:7–8 (KAR 33).

[39] *Ugaritica* V 7:61–76.

[40] Astour ("Ugaritic Serpent Charms," 26) tentatively suggests that *ḥt* is a word meaning "life, vitality," but agrees with Virolleaud that a more concrete meaning was probably intended. C. H. Bowman and R. B. Coote emend to *ḥ*<*m*>*t*, "heat," and draw a parallel between the "heat" of the snake bite and the "heat" of male erection and orgasm (cf. *nēḥāmîm*, Isa 57:5); "A Narrative Incantation for Snake Bite," *UF* 12 (1980) 135.

[41] The parallelism between *mṭh* and *ḥṭr* was noted by Hoftijzer in the *editio princeps* (p. 205) and has since been almost universally accepted.

[42] "Cledomancy," in Caquot's words, is a form of divination which "consistant à tirer présage d'une parole entendue par hasard ou sollicitée," and occurs several times in the Bible (1 Sam 14:8–10; 1 Kgs 20:30–35; Gen 24:12–21; cf. "La divination dans l'ancien Israël," 96). Mesopotamian examples of cledomancy are cited by A. L. Oppenheim ("Sumerian *INIM.GAR*=Akkadian *egurru*=Greek *klēdōn*," *AfO* 17 [1954–1956] 49–55). Arabic examples are cited by T. Fahd (*La divination arabe*, 460–464). The Talmudic portrayal of Balaam as divining by means of his male member (*bĕ'āmtô*) thus seems to be, as in the she-ass story, another deliberate satire on his divinatory abilities, then later perhaps on his moral behavior (*b. Sanh* 105a).

Canaanite myths is unavoidably deliberate and consistently articulated.

The loss of this regenerative power, for whatever reason, precipitated grave crisis. Myths were spawned to describe especially the cyclical loss of this power at the change of seasons. In Mesopotamia, this loss could be pictured as a descent of Tammuz to the Netherworld; i.e., a time when the earth lies dormant and animals and human beings lose their desire to procreate.[43] In Anatolia, it could be described as Telepinus' getting lost in the steppes. Persuading him to return involved hiring a specialist (Kamrusepas) to perform a complicated exorcistic ritual to remove the god's anger:

> Just as (water in) a pipe does not flow upward,
> Even so let Telepinus' [rage, anger (and)] fury not
> [come] back![44]

Magico-religious rituals, like those recited by the "old woman" Allaituraḫ(ḫ)i from North Syria, were often deliberately set in the context of these myths, the Šaušga cycle being one of the most popular.[45]

An Assyrian ritual (KAR 33), already mentioned, employs a "rod" (*ḫaṭṭu*) and a "beaker" (*kāsu*), presumably as symbols for the genitalia,[46] in an involved attempt to rescue a sick client from the power of an evil god (*ilu raṣmu*). At the climax of this ritual, the client is required to eat the flesh of a sacrificed animal after its homeopathic substitute has been buried in a pit representing the Netherworld. The homeopathic substitute for this dying man is an "almond branch" (?) clothed in the skin of the slaughtered animal.[47] After transferring the sickness to the homeopathic substitute and banishing it from the world of the living, the client then "comes back to life" (*iballuṭ*) on the day something (presumably this "rod") is "taken up" (*e-lu-ú*) from the grave.

At Ugarit, the loss of regenerative power is corroboratively explained in one mythical cycle as Baal's "Descent to the Netherworld." While making preparations for this descent, Baal mentions a possible deity named *šgr* in one of his

[43] ANET 108:76–80. Thorkild Jacobsen uses the phrases "fecund power" and "ruttish powers of fecundation of the herds" to describe this power of regeneration; cf. *The Treasures of Darkness* (New Haven: Yale, 1976) 47, 143.

[44] ANET 128.

[45] Haas & Thiel, *Allaituraḫ(ḫ)i* 140:19–27. This is the ritual where the rubbing of a medicinal drug into a client's skin is paralleled to the revival of Šaušga.

[46] TuL 74:5–6 (KAR 33). E. Ebeling suggests that: "Stab und Becher die Geschlechtsteile des Mannes und des Weibes darstellen sollen, das Wasser aber den Samen" (TuL, p. 74).

[47] *lammu*, CAD *L*, 67–68. Cf. the homeopathic function of the grapevine adorned with strips of cloth and grapes, then lowered into the "dish of the dead" on the twelfth day of *šalliš waštaiš* (HT 32:9–14). The Netherworld is elsewhere described as a place where "the worm grows fat" (*tul-tú i-kab-*[*bi-ir*], TuL 75:28), a description which is substantially echoed in Isa 66:24 ("their worm shall not die," *twl'tm l' tmwt*) and DAT II:8 ("worm from a grave," *rmh mn gdš*); see further Hoftijzer, *editio princeps*, 226.

speeches,[48] but this deity's function has unfortunately been obscured by damaged lines. In a Yahwistic form, however, we may catch a glimpse of *šgr*'s magico-religious function in a biblical phrase which reads *šěgar 'ălāpekā we'aštěrōt ṣō'nekā* ("the *šgr* of your herds and the *'štrt* of your flocks," Deut 7:13). *Šgr* was more than likely a minor Canaanite deity charged with catalyzing and protecting the fertility of domesticated animals, a very important function in economies dependent upon herds and flocks for survival.[49] In other words, *šgr* might well be, as many argue, locked with *'štr* in a hypostatic union parallel to that found in DAT I:14 (*šgr w'štr*). As is well-known, combined deities are not uncommon to mixed populations like those continuously melding in Transjordan.[50]

Whether these texts speak of the animal, human, or divine spheres, the mysterious power of regeneration is always treated as a matter of profound concern. Without it, there is famine, loss of posterity, sickness, and death.[51]

Syro-Palestinian rhabdomancy may also underlie a famous story in the biblical patriarchal traditions. In Gen 30:37–43, the Israelite hero Jacob triumphs over Laban the Aramean by means of an obscure practice which has been preserved in Israelite tradition, perhaps ultimately by way of Transjordan.[52]

[48] KTU 1.5 III 16–17 lies in a very damaged portion.

[49] R. de Vaux emphasizes the foundational roles enacted by shepherds and herdsmen in the Transjordanian economy, noting also several parallels between Jacob's treatment of Laban's flocks in Gen 30 and the laws regulating the wages and duties of shepherds in Hammurapi's Code, *The Early History of Israel* (Philadelphia: Westminster, 1978, trans. from 1971 ed.) 254–255; cf. ANET 177:261–267. The biblical tradition explicitly calls lower Transjordan a "place for cattle" (Num 32:1).

[50] *Šgr wiṯm* appears in *Ugaritica* V 9:9'; *Iṯm* appears in KTU 1.5 III 24, seven lines down the tablet from *šgr* (KTU 1.5 III 17). *Šgr* also survives in a Punic personal name from Carthage: *'bdšgr*, "servant of *šgr*"; cf. F. L. Benz, *Personal Names in the Phoenician-Punic Inscriptions*, SP 8 (Rome: Pontifical Biblical Institute, 1972) 163. Meša the "sheep breeder" (2 Kgs 3:4, *nqd*) devoted booty to *'štr kmš* (KAI 181:17). Hoftijzer has a full discussion in the *editio princeps*, 273–274.

The Akkadian counterpart to Ugar. *šgr* may have been the deity *Šakkan*, one of whose functions was to protect the herds of the dark-headed people from the Sibitti (Erra I:43).

[51] Death signifies not only the loss of temporal life, but the loss of free movement, the loss of living community, and the loss of vitality due to sickness, misfortune, or calamity; cf. C. Barth, *Die Erretung vom Tode in den individuellen Klage- und Dankliedern des alten Testaments* (Basel: Zollikon, 1947) 53–67.

[52] C. Westermann (*Genesis 12–36* [Minneapolis: Augsburg, 1985, trans. from 1981 *BK* edition] 480) calls this a "professional" narrative originating among Transjordanian herdsmen and preserved by J in order to balance the story of Jacob's outwitting by Laban (Gen 29:25) with a story of Laban's outwitting by Jacob. According to Westermann, J accomplishes this by preserving "the execution of a trick with sheep and goats." H. Gunkel (*Genesis*, HKAT I/1 [Göttingen: Vandenhoeck und Ruprecht, 1917] 338) had earlier postulated that this "saga" originated "ursprünglich im Kreisen von Hirten," claiming that "solche Züchtungsmittel waren den Antiken bekannt" (339).

Older commentators like C. F. Keil in Keil & F. Delitzsch (*Biblical Commentary on the Old Testament I: Pentateuch* [Grand Rapids: Eerdmans, 1964, trans. from 1899

Although the precise contours of this praxis are, as with most biblical memories about magico-religious practices, deliberately blurred,[53] enough remains intact to suggest a number of striking parallels between the roles enacted among Laban's Transjordanian herbs and the roles enacted in DAT.

Like the "rod" which is "lowered" (*nḥt*) and "chanted over(?)" (*ymnn*)[54] at Ugarit to increase the size of El's divine "flock," Jacob also "lays down" (*yāṣag*)[55] specially prepared "rods" in order to increase the size of his flocks. Portraying Laban as the "deceived deceiver," the Israelite narrator focuses his point considerably by offering a subtle play on the root *lābān* ("white") in order to show that the white streaks on these rods are somehow responsible for Laban's ultimate defeat.[56] Just like the necromantic oracle in 1 Sam 28, furthermore, the biblical tradent here shows profound disinterest in preserving either the praxis or the incantational elements connected with this magico-religious activity.

German ed.] 293) and J. P. Lange (*Genesis* [New York: Scribner, 1868] 537) explained this "well-known" practice as the folkloristic belief that the striped rods produced striped lambs because of a direct visual impression left on the ewes' brains while rutting in front of them. Later commentators, however, have been slow to perpetuate this explanation. Westermann (*Genesis 12–36,* 483) only goes so far as to state that "there are signs here of an earlier transition from magical to scientific thinking," while E. A. Speiser (*Genesis,* AB 1 [Garden City, NY: Doubleday, 1964] 239) cites a Mesopotamian omen-text regarding the coloring of animals at birth as a parallel.

[53] Speiser (*Genesis,* 239) suggests that the biblical editors collecting these old stories were simply unfamiliar with these ancient practices because they lived in a "different cultural environment." Westermann emphasizes (*Genesis 12–36,* 483) that "what is peculiar to Jacob's artifice is not the notion behind it, but its deliberate *manipulation* (emphasis added) with the intention of producing a particular breeding effect."

[54] Several possibilities for *ymnn* have been suggested. Cross (*Canaanite Myth and Hebrew Epic,* 23, n. 58) derives *ymnn* from *yamīn,* "right hand," translating "he drew." See G. del Olmo Lete, *Mitos y Leyendas de Canaan* (Madrid: Ediciones Cristiandad, 1981) 560, for other possibilities. On the basis of the parallel with *nḥt* in KTU 1.23 37, Gordon (UT 19:1505) translates "to lower," but it is interesting to note that *nḥt* is used in conjunction with a verb for "speaking" in KTU 1.2 IV 11 (*p'r,* "to proclaim"). The translation proposed here reads *mnn* with a reduplicated second radical, like *ḥrr* in KTU 1.23 48, seven lines down the tablet from *mnn.* For an analogy, Heb. has two forms, *ḥrh* and *ḥrr,* for the same basic concept ("to burn"). We have already noted above the specialized translation "(to recite an) incantation" for Akk. *manû* (TaanL I:21) and NW Semitic *mnt* (*Ugaritica* V, 7:4; Arslan Tash II:13).

[55] It is interesting to note how often *yāṣag* is employed in explicit magico-religious contexts: Gideon "lays down" his fleece to divine the will of *'ĕlōhîm* (Judg 6:37); Gideon makes an ephod and "sets" it in his city (Judg 8:27); the ark of *'ĕlōhîm* is captured by the Philistines and "set down" beside an image of Dagon (1 Sam 5:2); when the ark finally returns to Jerusalem, it is "set" in its place (2 Sam 6:17); Jacob "lays down" the *maqqĕlôt* before the eyes of his sheep (Gen 30:38). Thus we see a (magical) "lowering" of a "rod" in Anatolian (HT 32:14), Mesopotamian (TuL 75:26), Canaanite (KTU 1.23 37) and Israelite (Gen 30:38) tradition.

[56] See Gunkel (*Genesis,* 339); Westermann (*Genesis 12–36,* 483); Speiser (*Genesis,* 237).

Perhaps these elements were deliberately censored from the tradition, as Caquot suggests for the material in 1 Sam 28.[57]

The narrator chooses instead to emphasize that Jacob's rhabdomancy could not be thwarted by Laban, who is, like Joseph (Gen 44:5), portrayed without comment as a practitioner of *naḥaš* (Gen 30:27).[58] Jacob's triumph over Laban, moreover, is not merely a matter of coincidence, but divinely sanctioned by God. In a parallel version of this story (Gen 31:10–13),[59] Jacob enacts a role closer in keeping with Joseph's role as *pōtēr* (Gen 40:8; cf. 41:13), since here Jacob enacts a role as a "diviner/seer" who "sees in a dream" (*wa'ēre' baḥălôm*, Gen 31:10) a vision of his growing flocks in an oneiromantic oracle.[60] Like Joseph, who enacts multiple roles as lecanomantic (Gen 44:4–5) and oneiromantic (Gen 40:8; 41:13) in the tradition, Jacob also enacts multiple roles as rhabdomantic (Gen 30:37–42) and oneiromantic (Gen 31:10–12).

Alongside these continuities, however, stands a major discontinuity. Jacob's manipulation of his "rod" is spectacularly successful in the biblical tradition, but the rod in DAT I:9 can only "bring forth" (*yybl*)[61] "wild rabbits" instead of "ewes." Though the language here seems very bizarre, it may be more hyperbolic than literal and more standardized than one might guess without more Syro-Palestinian parallels. The series *šumma izbu*, for example, a series filled with similarly bizarre language, is a creation of scribal "logic" designed to elicit

[57] Caquot, "La divination dans l'ancien Israël," 100.

[58] Several references to *naḥaš*-divination, though outlawed in the Deuteronomic code (Deut 18:10; cf. Jer 27:9), are nevertheless preserved by editors of varied stripes (Gen 30:27; 44:5, 15; 1 Kgs 20:33) as an integral part of Israelite tradition.

[59] The formulaic "God of Bethel" saying in Gen 31:13 has long been suspected as an interpolation (e.g., Wellhausen, *Die Composition*, 38). Gunkel (*Genesis*, 342) argued that whereas the J narrative emphasized Jacob as trickster, E emphasized that he stood under divine care. Westermann (*Genesis 12–36*, 491–492) also sees two distinct dream narratives in 31:10–13, one emphasizing the mating of Jacob's flock, the other the call by God to return home, both as "additions." Speiser, however (*Genesis*, 238), while admitting that there may be "later ethical reflections" in E's narrative, nevertheless insists that both J and E rest "on sound traditional data."

[60] From a literary-critical point of view, any connection between Jacob's roles as rhabdomantic and as oneiromantic is usually viewed as secondary; so the majority of commentators, with the notable exception of Speiser. From the point of view of role theory, however, Jacob simply enacts, like most of the magico-religious specialists examined in this study, multiple roles. J and E, from this perspective, may well have split up an originally seamless narrative (Noth's *Grundlage*) in order to emphasize their own distinctive agendas (see Noth, *A History of Pentateuchal Traditions*, 38–41, 76).

[61] The present translation takes *yybl* actively, with Hoftijzer (*editio princeps*, 205–206), Caquot & Lemaire ("Les textes araméennes," 199), Ringgren ("Balaam and the Deir 'Allā Inscription," 94), Müller ("Die aramäische Inschrift," 226), Rofé (*Spr Bl'm*, 66), and the Weipperts ("Die 'Bileam' Inschrift," 96). In support of the semantic parallel here between *yld* (Gen 30:39) and *ybl* (DAT I:9), N.B. the parallel between *ybl* and *yṣ'* in Job 10:18–19: *mrḥm hṣ'tny//mbṭn 'wbl*, "from the womb you brought me forth//from the womb I have been brought forth."

answers from the gods by "reading" them in the peculiarities associated with malformed births.[62]

At any rate, "rod" and "staff" in DAT I:9 may preserve remnants of a rhabdomantic technique in a religious tradition which may be somewhat similar to the strange practice preserved in the biblical folktale of Gen 30:37–42. Assuming that the association of both traditions with the Transjordan is more than mere coincidence, the surface parallels between the two may well reflect, as Hackett has argued, part of a recognizable religio-cultural "pattern,"[63] particularly since both may also come from a region where demonic beings were predisposed to nocturnal attacks, at least according to the biblical tradition of the Penuel encounter (Gen 32:22–23).[64]

Most importantly for this study, DAT I:9 and Gen 30–31 appear to preserve role-sets which are strikingly parallel.[65] From a role theory perspective, the Balaam portrayed in DAT I:1–9, like Jacob and Joseph in the Israelite traditions, enacts closely complementary roles within a common Syro-Palestinian "diviner/seer" role-set. As augur/ornithomantic, the DAT Balaam appears to have read

[62] E. Leichty, *The Omen Series šumma izbu* (Locust Valley, N.Y.: J. J. Augustin, 1970). This statement (and those that follow in DAT I:9–19) might well be intended to be hyperbolic, as are many of the statements in *šumma izbu.* Nougayrol cites an illustrative example of physiognomic divination in which omens are drawn from the shape of a man's head; i.e., whether it looks like that of a chameleon, a marten, a deer, a falcon, a bat, an ox, an ass, a dog, or a pig. The shape itself communicated a message from the gods. Nougayrol calls this method of divination "assez ingenieuse et imagée" ("La divination babylonienne," 56), adjectives not inapplicable to the material in DAT I:9–16.

In the dream of Dumuzi (Oppenheim, *Dreambook,* 246) there is a similar list of negative omens "seen" by Dumuzi in a dream. In this list, it is quite interesting to note that images of an owl and a falcon, each holding something in their claws, are immediately followed by goats and sheep in severe distress. Moreover, these visions are uniformly interpreted by Dumuzi's sister (Geštinanna) as negative omens. Balaam's oracles in DAT I might well have been constructed according to a mythical pattern common to fertility cults elsewhere in the ancient Near East.

[63] Hackett, "Some Observations on the Balaam Tradition," 220.

[64] The Penuel encounter is interesting because it takes place on the Jabbok (Zerqa), in the precise vicinity of modern Deir 'Allā. Jacob was accosted here by a demonic being very much like that which confronts Balaam in Num 22:21–35 (cf. H. Gressmann, *Mose und seine Zeit,* 325). The appearance of the *šdyn* in a similar demonic role (DAT I:6; cf. the *śāṭān* in Num 22:22) lends credence to Rudolph's assessment of the she-ass story's relative antiquity (*Der "Elohist" von Exodus bis Josua,* 106–111; contrast Rofé, *Spr Bl'm,* 51).

[65] In support of the hypothesis that J and E split up an originally seamless G narrative portraying Jacob in complementary divinatory roles, note several examples in which oneiromantic oracles are sent by the gods to confirm or deny the validity of other oracles. In KUB XXIV 3 ii 42, for example, Muwattili asks that the Storm-god confirm a *GIŠḪUR* oracle via a dream (Kammenhuber, *Orakelpraxis,* 24). In KUB VII 5 iv 1–10, the success of a ritual against impotence is determined by whether or not an erotic dream is experienced (cited in G. M. Beckman, *Hittite Birth Rituals,* 170–171). At Ugarit, El's hopes for Baal are confirmed via a cledonomantic omen seen in a dream (KTU 1.6 III 1–24).

a number of bird-omens clearly parallel to those in Anatolian and Mesopotamian sources. As rhabdomantic/oneiromantic, the DAT Balaam apparently also enacted a role-set identical in form (if not precisely in function) to that enacted by a Hebrew patriarch in the Bible.

Balaam as Oneiromantic

The oracle responsible for generating all this ancillary divinatory activity came to Balaam in a nocturnal vision/audition. It may well have been solicited. Formal incubation is attested as early as the Old Hittite period in Anatolia,[66] and is a practice common to several ancient cultures.[67] In Syria-Palestine, Samuel, a *rōʾeh* and *nābîʾ*, *inter alia,* received his initial "vision" (*ḥzwn*) in an incident that contains all the essential elements of an incubation.[68] In Anatolia, moreover, incubation can be linked directly to ritual purification: a pregnant woman, for example, is pronounced ready to bear a child only after receiving a favorable dream.[69]

On the other hand, it is entirely possible that Balaam's dream came unsolicited (though this appears unlikely, given the "professional" context in which it is found). Joseph the *pōtēr* could receive unsolicited dreams (Gen 37:5–11) as well as interpret the dreams of others (Gen 40:8). So could Daniel (Dan 7:1; 2:28).[70]

[66] Kammenhuber, *Orakelpraxis,* 38–39.

[67] For Mesopotamia, note Gudea's dream (*Dreambook,* 245–246), provoked in order to ascertain when to begin temple construction (M. Leibovici, "Les songes et leur interpretation à Babylone," dans *Les songes et leur interpretation,* SO 2 [Paris: Editions du Seuil, 1959] 80–81). Note also the description of Addu-duri's dream in the temple of Bēlet-ekallim (ARM X 50:8–13; cf. Noort, *Untersuchungen,* 27). In Greece, incubation was especially popular in Aesclepian temples; cf. C. A. Meier, "The Dream in Ancient Greece and Its Use in Temple Cures (Incubation)," in G. E. von Grunebaum & R. Caillois, eds., *The Dream and Human Societies* (Berkeley: Univ. of California, 1966) 303–320. In Egypt, incubation comes rather late; see A. Erman, *Die Religion der Ägypter* (Berlin: de Gruyter, 1934) 388, probably because of Hellenistic influence; see S. Sauneron, "Les songes et leur interpretation dans l'Egypte ancienne," dans *Les songes et leur interpretation,* 40–41.

[68] Incubation is suspected whenever a dreamer receives a nocturnal vision while sleeping in a sanctuary. An image or icon representing the deity is usually nearby (the absence of which occasions Addu-dūri's weeping in ARM X 50:12), and often a divine voice calls out to the sleeper. All these ingredients are present, for example, in 1 Sam 3:3–4 (cf. A. Caquot, "Les songes et leur interpretation selon Canaan et Israël," in *Les songes et leur interpretation,* 110–111), but both the DAT and biblical Balaam traditions are somewhat ambiguous.

[69] "The next morning the woman washes, and if she is (shown) by a dream (to be) pure, then the *patili*-priest takes her in to the birth-stool" (KUB IX 22 iii 30, 35, cited in G. Beckman, *Hittite Birth Rituals,* 94–97, 114; cf. Kammenhuber, *Orakelpraxis,* 40).

[70] Caquot, "Les songes et leur interpretation selon Canaan et Israël," 120–122.

The text does say that Balaam "saw" (*ḥzh*) this vision, and the scribe recording this important event in red ink ascribed to it the authority of El himself, the supreme god of the Canaanite pantheon, because Balaam appears to have seen this vision *kmś*' *'l;* i.e., "in a manner similar to the way one receives a *mś*' of El" or "according to a *mś*' of El" (DAT I:2), a statement evidently intended to refer the reader to a known means of receiving divine revelation.[71] From the biblical parallels (which are the only other examples of *mś*' oracles at our disposal),[72] we know that the oracles delivered under the superscription *mś*' were typically "seen," usually judgmental, and linked directly to the Jerusalem cult, a form of Yahwism which maintained close ties to Canaanite religious forms and practices.[73]

Should the phrase *mś*' *'l* have been stereotypical, then we must consider seriously whether this particular "diviner/seer" was portrayed here as receiving a nocturnal vision by means of a well-known Syro-Palestinian praxis essentially no different from that of "diviners/seers" operating elsewhere.[74] The *mś*' form appears to have remained the same. While certainty is impossible, the only major difference to surface so far is the name of the deity who authorizes it.[75]

This possibility seems more attractive when we note the continuing presence of *ḥzh* seers in some biblical circles and contrast this with the reactionary

[71] Although the *ś* is not completely clear, it seems epigraphically preferable to *l;* cf. B. Levine ("The Deir 'Allā Plaster Inscriptions," 196), following a suggestion by E. Puech, who examined the fragments personally. J. Hackett, who also examined the fragments personally (*The Balaam Text,* 25), A. Rofé (*Spr Bl'm,* 61), and the Weipperts ("Die 'Bileam' Inschrift, 82) all concur with this reading.

[72] See the discussion in M. Saebø, "Excurs: der Begriff *maśśā*' als Überschrift und Fachwort in den Prophetenbüchern," *Sacharja 9–14,* 137–140.

[73] The dovetailing of Yahwistic belief with Canaanite praxis is concisely discussed by G. von Rad (*Old Testament Theology* I:40–48) and G. Fohrer, *History of Israelite Religion* (Nashville: Abingdon, 1972), para. 3 & 4.

[74] Thus we cannot limit the *maśśā*' only to "a specialized oracle that was peculiar to Judah" (R. Wilson, *Prophecy and Society,* 258).

[75] B. A. Levine surveys the historical, archaeological, epigraphical, and biblical evidence to argue that the Iron Age temple at Deir 'Allā was an El temple. He is careful not to assert that Israelite Yahwism was not established in Gilead, "but only that it coexisted, in this case, with an autochthonous El cult of probable great antiquity." Levine further argues, from a comparative analysis of the biblical and DAT Balaam traditions, that there likely existed an "El repertoire, emanating from centers of the El cult, upon which biblical writers drew for their materials." A major biblical tradition-complex characterized by this "El repertoire" is the Balaam complex, but it does not stand alone: cf. also Isa 14:12–20 and much of the book of Job, *sans* prologue and epilogue. Cf. Levine, "The Balaam Inscription from Deir 'Allā: Historical Aspects," in *Biblical Archaeology Today,* 334–335. Cf. also C. E. L'Heureux, *Rank Among the Canaanite Gods,* 67: "There is no evidence that El was in decline during the Israelite period. On the other hand, there are a number of indications that throughout the time in which the Hebrew Bible was being formed, there was periodic contact with El traditions which continued to be alive outside of Israel."

emphasis against "visions" (*ḥăzônîm*) characteristic of others, where "audition" —the "word" (*dābār*)—gradually became, according to some, the "orthodox" mode of revelation.[76] Positing a close relationship between divination and *mśʾ*-oracle would also help us to explain why a tradent from something resembling this latter circle so vigorously attacks its Yahwicization (Jer 23:33–40).[77]

From the perspective of role-theory, Balaam, like all the other magico-religious specialists examined in this study, simply enacts a set of complementary roles at Deir ʿAllā. What is "complementary" to one audience's view of an "appropriate" role-set, however, can be "divergent" to another's. This is a matter of utmost delicacy within Israelite tradition, particularly with regard to the defining parameters of the terms "prophecy" and "divination."[78] Without discounting the pervasive influence of the deuteronomistic editors on Israel's literary traditions, role theory helps us not only to explain the contours of these often shifting parameters, but also to understand better the severity of the intrarole conflict in Israel over the nature and authority of these differing types of divine revelation.[79] *Mśʾ ʾl*-revelation may well have been at the center of its own distinctive intrarole conflict.[80]

[76] Wilson, *Prophecy and Society*, 249–250; Petersen, *The Roles of Israel's Prophets*, 85–86.

[77] Wilson, *Prophecy and Society*, 249–250. Cf. also W. McKane, "*Maśśāʾ* in Jer 23:33–40," in *Prophecy: FS G. Fohrer*, 35–40.

[78] H. B. Huffmon defines "prophecy" as "(a) a communication from the divine world, normally for a third party through a mediator (prophet) who may or may not identify with the deity; (b) inspiration through ecstasy, dreams (apart from induced dreams in most instances), or what may be called inner illumination; (c) an immediate message, i.e., a message that does not require a technical specialist to interpret it; (d) the likelihood that the message is unsolicited (unlike divination except in the case of unusual natural phenomena); and (e) the likelihood that the message is exhortatory or admonitory"; cf. "Prophecy in the Mari Letters," *BA* 31 (1968) 103.

A. de Waal Malefijt defines "divination" as "a form of religious communication in which supernatural powers give, or are coerced into giving, direct information . . . . Moreover, divination differs significantly from other forms of religious communication in that it does not generally attempt to alter the behavior or judgment of the supernatural powers, but merely to discover their opinions. It tries to discover the will and intention of the gods, and thereby to foretell the future, or explain past events"; cf. *Religion and Culture*, 215.

For Max Weber, the "ethical prophet" is predominantly an instrument for the proclamation and will of a deity, while the "exemplary prophet" is a person, who, by his/her personal example, shows the way to religious salvation. "Priests" are predominantly interested in maintaining the religious *status quo*, but "prophets . . . do not receive their mission from any human agency." This sentence reflects Weber's concept of "prophetic breakthrough" (*Sociology of Religion*, 51, 55), yet he also recognizes that there is significant role overlap between "prophecy" and "divination": "prophets very often practiced divination as well as magical healing and counseling" (ibid., 47).

[79] Cf. Petersen, *Roles of Israel's Prophets*, 93–97.

[80] Cf. Petersen, *Late Israelite Prophecy*, 97–102.

At any rate, Balaam's nocturnal dream/vision was both a revelation from the gods and a mantic glimpse into the future, to define it by means of the dream categories carefully framed by Oppenheim. With some dreams, the meaning lay hidden until "released" (*pšr*) by a professional oneiromantic: witness the extensive collection of omens in the Assyrian series *Ziqīqu* (the god of dreams) used by professional oneiromantics in Mesopotamia.[81] In Anatolia, Hattušili III grew quite famous for his dream collections, many of which starred Šaušga, his favorite goddess.[82]

In Syria-Palestine, Joseph unravels symbolic dreams needing an interpretation (Gen 40:9–19; 41:25–32). Apart from this interpretation, Egypt's future would have remained a mystery, and the famine looming over the horizon would have devastated the country. Moreover, the tradent responsible for relating this narrative would have lost an opportunity to exalt his hero's oneiromantic prowess over against that of his Egyptian antagonists (Gen 41:8).[83]

Balaam's night-vision at Deir 'Allā, however, is more like Joseph's dreams of the sheaves and heavenly bodies (Gen 37:8, 10), dreams which were clearly understood by Joseph's family without the aid of an interpreter.[84] We can see from the DAT Balaam's sorrowful reaction in DAT I:3–4 that he understood immediately the tragic import of the divine council's decree.[85]

With regard to the formal elements in Balaam's night-vision, reference to other dreams from the ancient Near East may prove to be informative. One of the most obvious problems in interpreting this vision in DAT is a lack of context. What we have on the surface of this text, hovering about this night-vision/audition, is a swarm of fragmentary details that need to be pulled together into a broader perspective. We will attempt to illuminate this perspective by examining Balaam's "divine council" encounter against other well-known "divine council" encounters.[86]

[81] *Dreambook,* 307–344.

[82] Ibid., 254–255; Gurney, "Babylonians and Hittites," 143; M. Vieyra, "Les songes et leur interpretation chez les Hittites," 92–94.

[83] Caquot, "Les songes et leur interpretation selon Canaan et Israël," 112–115; Oppenheim, *Dreambook,* 204–208. Some have suggested, since the motif of celestial bodies paying homage to a great person is known elsewhere (e.g., Sennacherib), that Joseph's dream in Gen 37:9 is an interpolation, and the "sheaves" dream is "more original." Against this possibility one must weigh the ancient Near Eastern phenomenon of "dream-doubling" (as in Gen 41:32); cf. D. B. Redford, *A Study of the Biblical Story of Joseph,* 70.

[84] Ibid., 70–71.

[85] "And Balaam arose on the morrow . . . and wept bitterly" (*wbkh ybkh,* DAT I:3–4). Balaam's "people" (*'mh*) then ask him, "why do you fast (*ṭṣm*); (why) do you weep?" (*tbkh,* DAT I:4).

[86] E. T. Mullen (*The Assembly of the Gods: The Divine Council in Canaanite and Early Hebrew Literature,* HSM 24 [Chico, Ca.: Scholars, 1980] 228) notes that the "major function" of the divine council in all the Near Eastern sources "is to decree the fate or destiny of a group or an individual."

In Enkidu's dream in Tablet VII of the Epic of Gilgameš (Hittite version), for example,[87] Anu, Enlil, Ea, and Šamaš come together in council to solve an immediate crisis,[88] viz. the killing of the Bull of Heaven. As "presiding officer," Anu[89] opens this heavenly meeting with a demand for justice. The role of "prosecuting attorney" is enacted by Enlil, an old Sumerian god with a chthonic past.[90] Šamaš serves as "defense counsel" on Enkidu's behalf, a role well in keeping with his character as the primary deity before whom men cry out for justice elsewhere in Mesopotamian myth and ritual.[91] Over Šamaš' protests, Enlil argues strenuously for Enkidu's death. Enlil's position prevails, and the council reveals its decision to Enkidu through a mantic dream which needs no interpreter. Enkidu responds to this judicial decision with bitter weeping.

In Job 1:6–12 and 2:1–6, another famous divine council convenes. In this scene, a prosecutor-figure (*hśṭn*) "takes a stand" (*htyṣb*)[92] before Yahweh, who grants the request to afflict Job. Like the terrors unleashed by the Sibitti (the demons spawned by Anu to serve at Erra's bidding),[93] "the satan's" afflictions are launched against Job and his house through several traditionally "demonic" channels: fire, wind, war, and sickness.

[87] Oppenheim, *Dreambook,* 248 (Hittite version); ANET 85–86.

[88] T. Jacobsen has argued that the council motif in Mesopotamia goes back to a time when the assembly convened only to deal with immediate crises; cf. "Primitive Democracy in Ancient Mesopotamia," in W. L. Moran, ed., *Toward the Image of Tammuz* (Cambridge: Harvard, 1970) 157–180.

[89] Like El in the Šaḥar/Šalim cycle at Ugarit (KTU 1.23 49–51), Anu is the "king of the gods" (*šar ilāni*) who "impregnates" a consort (*ir-ḫe-e-ma,* Erra I:28). On El's continuing sexual potency and primacy even into old age, cf. L'Heureux, *Rank Among the Canaanite Gods,* 7–12.

[90] See Oppenheim, *Ancient Mesopotamia,* 194–195. Enlil's area of expertise includes the "oracular decisions (which affect) humankind" (*te-rit nišê,* AGH 20:23). His command in this regard is even styled "unalterable" (*lā uttakkaru,* AGH 20:24, 30).

[91] Šamaš is the "lord of justice" (*be-el dinim,* HSM 7494:141, cited in Starr, *Rituals of the Diviner,* 36, 44) and "lord of the (judicial) decision" (*bēl purussû,* BBR 1–20:124). One of Šamaš' jobs is to open "the bolts on the gates of heaven" (*si-ik-ku-ri da-la-at ša-me-e,* HSM 7494:9, cited in Starr, *Rituals,* 30, 37), and "judge humankind's case" (*ta-di-in di-in te-ni-ši-tim,* HSM 7494:11, cited in Starr, *Rituals,* 30, 37).

[92] In Job 2:1, "the satan" enters with the other divine beings "to take a stand" (*lhtyṣb*) for the express purpose of beginning formal prosecution. In DAT I:6, the *šdyn* "take a stand in the assembly" (*nṣbw šdyn mw'd*) for the same reason. Mullen (*The Assembly of the Gods,* 231) reviews the divine council scenes in 1 Kgs 22:19–23; Isa 6:1–2; Psa 29; 82:1–8; 89:6–9; Job 1:6; 2:1, and concludes, among other things, that *yṣb* is a "technical term for participating in the assembly." Its counterpart in the Mesopotamian divine council is *uzuzzu* ("to stand"), as noted by T. Jacobsen ("Primitive Democracy in Ancient Mesopotamia," 401). Oppenheim notes that this formal "taking a stand" is typical for dream experiences well into the Hellenistic period (*Dreambook,* 187–189).

[93] Erra I:28–44. N.B. that the Sibitti are held in check by Išum, who is metaphorically called a "door bolted before them" (*dal-tùm-ma e-dil pa-nu-*[*uš-šú-u*]*n,* Erra I:27).

Unlike Enkidu, however, Job is never told why all this has happened to him, nor does a deified defense counsel "take a stand" on his behalf. The deliberate omission of these elements thus helps to set the stage for the several dialogues about human suffering which follow, dialogues in which Job weeps (Job 16:16), and, significantly, insists that a vindicator/"defense counselor" will eventually arise (Job 19:25).[94]

DAT I presents clear parallels to these "divine council" judgment scenes. The supreme Canaanite deity El is not specifically cited as presiding over the "assembly," but an "assembly" (*mw'd,* DAT I:6) of "divine beings" (*'lhn,* I:2, 5)[95] convenes. El does appear as the primary deity in DAT II:6.[96] Moreover, Balaam does apparently see a vision "according to an oracle of El" (*kmś' 'l,* DAT I:1–2).[97] When these references are taken together, it becomes very difficult to imagine any other deity in control of these heavenly proceedings. At any rate, the DAT *šdyn* "take a stand" (*nṣbw,* DAT I:6), apparently to prosecute someone, in this *mw'd* assembly; i.e., they apparently enact a role similar to that enacted by Enlil in Enkidu's dream and by the *śṭn* in Job 1–2.

The sun, moon, and stars, while overtly recognized as part of Yahweh's heavenly host (cf. Josh 10:12b–13a; 2 Kgs 21:2–5),[98] nevertheless enact no role in the Yahwistic cultus (Deut 4:19; 17:3), and there is no heavenly "defense counsel" in Job's version of this judgment scene. In light, however, of the role enacted by Šamaš in Enkidu's dream, and the rather prominent role enacted by the Sun-goddess of the Netherworld in Anatolian ritual (HT 22:7; 26:1; 28:16, 18; 30:5; 32:3; 34:39), it is very tempting to follow Caquot and Lemaire[99] in restoring *š[m/pš]* in DAT I:6 and to identify the "defense counsel" in this Transjordanian dream with a solar deity.

Several texts from Ugarit support this suggestion. The solar goddess there skillfully counsels Baal as together they conspire to outwit his Netherworld

[94] N. Habel believes that the *g'l* of Job 19:25 refers to a non-Yahwistic "redeemer"; *Job,* OTL (Philadelphia: Westminster, 1985) 306–307.

[95] The activities of the attendant deities in the Canaanite divine council are little known compared with the Mesopotamian council (Mullen, *Assembly of the Gods,* 178).

[96] Hoftijzer, Müller and Levine read *'l* twice in DAT II:6 as the Canaanite deity El. Hackett reads the first *'l* as the Canaanite deity and the second *'l* as a preposition. Caquot & Lemaire take both occurrences of *'l* in DAT II:6 (plus the *'l* in DAT I:2) as plural demonstratives.

[97] Levine notes ("The Balaam Inscription: Historical Aspects," 333) that G. Hamilton and E. Puech independently proposed the restoration (*wyḥz mḥzh*) *kmś' 'l* in DAT I:1–2. Hackett accepts this (*The Balaam Text,* 33).

[98] Cf. the discussion in Mullen, *Assembly of the Gods,* 196–197.

[99] "Les textes araméennes," 196. Should the careful positioning of the fragment-combinations by the Weipperts ("Die 'Bileam' Inschrift," 80) and A. Lemaire ("L'inscription de Balaam trouvée à Deir 'Allā: épigraphie," 319) be taken seriously, there is not enough room in the join between Combinations Ic and Id for a reconstruction as long as *š[gr w'štr]* in DAT I:6.

nemesis.[100] She boldly argues before Mot that El is really on Baal's side, and Mot is convinced by her argument; persuaded that Baal's ultimate victory is certain, Mot decides to retreat.[101] Šapaš also knows how to keep a client's confidence, a detail in the text consequent to a "defense counselor" role-set. (Baal's own sister Anat is not informed of their ingenious homeopathic scheme to trick Mot into thinking Baal has already died.[102]) For her successful efforts in defending Baal against Mot's "prosecution," Šapaš is finally lauded in song, like Šamaš in Mesopotamia.[103]

Whether or not the sun-deity enacts a role in this tradition, Balaam's response to the council's decree is not at all obscure. Like Enkidu and Job, Balaam weeps bitterly after hearing the council's decision (*wbkh ybkh,* DAT I:3–4), a fearful response which becomes highly institutionalized in later Jewish apocalyptic.[104] We have no way of knowing for sure how his client—if any—reacted, but the immediate appearance of a series of counterchecking (?) measures seems a telling indication.

In addition to these parallels, the doomsday oracle of the *šdyn* (DAT I:6–7) is clothed in cosmic metaphors very similar to those used in anti-demonic incantations from Mesopotamia. "Heavenly bolts" (*skry šmyn,* DAT I:6)[105] and impenetrable "clouds" (*'b,* I:6) are like metaphors used by *āšipu* exorcists. In the exorcists' incantations and prayers, moreover, Šamaš repeatedly emerges as the deity primarily responsible for controlling access to the bolt on the heavenly doors,[106] although Ištar, as Morning Star, can also perform the necessary

[100] KTU 1.5 V, assuming, with J. C. L. Gibson, that Šapaš is the speaker on this fragmentary tablet; cf. *Canaanite Myths and Legends* (Edinburgh: T. and T. Clark, 1977) 15–16. In KTU 1.161 Šapaš is adjured to descend to the Netherworld in a ritual designed to bring "peace to Ugarit"; this text was discussed by T. J. Lewis, "The Role of Šapšu in the Ugaritic Funerary Text," paper presented to Ugaritic Studies Group, Annual Meeting of the Society of Biblical Literature, Chicago, Illinois, Nov 20, 1988.

[101] KTU 1.6 VI 22–35.

[102] KTU 1.6 I 8–15.

[103] KTU 1.6 VI 45–53. Cf. BWL 126–138 (Šamaš).

[104] Cf. Dan 8:27; 1 Enoch 90:41; 2 Esdras 6:36–37.

[105] The nominal form + fem sg suff *skrky* ("your bolt") in DAT I:7 probably means that *skry* in DAT I:6 should also be taken nominatively ("bolts"). Other viewpoints are expressed in Levine, "The Deir 'Allā Plaster Inscriptions," 198, and Hackett, *The Balaam Text,* 43. *Skry šmyn* is recognized as a stock metaphor by Hoftijzer (*editio princeps,* 194), S. Kaufman ("Review of Hoftijzer & van der Kooij," 73), Dahood ("Review of Hoftijzer & van der Kooij," 125), and the Weipperts ("Der 'Bileam' Inschrift," 92).

[106] "You (Šamaš) open the locked bolts of heaven" (*ed-lu-u-ti sik-kur šamê,* AGH 48:107). As "defense counsel," Šamaš is often petitioned as the savior of humankind from darkness, but in his role as "impartial judge," note that Šamaš is able not only to "dispel the darkness," but also to "shorten the days and lengthen the nights" (BWL 135:177, 180). He can even "open wide the doors of the earth," while he "(locks?) the bolt of the heavens" (BWL 136:182).

This impartiality is also reflected in Anatolia. The Sun-goddess of Arinna is described

task of opening it.[107]

That this is indeed a necessary task becomes clear once we consider the alternative. Should the heavenly doors remain locked, the forces of darkness could roam freely over the earth, afflicting humankind at their whim and will—precisely what the *šdyn* have in mind! Accordingly, at least one exorcist's ritual cannot begin until the earthly doors are securely locked and the heavenly doors are thrown open; i.e., when the exorcist as "healer" has been given direct access to the heavenly realm where the "great gods of the night" reside.[108]

Similar "cloud" metaphors are picked up and elaborated in later, predominantly astrological texts,[109] but the *combination* of "heavenly bolts" and "dark cloud" metaphors in DAT I:6–7 also has a striking parallel in the *āšipūtu* literature, specifically Maqlû VII 1–22, in that these prayer-requests of the macrocosmos have their microcosmos in the rituals, apotropaic and otherwise, designed to protect and purify the entranceways of houses and temples from demonic attack.[110] Note in Maqlû VII that the sorceress' machinations are described as "your sorcery" (*kiš-pi-ki*), "your weather" (*ûm-ki*), and "your dark cloud" (*urpata-ki*)[111] while the *āšipu*-exorcist chants an incantation about the "locked doors." In this chant, the exorcist points out, together with Siris, that Ningišzida, the constable of the Netherworld, has matters firmly under control: no demon can escape because "the locks are placed on door and bar, as well as the

---

as one who "opens the doors of heaven" (Goetze, *Kleinasien,* 136, citing KUB XXIV 3 i 50), but, at the Storm-god's command, can also "open the door of the Netherworld" (Haas & Wilhelm, *Hurritische und luwische Riten,* 52, citing KBo X 45 i).

McCarter argues ("The Balaam Texts," 53–54) against Caquot & Lemaire's restoration partially on the grounds that it is difficult to conceive of the solar deity *obscuring* the sky, but it is not unusual for the Anatolian Sun-goddess of the Netherworld to enact such a role. Neither is it particularly unusual in Canaanite/Phoenician religion to see inversions where, e.g., prayers are offered to *ršp,* god of pestilence, in order to insure good health (cited in W. F. Albright, *Archaeology and the Religion of Israel* [Garden City, N.Y.: Doubleday, 1969] 77–78).

[107] "Ištar . . . opens the way like the sun-disk" (AGH 128:7–8).

[108] "Quiet is the steppe-land, closed are the doors, locked are the bolts (*ši-ga-ru*), silent are the gods of the Netherworld (*irṣiti*); open are the doors of the wide heavens" (TuL 163:8–10). See further W. Mayer, *Untersuchungen zur Formensprache der babylonischen "Gebetsbeschwörungen,"* 180, 211, n. 4, and esp. 427–428.

[109] For example, see ACh (Adad) 35:48: "If the night is obscured, there will be disease and pestilence in the land" (cited in Levine, "Plaster Inscriptions," 203, n. 29).

[110] Maqlû VII:14 reassures the exorcist's client that no evil can "enter through the door into the house" when the house's (Netherworld's) doors are "locked" and "bolted," language essentially identical to that found in Arslan Tash I:21, and indeed, in all apotropaic portal inscriptions. N.B. that the incantation in Arslan Tash I also appeals to "all the sons of El" (*kl bn 'lm,* taking *m* as enclitic) and "all the holy ones" (*kl qdšn,* KAI 27:11–12), NW Semitic epithets used elsewhere for the "divine council" (cf. Psa 29:1; 89:6, 8).

[111] This sequence is found twice, in Maqlû V:86–87 as well as VII:5–6.

incantation of Siris and Ningišzida."[112]

The *šdyn* in DAT I:6–7 want not only to inflict punishment on Balaam's client, but also to insure that the other members of the heavenly council do nothing to interfere with the afflictions they have planned:

> Sew up the bolts of heaven (*skry šmyn*) . . .
> With your cloud (*'bky*) ordaining darkness and not eternal light!

The oneiromantic role enacted by the DAT Balaam thus appears to stand within a broader ancient Near Eastern trajectory and corresponds rather closely to that of other "divine council" messengers (cf. Jer 23:8; also Job 15:8).[113] Having witnessed the council's decree, Balaam then "tells" it (*'ḥwkm,* DAT I:5)[114] to its intended recipient (presumably his client), even introducing the conciliar decree with a stereotypical epithet ("Come, see the works of the gods!," DAT I:5)[115] and reporting the *šdyn*'s prosecutorial decrees in cosmic metaphors habitually found in the incantation literature.

[112] "Door" (*daltu*), "bolt" (*sikkūru*), and "cloud" (*urpatu*) are all linked with "sorcery" (*kiš-pi*) in Maq VII:1–22. On Ningišzida's function as "sheriff," see Jacobsen, *Treasures of Darkness,* 228–229.

[113] Building on the suggestions of H. W. Robinson ("The Council of Yahweh," *JTS* 45 [1944] 151–157), and F. M. Cross ("The Council of Yahweh in Second Isaiah," *JNES* 12 [1953] 274–277), Mullen argues for a type of "prophecy" where "the prophet is the herald of the divine council," even suggesting, on the basis of Nathan's reception of Yahweh's word at night (2 Sam 7:4–5), an oneiromantic praxis underlying this type of "prophecy" (*Assembly of the Gods,* 216–226).

N.B. the "returning" of divine/human messages in Syria-Palestine follows a stereotypical pattern. Baal "returns/replies" (*y[t]b// 'dd*) to Anat regarding the poor treatment accorded him by the divine council (KTU 1.4 III 10–11). Gad the *ḥōzeh* asks David what "word" he should "return" (*'āšîb*) to Yahweh (2 Sam 24:13). A royal servant named *Tlmyn* asks a Canaanite queen to "return a word to your servant" (UT 89:14–15). Habakkuk "takes a stand" (*'etyaṣṣēbâ*) to see what Yahweh will say and what he (Habakkuk) will "return/answer" (*'āšîb,* Hab 2:1).

Balaam "returns" a "word" (*hăšibōtî 'etkem dābār,* Num 22:8) to Balak's messengers. Since the word of the council's herald is equivalent to the word of the council itself, Balaam "answers" (*'ānāh,* Mic 6:5) Balak with this word.

[114] The root *ḥwh* is found five times in Job (13:7; 15:17; 32:6, 10, 17; 36:2) and once in Psalms (19:3). Job 15:17 is set in a "divine council" context, since 15:15 expressly states that God puts no trust in "his holy ones" (*biqdōšāw;* cf. Psa 89:6–9). Job expressly states, "I will tell you what I have seen"; cf.

Job 15:17	*'ḥwk . . . zh ḥzyty*
DAT I:5	*'ḥwkm . . .*
I:1	*ḥzh 'lhn*

[115] Hoftijzer (*editio princeps,* 192) points out the exact parallels between the following epithets:

Psa 46:9	*lkw ḥzh mp'lt yhwh*
Psa 66:5	*lkw wr'w mp'lt 'lhym*
DAT I:5	*wlkw r'w p'lt 'lhn.*

See also McCarter, "The Balaam Texts," 53.

BALAAM AS "EXORCIST"

Accurately reflecting the present nebulous state of Syro-Palestinian evidence for the roles enacted by "diviners/seers" vs. those enacted by "exorcists," the evidence for positing exorcistic activity in DAT is rather sketchy, at least when compared with the evidence for postulating complementary ornithomantic, rhabdomantic, and oneiromantic roles for the DAT Balaam as "diviner/seer." Nonetheless, a number of telltale signs, recognizable from comparison with Anatolian, Mesopotamian, and Syro-Palestinian texts, need to be examined carefully.

However one might approach the etymological origins of the *šdyn,* it seems clear that they enact a demonic *role* in the "divine council" judgment scene in DAT I, a chthonic function repeatedly exercised by the much-feared Sibitti in Anatolia and Mesopotamia,[116] the "Satan" (Job 1:7–12; cf. Num 22:22) and perhaps the *rûaḥ šeqer* ("lying spirit," 1 Kgs 22:22) in biblical conventions of the divine council, and the *šydyn* in later Aramaic bowl incantations.[117] The winged creature sketched on Combination I, moreover, looks very much like the winged creature sketched on the apotropaic portal plaque from Arslan Tash. The functional exorcistic parallels between the two have already been noted above in light of the winged demons sketched (on plaster!) elsewhere in Mesopotamian *āšipūtu* incantations.[118]

Further, the cosmic language employed by these *šdyn* in DAT I:6–7 preserves the same *combination* of metaphors about "(dark) clouds" and "(heavenly) bolts" found on the lips of *āšipu* exorcists in stereotypical exorcistic formulae designed to ward them off (Maqlû V:86–87; VII:5–6; see above for discussion). The speaker in DAT I:6–7 was evidently perceived as possessing more than just a passing acquaintance with this technical literature.

The presence of both winged (demonic?) figures and stereotypical language in DAT I, in other words, points toward the observation that the role-set of the magico-religious specialist responsible for generating this tradition, like that of the "old woman" in Anatolia,[119] encompassed both ends of the magic-religion continuum; i.e., both "exorcist" as well as "diviner/seer." Some of the usual complementary roles associated with the "exorcist" role-set ("purification-priest,"

[116] For Anatolia, cf. the portion of KUB XXVIII 5 cited by Kammenhuber (*Orakelpraxis,* 48–49). For Mesopotamia, see Erra I:23–44.

[117] Cf. CAI 3:14; 7:17; 47:2; 48:1 and *passim.*

[118] Cf. the plate of Arslan Tash I (Comte du Mesnil du Buisson, *Mélanges syriens offerts à M. René Dussaud,* p. 422), the plate of DAT I (Hoftijzer, *editio princeps,* plate 15), and BBR 53:16; 54:12.

Victor Sasson argues similarly that "the *'lhyn* and the *šdyn* are two separate and opposing groups of gods," "The Language of Rebellion in Psalm 2 and in the Plaster Texts from Deir 'Allā," *AUSS* 24 (1986) 148.

[119] Cf. the discussion of Anatolian specialists above in chapter 1.

"healer," "sorcerer") cannot be as readily traced in DAT as they can in the biblical Balaam tradition, but there does seem to be evidence for positing at least two other supplementary roles, about which more will be said below.

The evidence for positing these supplementary exorcistic roles, however, emerges from a comparative phenomenological analysis of Combination II, one of the more fragmentary texts discovered at Deir ʿAllā, and certainly one of the most controversial. Before entering this textual minefield, two qualifying remarks seem warranted. First, no convincing criteria exist for segregating the activity of Balaam in DAT I from the activity recorded on Combination II. Indeed, most interpreters feel that Combinations I and II preserve material cut basically from the same cloth, though there are still questions, of course, over how uniform the texture of this cloth might be.[120]

Second, Combination II is poorly read as entirely ritual or as entirely myth, but probably better read as a hybrid of both ritual and mythological narrative, like the Šaḥar/Šalim cycle at Ugarit (KTU 1.23). Several scholars, in fact, perceive the term *nqr* (repeated in DAT II:5, 12, & 14) to be a key ingredient in this ritual/narrative. J. Hoftijzer, for example, first interpreted *nqr* as a passive participle, "the one bored out" (i.e., "blinded": cf. Num 16:14; Judg 16:21), then set it in a framework of "curses" on Combination II.[121] Caquot and Lemaire, however, suggested that the middle radical *q* was really a grapheme for *ṣ*,[122] a linguistic peculiarity which resulted from phonological development over time (viz., proto-Semitic *ḏ* > *ṣ*).[123] In addition, they read *nqr* as a noun instead of a passive participle ("sprout"; cf. Arab. *nḏr*//Heb. *nṣr*).[124]

P. Kyle McCarter and Jo Ann Hackett developed both the phonological and lexical cues offered by Caquot and Lemaire and proposed intriguing hypotheses about the possible ritual scenario being played out on Combination II. McCarter proposed that *nq/ṣr* represented the "sprout" in an Adonis-type revivification

[120] Both McCarter ("The Balaam Texts," 49) and Müller ("Die aramäische Inschrift," 231) point out that the audience in both Combinations, (Balaam's) "people" (*ʿm*, DAT I:4; II:17) is apparently the same.

[121] J. Hoftijzer, *editio princeps*, 237. Apparently Hoftijzer extrapolated the "sorcerer" role enacted in a strand of the biblical Balaam tradition (Num 22:6) to the DAT Balaam, interpreting DAT II accordingly. While this methodology is suspect, Hoftijzer's view at least harmonizes with the view argued here in that the role of "sorcerer" is set within an "exorcist" role-set.

[122] R. Degen, *Altaramäische Grammatik* (Wiesbaden: Steiner, 1969) 36–37. Cf. *ʾrq* ("earth, land") in KAI 202B:26; 216:4; 222A:26, 28.

[123] Opinions are divided over whether the graphemes for the interdentals in the most ancient Aramaic inscriptions are due to dialectal influences ("Canaanisms") or instead represent the proto-Semitic interdentals, following upon the adoption of an alphabet (the Phoenician) which had no graphemes for them. Cf. the discussion in Moscati, ed., *Comparative Grammar of the Semitic Languages*, 29–30.

[124] Caquot & Lemaire, "Les textes araméennes," 202.

ritual,[125] while Hackett, following a suggestion by F. M. Cross, interpreted *nq/ṣr* as the "sprout/scion" offered in child sacrifice ritual.[126] B. A. Levine agreed with Caquot and Lemaire's reading of *nq/ṣr* as a noun, but translated "corpse" instead of "sprout" in an effort to develop an interpretation which takes into account more specifically the explicit Netherworld context intimated by the various *byt*-epithets found in DAT II:6–7.[127]

Since this text is far too fragmentary for any interpretation to claim exclusivity, none will be claimed here. Still, since radically pessimistic refusals to learn anything at all from this text seem neither warranted nor appropriate, and since few have sought to interpret this text against the backdrop of other ancient Near Eastern ritual texts, perhaps a comparative phenomenological approach might at least help us toward proposing a plausible ritual context.

Balaam as Craftsman of Homeopathic Images

However one reads *nqr*, it is to be noted that in DAT II:5 *nqr* stands in conjunction with *mdr* (*nqr wmdr*). The latter term can designate a "circumscribed" cultic area connected with "burning."[128] Further, the presence of the terms *kl*

[125] McCarter, in a sketch of unpublished lectures (cited in Hackett, *The Balaam Text*, 78–80). Interpreting McCarter's proposal from a role theory perspective, the specialist responsible for nurturing the "shoot" (taking *nq/ṣr* as a metaphorical representative of Adonis) would probably better be labelled an "exorcist" than a "diviner/seer," especially since most vegetation ceremonies connected with revivification of the "dying god" are heavily dependent on homeopathic magic. On Adonis rituals, see J. Frazer, *The Golden Bough*, abridged ed. (New York: MacMillan, 1922) 396–403.

[126] Hackett, *The Balaam Text*, 80–85. H. Ringgren suggests that *nq/ṣr* functioned metaphorically in DAT II in a manner analogous to the way in which *ṣmḥ* ("shoot, sprout") functions in Zech 3:8, "Bileam och inskriften från Deir 'Allā," *Religion och Bibel* 36 (1977) 85–89 (cited in Hackett, *The Balaam Text*, 5). Hackett's interpretation presupposes that the magico-religious specialist directing this child-sacrifice ritual enacted a rather complex set of exorcistic roles, at least as "reciter of incantations" and probably also as "purification priest."

[127] Levine, "The Deir 'Allā Plaster Inscriptions," 201. Levine argues that a magico-religious specialist was responsible for successfully freeing the goddess *šgr w'štr* from the Netherworld, and that he did so by "execrations and other forms of magic." The most plausible candidate for this exorcistic role-set had to be Balaam himself (ibid., 196). Although Levine does not pretend to analyze DAT from a role theory perspective, his interpretation is nevertheless highly congruent with the results of the present study, particularly when he implies that the DAT Balaam engaged in multiple role enactment, and further, that these roles included the role-sets encompassed by the labels "exorcist" *and* "diviner/seer."

[128] The *mědûrāh* in Isa 30:33 and Ezek 24:9 has analogues in the Mesopotamian *abru*- "pyre" (BBR 26 II:25), the *nappaṭu/ḫuluppaqu* (Šur I:1; Maq IX:22), and the Anatolian *ukturi* (HT 66:1, 10, 20). The root of the Heb. term *mědûrāh* (*dwr*) can mean "ball" in the

("provided")[129] and *rṭb* ("foliage")[130] leave the distinct impression that whatever this *nqr* might represent, it has something to do with the preparation of an area for (cultic) burning. Similar preparations are found at the beginning of a number of ritual texts, e.g., Šurpu I:1–5:

> When you perform the rituals for the Šurpu (-series), you set up a brazier,
> you put trimmed reeds crosswise on top of the brazier,
> you surround it with a magic circle of flour.
> You recite the incantation "I am a pure man," sprinkle water (around),
> light a torch from a sulphur-flame . . . .[131]

When next we find the term *nqr*, it is in the phrase *nqr blbbh n'nḥ* ("the *nqr* moans in its heart, DAT II:12). Though lodged in a context that is quite unclear, this phrase may be paralleled by the one which immediately precedes it, *blbbm n'nḥ* ("in their heart it moans" [?]), the plural suffix apparently indicating the presence of a group. It must be emphasized, however, that this is only one of several conceivable possibilities for translation.[132]

Nevertheless, the "moaning"[133] of the *nqr* in *its* heart (*blbbh*), should it be

---

nominative form (Isa 22:18; cf. 29:3) and "to encircle, heap up" in the verbal form (Ezek 24:5). Cf. the "magic circle" (*zì-su-ra-a*) delineating the exorcist's sphere of activity at the beginning of *Šurpu* (Šur I:3; cf. also TuL 117:3).

[129] Regarding *kl* ("to prepare"), one of the *āšipu*'s roles is to "prepare the house for the *rābiṣu*-demon" (*bît rābiṣi u-kal,* TuL 17:20). When a person is seized by a dead spirit, the exorcist must "consecrate the prepared place" (*kul-la-ta tu-qad-daš,* BBR 52:2; von Soden translates *kul-la-ta* "*Lehmterrasse*" [AHW 502]). For a discussion, cf. Hackett, *Balaam Text,* 58.

[130] On *rṭb* ("foliage"), cf. the "trimmed reeds" (*GI.MEŠkar-tu-tì*) which are laid out on the *nappaṭu* at the beginning of the *Šurpu* series (Šur I:2).

[131] Translation by E. Reiner. See also the ritual preparations in BBR 26 I:20–32, II:17; TuL 118:18–19.

[132] For the epigraphical and syntactic possibilities, see Hackett, *The Balaam Text,* 68.

[133] Several texts allude to "moaning" in the course of exorcistic ritual praxis. In a complex ritual for purifying a defiled temple (Racc 44:1–5), several magico-religious specialists engage in what appear to be specific cultic activities associated with their respective offices. The *bārû* "opens" (*uš-šar*) the ritual, and an *abru*-pyre is lit at night. Then a *kalû* priest "lays an intercessory offering" (*taqribta išakkan*) upon this pyre while a *zammāru* singer "moans loudly" (*in-ḫa in-ni-iḫ*). Elsewhere an *āšipu* priest opens an exorcistic ritual for the king by "moaning" (*uš-ta-ni-iḫ,* BBR 26 I:11; cf. TuL 118:17). The client, furthermore, can allude to a "heart full of tears and moaning" (*ta-ni-ḫi,* AGH 132:47) while petitioning Ištar for help. Ritualistic "moaning" was evidently an integral part of exorcistic praxis, at least in Mesopotamia.

The homeopathic "moaning" of a client and an animate image is well illustrated by the praxis of a Borneo wizard who straps a large stone to his abdomen and mimics every move and sound of his pregnant client in order to facilitate the birth of her child (Frazer, *The Golden Bough,* 16). Should the ritual in DAT II be intended to restore fertility to

in parallel with the "moaning" of some group "in *their* heart" (*blbbm*), could well be a homeopathic indicator of the sort common to exorcistic ritual. Perhaps we have to do here with the simultaneous "moaning" of a homeopathic image and its human referent (viz. Balaam's "people"). Should this be the case, then such a "moaning" could have been intended to confirm that the evil perpetrated against the client by the *šdyn* in DAT I has now been successfully transferred from (Balaam's?) client to a homeopathic image specially constructed for this purpose (as an example of this process, cf. the Maštikka ritual, ANET 350–351, examined above).

In DAT II:14, one could read the phrase *lbb nqr šhh* as "the heart of the *nqr* died out."[134] Following the hypothesis that an exorcistic ritual lay at the root of this text, this phrase could be an indication that as the image "dies," so does the *šdyn*'s evil curse, presumably on a cultic brazier set up for this purpose.

One of the exorcist's most important roles in the ancient Near East involved the ritual construction and destruction of homeopathic images.[135] Several terms for "craftsman/artisan" are preserved in Syria-Palestine, and many of these are on occasion closely bound to the actual crafting of magical images.[136] The terms *GUL-(a)š* in Anatolia (HT 66:23), *eṣēru* in Mesopotamia (BBR 53:16; 54:12), and *yṣr* in Syria-Palestine (KTU 1.16 II 25-26; cf. Isa 43:10; 54:17) all orbit within the same semantic field of "forming/sketching."

In one Anatolian death-ritual, for example, a human image formed out of figs, raisins, and olives substitutes for the deceased in order that the deceased, by this homeopathic means, might silently participate in a dialogue between two "old women" regarding the most appropriate way to conduct his remains to the "stone-house" (mausoleum).[137] In Mesopotamia, exorcists sketched images of Nergal and *urigallu*-huts on plastered walls in sanctuaries. Beside these images were often sketched "seven winged images at the front of the sanctuary" (elsewhere expressly called "the Sibitti with fearful wings.")[138]

---

cattle, the "moaning" here might even be intended to mimic the "moaning" of dying cattle. Cf. the phrase, "How the beast moans!" (*māh ne'enḥâ bĕhēmâ*) in Joel 1:18.

[134] Even as *mnn* might be a variant of *mnt* in KTU 1.23 37, *šhh* may be a variant of *šh'* here. In the Targum to Isa 37:26, Aram. *šh'* refers to the desolation of cities after war. Syr. *šh'* can explicitly refer, however, to the "dying out" of a fire, as in the expression "the fire burnt low" (*šh' nwr'*, PSSD 561).

[135] See Goetze, *Kleinasien*, 158; Reiner, "La magie babylonienne," 78; G. Vajda, "Israel et la judaïsme," 130–133.

[136] Cf. *ummânu* ("craftsman") in TaanL I:20 (ANET 490, translated "wizard"); *gāzĕrîn* ("cutters" in Dan 2:27; 5:11); *ḥarṭummîm/n* ("engravers" in Dan 1:20; 2:2, 27; 5:11).

[137] HT 66–68:21–36.

[138] BBR 53:14, 16; 54:12. Cf. the phrases "I have formed a design" (*e-ṣir uṣurta*) in BBR 83 III:22, and "he has formed a design" (*uṣ-ṣir* ^{GIŠ}*uṣurta*) in Racc 142:379, passages set in exorcistic/purification contexts. Referring to the great number of these "sketches" throughout Mesopotamia, an *āšipu* exorcist asks Ištar in AGH 130:16, "Where are thy images not sketched?" (*e-ki-a-am lā uṣ-ṣu-ra* ^{GIŠ}*uṣurāti*^{meš}*-ki*).

We suggested above a parallel between BBR 53:16; 54:12 and the iconographically-

Exorcists in the ancient Near East often used a temporary, disposable structure to represent the Netherworld in chthonic ritual. In Anatolia, for example, a "grapevine" is lowered into the "dish of the dead" within the confines of a "movable tent" (HT 32:10–14; 46:30–31). A homeopathic image of a dead king or queen is set up for a short time (HT 52:7) on a golden "throne/footstool" within this tent (HT 60:14–16), before continuing on to the "stone-house" (HT 34:61).

In Mesopotamian ritual, the Netherworld could be represented by a structure called an *urigallu*-hut. In one ritual, a "magic circle" is "formed/scratched" (*zì-sur-ra-a teṣṣir*) and a god's image placed within this sanctified space.[139] The exorcist then builds an *urigallu*-hut, "forms" (*teṣṣir*) a "house of confinement" within it, then places a pedestal (exactly like the one supporting the image of the deity) for the afflicted client within this space.[140] The *urigallu*-hut must be of some size because the afflicted client (or symbol/image thereof) then enters it and sits upon the pedestal inside it. At this juncture of the ritual both deity and client wait expectantly upon their respective pedestals.

Seven tallow images are then burned on a cultic brazier (*nappaṭu*), along with four images of the client.[141] After this, the exorcist takes the hand of the sick man and leads him out of "the Netherworld" (homeopathically portrayed). As the man rises from "the Netherworld," his god is reconciled to him and made ready to protect him from further demonic attack.

The same pattern is also intimated in the Kirta legend at Ugarit. The hero Ilḥu upbraids Thitmanat for failing to inform him of Kirta's illness, but she can save him by "forming a grave" (*qbr tṣr*, KTU 1.16 II 25–26), complete with "protected area" (*nkyt*, line 27),[142] and "gate" (*ṯǵr*, line 27).[143] Probably this *qbr* is

---

similar winged creatures sketched on plaster at Arslan Tash and Tell Deir ʿAllā. Note also that El's retinue of attendant deities, according to the Phoenician account of Sanchuniathon (Philo Byblius, *Praep. Evang.* I 10:20) were also winged, as was El himself (cited from Mullen, *Assembly of the Gods*, 184–185).

[139] TuL 117:3–5 (lit. "you shall scratch out a magical circle"). This "magic circle" (*zì-su-ra-a*) also appears at the beginning of the *Šurpu* series (Šur I:3).

[140] TuL 118:18–19.

[141] TuL 118–119:5′–7′. E. Reiner notes (*Šurpu*, p. 54) that *nappaṭu* is a close synonym to *ḫuluppaqqu*, translating both "cauldron/brazier." Tallow, bitumen, wood, clay, and wax images were burnt in this *ḫuluppaqqu* after evil had been magically transferred to them (cf. Maq IX:22, 27; cf. also KAI 222A:37–39).

[142] The Arab. verb *nakata* can mean simply "to scratch up" (Wehr-Cowan, *A Dictionary of Modern Written Arabic*, 997), a connotation which resonates well with the ritual nuances of KTU 1.16 II 27. G. del Olmo Lete's translation of *nkyt*, "una cámara de tesoro (?)," is based on Heb *bêt nĕkôt* (Isa 39:2), a phrase which may be borrowed from Akk. *bīt nak(k)amti* (cf. AHW 722); cf. *Mitos y Leyendas de Canaan*, 314.

[143] The house in which El celebrates *mrzḥ* has a "gate" (*ṯǵr*, *Ugaritica* V 1:11), as does Sheol (*šaʿărê šĕʾôl*, Isa 38:10) and the Netherworld (TuL 163:8). A tomb is designated a "grave house" (*bt qbwrʾ*) at Palmyra (Ephem I:199) and a "sepulchre" (*byt qbwrt*) appears

a Canaanite parallel to the *urigallu*-hut in Mesopotamia and the "tent" (^{GIŠ}*ZA.LAM.GAR*) in Anatolia. Perhaps also the "eternal house,"[144] "the house the traveller cannot enter,"[145] and "the house the bridegroom cannot enter"[146] in DAT II:6–7 are all *primarily* epithets for a homeopathic *image* of the Netherworld, and only *secondarily* referents for the Netherworld itself.

In other words, while no hypothesis can aspire to becoming dogmatic when dealing with such a fragmentary text like DAT II, there may be enough evidence left here to hypothesize that DAT II preserves an exorcistic ritual performed to remove the evil set loose in DAT I. Instead of focusing on the etymology or philology of the term *nqr,* we would suggest focusing instead on the *sequence of events* with which it appears to be bound. In DAT II:5, it appears to be lodged in a context of preparation. In II:12, it appears to be connected with what looks to be a "moaning" ritual of some kind. In II:14, it appears to be destroyed. This standard sequence—construction, transferral of evil, destruction—appears to reflect an exorcistic ritual sequence which is quite common to rituals of this type throughout the ancient Near East, and indeed, the world.[147]

in the Targum to Qoh 12:5 (cited from S. A. Birnbaum, "The Kephar Bebhayu Marriage Deed," *JAOS* 78 [1958] 12–18).

[144] *byt 'lmn* (DAT II:6). Cf. the Phoen., Heb., and Aram. parallels cited by Birnbaum, "The Kephar Bebhayu Marriage Deed," 12–18.

[145] *byt ly'l hlk* (DAT II:7). Cf. "the house which none leave who have entered it" (ANET 107). Similar descriptions are found in Enkidu's Death-Dream (*Dreambook,* 249).

[146] *byt . . . ly'l ḥtn* (DAT II:7). As Hackett suggests on the basis of Psa 19:5 (*The Balaam Text,* 61), *ḥtn* ("bridegroom") might well be a metaphor for the solar deity, an equation which makes particular sense in view of the "light vs. darkness" imagery in DAT I:6–7. O. H. Steck argues that Psa 19 is a text in which several stock paeans to the Sun are subsumed to the authority of the Canaanite deity El; *Wahrnehmungen Gottes im Alten Testament. Gesammelte Studien* (München: Chr. Kaiser, 1982) 232–239.

Some do not see Netherworld imagery here at all. Caquot & Lemaire ("Les textes araméennes," 203) see a "house (for the pleasure of) young men" (*byt 'lmn*) and the "bridegroom" (*ḥtn*), while Rofé links these epithets with an actual "house of prostitution beyond the Jordan" (*byt qdšwt b'br hyrdn, Spr Bl'm,* 69).

An obscure incantation text from Ugarit (Ras Ibn Hani 78/20) combines elements of both rhabdomantic and necromantic ritual, and would appear to confirm the interpretation offered here for DAT. Note lines 14–19:

	w<r>d. ḥṭm. larṣ.	Descend, (O) ghost, to the Netherworld.
	zrm. (15) *lbn. adm. . . .*	Thou art alien to humankind . . .
(18)	[*b*]*t. ubu. al. tbi.*	To the house to (which) I go, thou shall not go
(19)	[*aṯr. aṯb*]. *al. ṯṯb.*	And in the place I dwell, thou shall not dwell.

This translation, from Y. Avishur ("The Ghost-Expelling Incantation from Ugarit (Ras Ibn Hani 78/20)," *UF* 13 [1981] 13–25) takes *ḥṭ* ("rod") to have a homeopathic meaning in an overall incantational context attacking "sorcerers" (*kšpm,* line 9) and "binders" (*ḥbrm,* line 10).

[147] See, e.g., the homeopathic rituals used to combat the four female demons Me Teb, Me Srei, Me Keo and Me Koet in Cambodian culture (P. Bitard, "Le monde du sorcier au Combodge," dans *Le monde du sorcier,* 318–319).

Balaam as Reciter of Incantations

Attention has already been given above to the remarkable parallel between the *combination* of cosmic metaphors in Maqlû VII:1–22 and the *combination* of similar metaphors in DAT I:6–7, and we suggested there that the "diviner/seer" responsible for communicating the oneiromantic oracle in DAT I:6–7 was to some degree familiar with the idiosyncratic cadences of the incantational literature. Taken together, both arguments suggest that Balaam may have enacted a role as "reciter of incantations" at Deir 'Allā.

A supporting line of argument for this thesis emerges from a study of the function of the red-inked line in DAT II:17 compared with similar rubrics elsewhere in the incantation literature. McCarter has plausibly suggested that the red-inked lines in both Combinations consistently refer to the inscription itself: the rubric in DAT I:1 ("The sayings of Balaam . . .") being a title or heading to the inscription as a whole, while that in DAT II:17 (". . . to make known in writing the matter concerning his people . . .") likely refers to the reason for setting up this inscription in the Deir 'Allā sanctuary.[148]

DAT II is not the only ritual text to conclude with a rubric explaining its contents. At the conclusion of several incantations in Mesopotamia, rubrics sometimes appear which are designed to limit the accessibility of this magically powerful (therefore dangerous) material only to a "knowledgeable" elite (*mudû*).[149] The "unknowledgeable" (*lā mudû*) are warned in these rubrics not to attempt access to this secret lore because they were considered patently unable to understand or manipulate the powers of the chthonic world.[150] Only a select group of magico-religious specialists were allowed to have access to the "secrets of the gods" (cf. *pirišti ilāni,* TuL 37:26), probably preserving this access first by oral means.[151]

If Levine is correct in dating the plaster inscription at Deir 'Allā prior to

[148] McCarter, "The Balaam Texts," 49.

[149] The colophon to a priestly ritual commentary reads: "Secret of the great gods: let the 'knowing' (*mudû*) show it to the 'knowing' (*mudû*); the 'unknowing' (*lā mudû*) shall not see it" (TuL 37:26; cf. also 47:19). Analogous "safeguard" techniques are discussed by G. Offner ("À propos de la sauvegarde des tablettes en assyro-babylonie," *RA* 44 [1950] 135–139), cited in E. Leichty, "The Colophon," in *Studies Presented to A. Leo Oppenheim* (Chicago: Univ. of Chicago, 1964) 153.

[150] The New Testament relates how seven Jewish exorcists tried to manipulate a powerful, but unfamiliar word by means of a magical incantation. This story at least partially intends to satirize the ignorance of the "unknowing" (Acts 19:13–16).

[151] The knowledge of a *bārû* is called the "secret of divination" (*pirišti bārûti,* BBR 1–20:18), and his oracle is called a "secret word" (*tamīt pirišti,* BBR 1–20:18, 27, 119). For an interesting discussion of "professional secrecy," see J. L. Crenshaw, *Old Testament Wisdom: An Introduction* (Atlanta: John Knox, 1981) 58–59.

the Assyrian invasions under Tiglath-Pileser III,[152] perhaps the developing international crisis associated with Assyria's brutal assault on Syria-Palestine helped to catalyze the decision within the "professional" magico-religious circle responsible for preserving it "to make known an account of the matter"(*ld't spr dbr,* DAT II:17). It may be that the DAT scribe, writing against the backdrop of a volatile historical situation similar to that facing the apocalyptist of Daniel 10–12, was provoked by dire circumstance to write it down in order to inspire a battered, frightened people suffering the effects of imminent military and political oppression.[153]

On the other hand, perhaps a crisis similar to the one recounted in the tradition itself provoked the decision to record the tradition about the famous confrontation between the *'lhn* and the *šdyn* (via Balaam). As was pointed out above, we have no way of knowing for sure whether this crisis was international in scope, yet the mention of the "king's inquiry" (*š'lt mlk,* DAT II:15)[154] needs to be weighed carefully. Further, the mention of *šgr w'štr* in DAT I:14 might imply that the original crisis faced by Balaam had simply to do with the infertility of cattle and/or sheep. Whether a similar or even some other type of crisis may have led to the plaster inscription set up on the Jabbok cannot be readily determined.

For whatever reason(s), this "secret knowledge" was eventually passed on to broader circles of the Transjordanian populace, and there seems little reason to doubt that DAT in its written form helped to accelerate the dispersion of this particular Balaam tradition. This story of the celebrated Balaam bar Beor was apparently deemed important enough "to make known an account of the matter regarding his (Balaam's) people."[155] By reducing this tradition to writing, the account we know as DAT thus codified and standardized an "oral"[156] tradition

[152] Levine, "The Balaam Inscription: Historical Aspects," 332. A. Wolters argues (in a paper to appear shortly in *HUCA*) that the inscription might better be dated *after* the Assyrian invasion, and further, that it might essentially be the product of a colony of Aramean exiles deported to Transjordan after their Assyrian conquest ("The Balaamites of Deir 'Allā as Aramean Deportees," paper presented to the Northwest Semitic Epigraphy Group, Annual SBL Meeting, Boston, Mass., Dec 7, 1987). It is, of course, not at all certain that the epigraphical and paleographical evidence allows enough room for Wolters' intriguing hypothesis.

[153] J.G. Heintz, among others, notes the "serie d'assertions de style apocalyptique" in the written form of DAT I, "Review of Hoftijzer & van der Kooij," *RHPR* 60 (1980) 211. Levine has drawn parallels to DAT from the doomsday language in Zeph 1:14–17 & Ezek 32:3–8 ("Deir 'Allā Plaster Inscriptions," 204–205).

[154] Cf. Hackett, *The Balaam Text,* 72.

[155] DAT II:17, reading *ld't spr dbr l'mh* with McCarter and Hackett.

[156] The expression *'l lšn* in DAT II:17 may be idiomatic, especially since *lšn* is elsewhere highly idiomatic. Cf. Jer 18:18 (*nakkēhû ballāšôn,* "let us strike him with the tongue"; i.e., "slander, rebuke"); Qoh 10:11 (*ba'al hallāšôn,* "master of the tongue"; i.e., "charmer"); and KAI 224:21 (*ltšlḥ lšn,* "you shall not send forth [your] tongue"; i.e., "slander"). A. Millard argues, primarily from the red line framing the DAT text vertically and horizontally, that

(or traditions) about Balaam. Displaying it on the wall of a sanctuary certainly witnessed to an important event in Syro-Palestinian history—one of the few inscriptional witnesses, in fact, presently known. The discovery of other texts serving similar functions would seem to support this analysis.[157]

In sum, should Balaam be engaging here in as standard an exorcistic ritual as his divination praxis appears to be, the following sequence of events commends itself: Balaam's client finds himself/(themselves?) under a terrifying curse from demonic chthonic powers, a crisis which is communicated to Balaam while he is enacting a fairly complex role as "diviner/seer." Several divinatory procedures seem only to confirm the seriousness of this crisis. To remedy his client's problem, Balaam as "exorcist" then successfully transfers this curse away from his client onto a homeopathic image, apparently by way of some kind of mysterious "moaning" ritual. When the image is destroyed, so is the curse which has afflicted his client. The story of Balaam's successful divination/exorcism was then probably preserved in "professional" magico-religious circles orally until a written memorial to his triumph, perhaps in response to a specific crisis, was eventually recorded on the wall of an eighth-century Transjordanian sanctuary.

The advantage of this scenario, in contrast to the others which have already been offered in previous studies of the DAT tradition, is that it is based on a comparative analysis of several other ritual texts. This scenario tries to take seriously the oracles, incantations, and ritual praxes known to have been characteristic of other magico-religious specialists operating during this general period. By staying close to this phenomenological foundation, we have simply attempted to reconstruct a plausible scenario for the occult activity of another, certainly better-known, magico-religious specialist, Balaam bar Beor.

The Deir ʿAllā texts do not lend themselves to precise exegesis, but they do permit phenomenological analysis. From such an analysis, it seems probable that Balaam enacted a rather broad range of roles on the magic-religion continuum. While there will always be room for further study of the matter, it appears to us at this point in our study of the Balaam traditions that these roles were rather equally balanced between the role-sets of "diviner/seer" and "exorcist" at Deir ʿAllā.

---

the inscription "was a copy of a literary manuscript written on a papyrus scroll"; see "The Question of Israelite Literacy," *Bible Review* 3, 3 (1987) 29–30.

[157] Cf. the plaster texts found at Kuntillet ʿAjrud (Z. Meshel & C. Meyers, "The Name of God in the Wilderness of Zin," *BA* 39 [1976] 9), and those found in an Egyptian grave at *eš-Šeḫ Faḍl* (N. [Aimé-]Giron, "Note sur une tombe découverte pres de Cheikl-Fadl par Monsieur Flinders Petrie et contenant des inscriptions araméennes," cited in H. & M. Weippert, "Die 'Bileam' Inschrift," 79).

3
The Roles Enacted by Balaam Ben Beor in the Bible

Arguably the most important theme underlying the narrative in Numbers 22–24 is the terrifying fear of the Netherworld. This fear is apparent from the very outset. Our first glimpse of Moab finds the people trembling with "great dread,"[1] and "loathing"[2] before an imminent Israelite invasion. Balak, the Moabite king (and Balaam's client),[3] realizes immediately that the threat facing Moab does not consist merely of an opposing human army. Rarely does a military leader in the ancient Near East view an army apart from the supernatural forces which empower it.[4] Balak's instinctive response, therefore, is to "hire"[5] a well-known magico-religious specialist (1) to ascertain the will of the

[1] *wayyāgar . . . mĕ'ōd,* Num 22:3 (MT, Sam); OG, *ephobēthē . . . sphodra,* "be very afraid of"; Vulg, *pertimuissent,* "become very much afraid of" (cf. LAB 18:2, *timuit valde*); Syr., *dḥlw . . . ṭb,* "they were very much afraid" (sometimes used of "daimon-fearers," *dḥly šd',* PSSD 89); Neo, PsJon, Onk, *dḥylw . . . lḥd',* "they were very much afraid." *Gûr* is used in the OT to describe a profound "dread" before the deity (Deut 9:19; Psa 119:39), the enemy (Jer 22:25; 39:17), or the diseases believed to be under divine control (Job 3:25; 9:28). Cf. esp. the (seven) diseases "dreaded" in Deut 22:28, 60 and the Sibitti in Mesopotamia and Anatolia. Reflecting the diminished tone in much later interpretation of this fear, Josephus portrays Balak merely as "concerned" (*eulabeito*) by Israel's growing numbers (AJ IV:102).

[2] *wayyāqaṣ,* Num 22:3 (MT, Sam); OG *prosōchthisen,* "he was vexed in spirit"; Vulg, *et impetum eius ferre non possent,* "and (seeing that) he (Moab) was not able to withstand his (Israel's) attack" (apparently a departure from the MT altogether); Syr., *w'qt lhwn lmw'by',* "and there was anxiety among the Moabites" (so also Onk); PsJon, *w'ty'qw mw'b'y,* "and the Moabites (felt?) anxious (lit., 'hemmed in')." This verb (*qwṣ*) elsewhere describes intense antipathy between nations (Exod 1:12; 1 Kgs 11:25; Isa 7:16).

[3] Samuel Daiches was the first to recognize the specialist-client relationship between Balaam and Balak ("Balaam: A Babylonian *bārû,*" 62–63).

[4] Cf. the complex cursing rituals enacted by king and specialist together in KUB VII 60 and the *bît rimki* ritual in BBR 26. Both of these ritual texts are discussed above in chapter 1 at some length.

[5] The expected professional fee is specified once by *śkr* (Deut 23:5). Balak the king as the representative person here equals the Moabites.

gods regarding the future of his country at this moment of military crisis,[6] and (2) to exorcise ("drive out"),[7] via the appropriate apotropaic rituals, the foreign people with its foreign god(s)/daimon(s) threatening to violate the vulnerable door to his "house."

BALAAM AS "DIVINER/SEER"

At its base, Num 22:7–21 is built around a sequence of nocturnal auditions which Balaam receives from the deity:

> The elders of Moab and Midian came, divination objects (?)[8] in their hands. They came to Balaam and told him Balak's words. He said to them, "Lodge here tonight and I will bring you back a word[9]—

[6] Perhaps the best Syro-Palestinian example is found in the Zakkur inscription (KAI 202). See above.

[7] *gāraš*, Num 22:6, 11 (MT, Sam); OG, *ekbalō;* Vulg, *ejicere* (22:6), *abigere* (22:11); Syr, *nwbdywhy mn 'r'*, "I will cast him out (lit., 'cause to perish') from the land"; Neo, *'ṭrwd ythwn mn 'r'*, "I will expel them from the land"; Onk, *'trkynyh* (PsJon, *'tyrykynyh*), "to drive out, imprecate, curse." Onk uses his verb (*trk*) again in Num 23:7, the first Balaam "oracle": *tryk* (MT *z'm*) *ly yśr'l*, "Drive Israel out for me!," possibly an indication that Onk fundamentally understood Balaam's commission to be exorcistic in nature. Cf. the "old woman's" command to the foreign gods threatening the border of her Anatolian client: "Leave your lands!" (KUB VII 60, cited in Haas & Wilhelm, 236:32). *Grš* is also found on the lips of another Moabite king: Meša credits his god (Kemoš) with "driving him out before me" (viz. Israel, KAI 181:19, *ygršh kmš mpny*). To be understood properly, the numerous references to "cursing" throughout this narrative and the broader biblical Balaam tradition must be taken as indications of a "sorcerer" role within the parameters of an "exorcist" role-set—*not* as *sui generis.*

[8] *qĕsāmîm*, Num 22:7 (MT); Sam, *qsmyhm*, "their divination things" (cf. Syr, *qsmyhwn*); OG, *ta manteia*, lit., "the things pertaining to divination" (*manteios/mantikos* is often used in conjunction with divinatory *technē*); Vulg, *habentes divinationis pretium in manibus*, "having the divination fee in (their) hands"; Neo, *gryn dqsmyn ḥtymyn bydhwn*, "sealed divination stalks (?) in their hand"; PsJon, *gdyn dqysmyn ḥtymyn*, "sealing genii of divination"; FTNum (Klein), *'grn ḥtymyn*, "sealed wages"; FTNum (Ginsburger), *'gdn ḥtymn*, "sealed staffs." Alongside the tendency to view *qĕsāmîm* as "diviner's fees" stands the repeated mention of "sealed" (*ḥtm;* cf. *ḥt*[*m*], DAT I:7) paraphernalia associated with divination, perhaps a reflection of the primitive rhabdomancy encased in DAT I. It is difficult to see how these unusual interpretations of *qĕsāmîm* could have arisen otherwise. For a discussion of the targumic evidence, see R. Le Déaut, *Targum du pentateuque, tome III, Nombres* (Paris: Les editions du Cerf, 1979) 209. Inner-biblically, Balaam is specifically called a *qōsēm* in Josh 13:22, but not in Num 31:8.

[9] *hăšibōtî 'etkem dābār*, Num 22:8 (MT, Sam); versions all basically agree. As was pointed out above, the phrase *hšyb . . . (dbr)* seems to reflect a stereotypical formula for reciting divine oracles at Ugarit (probably via the *'dd;* cf. KTU 1.4 III 10) as well as Israel (cf. the *ḥōzeh* Gad, 2 Sam 24:13). The placing of a "word" (*dābār*) in Balaam's mouth is made specific four times in the Balaam cycle (Num 22:38; 23:5, 12, & 16), and the Baal

whatever Yahweh says to me." So the Moabite princes stayed with Balaam. Then *'lhym*[10] came to Balaam (Num 22:7-9a).

After a nocturnal dialogue between *h'lhym* and Balaam regarding Balak's request (22:9-12), Balaam "rises up in the morning"[11] to relay the divine response to the previous night's divinatory inquiry—just like the DAT tradition. Upon hearing the initial unfavorable response, Balak persistently sends another delegation of dignitaries, more prominent than the first, who convey to Balaam the king's intention to "honor" him far above his normal fee-scale (22:17). While the retelling of this story tended to focus attention on the confrontational aspects of the Balaam-Balak encounter, heightened by repetition (cf. 2 Kgs 1:9-15), Balak is essentially demanding here a confirmation of the first (negative) oneiromantic oracle.[12] To Balak's second, more serious proposal, Balaam "answers"[13] that no

---

Peor incident is described in Num 31:16 as having been provoked by the "word" (*dābār*) of Balaam. Further, the incidents preserved in DAT are summarily described as a "word" (*dbr*, DAT II:17—not Aram. *ml'*).

[10] We assume, with von Pákozdy, that *'lhym* in the Balaam cycle fundamentally denotes "den Wahrsage- und Zauberdämon des Bileam" ("Theologische Redaktionsarbeit in der Bileam-Perikope," 169). Cf. DAT I:1, *wy'tw 'lwh 'lhn blylh*, "and the gods came to him in the night." Inconsistency in the words employed for the deity may reflect the persistence of a non-Yahwistic tradition.

[11] Cf. Num 22:13 *wyqm bl'm bbqr*
& DAT I:3 *wyqm bl'm mn mḥr.*

J. de Vaulx finds in this narrative an example of "incubation," *Les nombres*, SB (Paris: Gabalda, 1972) 256, but this may be stretching the evidence too far. We still do not know whether Balaam receives these nocturnal visions/auditions in a sanctuary, whether he was asleep at the time, or whether an icon/deity stood close by—all necessary ingredients for genuine incubation (cf. Caquot, "Les songes et leur interpretation selon Canaan et Israël," 110-111).

[12] See the discussion above regarding the counterchecking of/via oneiromantic oracles in Anatolia, Ugarit, Israel, and Deir 'Allā. The frequent volitional changes by Balaam's divine authority have long occasioned great mental distress for readers of this narrative. Josephus' solution was to have God change his mind out of anger, then deliberately delude (*apatē*) Balaam into going on a doomed mission (AJ IV:107). Philo's solution was to transfer all caprice from the divine character to Balaam himself. God never said anything in these nocturnal encounters; Balaam only *claimed* divine guidance in order to "up the ante" on his fee (VM I:266-267). Wellhausen's solution was to posit different literary sources (*Composition der Hexateuch*, 110). A phenomenological approach simply recognizes divine caprice more or less for what it is: a fearful reality which must be endured, even expected by every specialist who is experienced in dealing with it.

[13] *wayya'an bil'am*, Num 22:18 (MT, Sam, Syr, Neo); PsJon & Onk (*'tyb*, "returned, replied") were perhaps influenced by the use of *hšyb* in 22:8 (MT). On the conveying of "answers" from the deity as a primary role of the "oracle-reciter," cf. the answering omens received from Šamaš to the prayers of the *bārû* (AGS *passim*), discussed above at length. Mic 6:5 draws particular attention to this "oracle-reciter" role:

zkr n' mh y'ṣ blq "Remember what Balak plotted,
wmh 'nh 'tw bl'm and what Balaam answered him."

amount of "silver and gold"[14] can bring him to transgress the deity's command ("mouth"),[15] employing language which literally pulsates with terms and phrases common to oracular recitation elsewhere in the ancient Near East.

Consequently, Balaam seeks a counterchecking divine oracle, telling the delegation:

> Now, please, you also[16] stay here[17] tonight, and I will make

[14] Twice Balaam reiterates his complete lack of mercenary motivation, insisting that a "house full of silver and gold" could not induce him to violate his professional integrity. Cf. the dialogue between the two "old women" in the Anatolian funerary ritual discussed above (HT 68:28–36). The first one tempts her comrade with the words "Take the silver and gold," but the second replies three times, "I will not take it!" Similar protest is echoed in Israelite prophetic legend (1 Kgs 13:8). Since greed was doubtless a constant temptation set before magico-religious specialists, protestations like these were likely routine.

[15] *lō' 'ûkal la'ăbōr 'et pî*, "I cannot transgress the mouth" (Num 22:18, MT, Sam); OG, *to hrēma*, "the word"; Vulg, *verbum*, "word"; Syr., *mlt pwmh*, "word of his mouth"; Neo, *pwm gzyrt mymryh*, "mouth of the decree of the word"; PsJon, Onk, *gzyrt mymr'*, "decree of the word." In Mesopotamia, strong emphasis is placed on the appropriate reception of the divine *tamītu*-answer by the "mouth" (*pî*) of the *bārû*:

> Overlook it if . . . in the mouth (*pî*) of the *bārû* an answer (*tamītu*) may have terrified him

(preserved whole or in part in AGS 1:6′; 3:2′; 16:4′; 19:5′; 22:5′; 29:3′; 31:3′; 35:5′; 77:3′; 78:7′; 91:5′; 97:5′; 106:2′; 119:2′; 126:4′; 130:5′). The knowledge of a *bārû* is called the "secret of divination" (*pirišti bārûti*, BBR 1–20:18), and his oracle is called a "secret answer" (*tamīt pirišti*, BBR 1–20:18, 27, 119).

[16] *gam 'attem*, MT, Sam; Syr, *'p 'ntwn*, "you also"; Neo, PsJon, Onk, *'wp 'twn*. The *maqqeph* after *gam* in MT indicates an early attempt to align *gam* with *hallāyĕlāh* (*contra* RSV). NJPS translates, "So you, too, stay here overnight." The emphasis is not on a second overnight stay, but on the second group of dignitaries. For them, this was their first oneiromantic inquiry of the gods by means of this specialist. The participle *yōsēp* in the second half of verse 19 indicates that this is Balaam's second, confirmatory inquiry.

[17] *šĕbû*, MT, Sam; OG, *hupomeinate autou*, "wait for him/it"; Vulg, *maneatis*, "remain"; Syr., *pwšw*, "stay"; Neo *sqwn tbw*, "light a fire (?), (and) sit down"; PsJon, *'sḥrw*, "mill around"; Onk, *'wrykw*, "wait." In spite of the versions' tendency to de-emphasize the primary meaning of MT *yāšab* (with the exception of Neo), note the parallel with DAT

Num 22:19	*šbw . . . 'd'h,*	"Sit down . . . I will make known. . . ."
DAT I:5	*šbw . . . 'ḥwkm*	"Sit down . . . I will tell. . . ."

PsJon's verb (*sḥr*) looks at first like a paraphrase, but may be attempting to reflect a known ritual praxis. In a context explicitly condemning a variety of magical practices (*ḥbr, kšp, brw, ḥzh*), note how an Israelite prophet mocks Babylon for "milling about" (*sōḥărayik*, Isa 47:15; RSV translates "trafficking") with all sorts of magico-religious activity "since her youth." J. L. McKenzie emends *sḥr to šḥr,* based on *šḥr* in v. 11. He sees both as related to Akk. *sāḫiru; Second Isaiah,* AB 20 (Garden City, NY: Doubleday, 1968) 90–91.

known[18] whatever else Yahweh says to me (Num 22:19).

To this second inquiry, however, the deity demonstrates a perplexing propensity for reversal—a disturbing divine characteristic which surfaces repeatedly in the Balaam cycle. The *'lhym* again come to Balaam at night (v. 20) and reverse their earlier oracle (v. 12). Now they command him to go to Balak, but only under the important stipulation that he remain completely faithful to the divine word.[19]

The divine unpredictability is highlighted and intensified in the she-ass story which immediately follows. As in the DAT tradition, again we see a prosecutorial figure (*mal'ak yhwh*)[20] "taking a stand" as "the Adversary,"[21] yet notably

[18] *wĕ'ēdĕ'āh,* MT, Sam; OG, *gnōsomai;* Vulg, *scire;* Syr., *'d'*; targumim all agree. Cf. the important red-inked phrase discussed above, *ld't spr dbr l'mh,* "to make known an account of the word to his people" (DAT II:17).

[19] Note the following references to Balaam as "seer" in the biblical tradition:

(1) *wayĕgal yhwh 'et 'ênê bil'ām wayyar',* "Yahweh uncovered Balaam's eyes and he saw" (Num 22:31, MT, Sam); Vulg, *oculos,* "eye" (sg.; cf. the difficult phrase *šĕtum hā'āyin* in 24:3, 15); Syr., Onk, *wḥz',* "and he saw." Cf. *ḥzh 'lhn,* "seer of the gods" (DAT I:1). Cf. also *gĕluy 'ênayim,* "eyes uncovered" (Num 24:4, 16). Prior to this point in the narrative (22:31) Balaam "brings back" and "answers" words, but "sees" nothing.

(2) *dĕbar mah yar'ēnî,* "the word which he causes me to see" (Num 23:3, MT, Sam); Syr., *ptgm' dmḥw' ly 'ḥwywhy lk,* "the word which he shows me I will show you"; Neo, *yḥwwy,* "(Yahweh) tells, reveals"; PsJon, *yḥwy.* Cf. the same root (*ḥw'*) in DAT I:5.

(3) *śĕdēh ṣôpîm,* "field of watchmen" (Num 23:14, MT, Sam); OG, *agrou skopian;* Vulg, *locum sublimem;* Syr., *lḥql dwq',* "to the field for gazing"; Neo, *lḥql skyyh,* "to the seers' field"; PsJon, Onk, *lḥql skwth,* "to the field for watching." It is difficult to tell whether the name of this field infers the "seeing" of human activity, superhuman activity, or both.

(4) *maḥăzēh šadday yeḥĕzeh,* "who sees a vision of *šdy*" (Num 24:4, 16, MT, Sam); Syr., *wḥzw' d'lh' ḥz',* "who sees a vision of God." Cf. again Balaam's title in DAT I:1, *ḥzh 'lhyn,* and the reading arrived at independently by G. Hamilton and E. Puech, *wyḥz mḥzh kmś' 'l,* "and he saw a vision like an oracle of El" (DAT I:1-2).

[20] Working without the Deir 'Allā texts, Rudolph tried to explain the divine caprice in the she-ass story as fundamentally Yahwistic, citing Num 11:33 as a parallel (where Yahweh's anger "burns" and he strikes Israel with a plague for eating quail-meat; *Der "Elohist,"* 111). Gressmann felt strongly (but without offering ancient Near Eastern comparative evidence) that the addition of *mal'ak* before *yhwh* in the she-ass narrative betrayed a later euphemism, "ursprünglich aber die Sage, wie zahllöse Parallelen lehren, unbefangen von Jahve selbst" (*Mose und seine Zeit,* 323).

[21] *wayyityaṣēb . . . lĕśāṭān,* Num 22:22 (MT, Sam); Syr., *wqm ml'kh dmry' b'wrḥ' dhw' lh sṭn',* "the angel of the Lord stood in the way to be his Adversary." On the basis of the divine council judgment scene common to Mesopotamia, Israel, and the DAT Balaam tradition (DAT I:5-6), MT *śāṭān* can be understood as "an adversary" from the divine council. In Job 2:1, "the Adversary" (*haśśāṭān*) "takes a stand" (*lĕhityaṣēb*) to begin formal prosecution. In DAT I:6, the *šdyn* "take a stand in the assembly" (*nṣbw šdyn mw'd*) for the same reason. Note also *nṣb* in Num 22:23. Peggy L. Day has recently suggested that we begin to think of the "satans" in the Hebrew Bible in plural, generic terms;

without the authorizing mechanism of a "divine council," in what has now evolved into a completely "monotheized" narrative.[22] Whatever else the she-ass story might have been designed to do, it functions here purely and simply as an entertaining satire on Balaam's entire "diviner/seer" role-set. By means of several direct and indirect contrasts, the author of this "burlesque"[23] narrates a splendid parody which asks, then answers several questions: (1) Will Balaam, the "seer" so famous for reading the will of the gods in the past, now "see" the danger looming in front of his own nose? (2) Will Balaam, the "oracle-reciter" so famous for conveying divine "answers" to divinatory requests in the past, have a "word" placed in his mouth? and/or (3) Should these traditional avenues fail, will Balaam use some other means, like, say, a "magic wand,"[24] to get himself out of this predicament?

Working within a marvelous economy of space, the narrator summarily answers all three of these questions in the negative, doubtless to his audiences' repeated delight. (1) Three times in this vignette we read the phrase "the she-ass sees,"[25] but Balaam never even comes close to "seeing" what is going on; that is, not until Yahweh opens his eyes. (2) Second, the deity opens the "mouth"[26] of the she-ass, but not Balaam's mouth! A more humiliating indictment of an "oracle-reciter's" abilities would be hard to imagine. In fact, Balaam has nothing oracular to say at all until Yahweh puts a word in his "mouth" and he lifts up his first *māšāl*.[27] (3) Third, three times Balaam beats his she-ass, using a "rod"

An Adversary in Heaven: śāṭān in the Hebrew Bible (HSM 43; Atlanta: Scholars Press, 1988) esp. pp. 45–67.

[22] For another biblical parallel, cf. the "lying spirit" (*rûaḥ šeqer*) who "stands" (*ʿāmad*) before Yahweh in 1 Kgs 22:22. D. S. Russell suggests that this figure "forms a real link between the popular demonology and the general idea of the accessibility of human personality to the invasive spirit of Yahweh," *The Method and Message of Jewish Apocalyptic* (Philadelphia: Westminster, 1964) 160, nt. 3. E. Würthwein argues simply that it is "ein Gemisch von volkstümlich Glauben und schriftstellerischer Reflexion," "Zur Komposition von 1 Reg. 22:1–38," in F. Maass, ed., *Das ferne und nahe Wort, FS L. Rost,* BZAW 105 (Berlin: de Gruyter, 1967) 250. Whether one views the she-ass story as early (Rudolph) or late (Rofé), the existence of a prosecutorial "Adversary" figure is quite ancient.

[23] Rofé, *Spr Blʿm,* 51.

[24] Admittedly, positing the existence of this third question presupposes that the Israelite narrator was aware of a rhabdomantic role like that enacted in DAT I:9.

[25] *wattēreʾ hāʾātôn,* Num 22:23, 25, 27 (MT, Sam); cf. Syr., Onk, *wḥzt/h ʾtnʾ/h.*

[26] *wayyiptaḥ yhwh ʾet pî hāʾātôn,* "Yahweh opened the mouth of the she-ass" (Num 22:28, MT, Sam). Of passing interest to this study is the comment of PsJon on this verse: "Ten things were created after the world had been fashioned: . . . the rod of Moses (*ḥwṭrʾ dmšh* [cf. *ḥṭr* in DAT I:9]), . . . the demons (*mzyqy*) and the speaking ass."

[27] Num 23:7 (MT, Sam); OG, *parabolēn;* Vulg, *parabola;* Syr., *mtl;* Onk, *mtyl.* Neo & PsJon "nabi-ize" Balaam's *māšāl* as *mtl nbwt(y)h,* "the *mtl* of his prophecy." See Num 23:18; 24:3, 15, 20, 21, 23 for a perfect "seven" *mĕšālîm* from Balaam. Eissfeldt has

(*maqqēl*)[28] as a riding crop, not as a magical source of power. For this Israelite narrator, all power comes from Yahweh, and Yahweh cannot be manipulated by any means. By deliberately, even crudely satirizing these well-known roles,[29] the roles themselves are circuitously, yet decidedly substantiated.

Analyzing this material within the same theoretical categories employed above, therefore, it seems that Balaam's first set of roles, enacted prior to the beginning of the ritual which follows, includes at least those of "seer," "oneiromantic,"[30] and "oracle-reciter" within the parameters of a rather standardized

---

shown that while it is probably useless to search for an underlying etymology for *māšāl*, one can divide it into separate semantic categories. Further, while he felt that the term might mean "Orakelrede" in the Balaam cycle, he was quick to state his uncertainty about it. In light of the newer evidence from DAT, a better category for Balaam's *māšāl* might now be found in the category Eissfeldt called "Spottlied." Note the more revealing parallels: *māšāl // tōpet* (Job 17:6); *māšāl // ḥerpāh* (Joel 2:17); *mōšělê hā'ām // 'anšê lāšôn* (Isa 28:14; note also the enigmatic parallel between those who *māšāl* the people and those who make a *ḥōzeh* with Sheol in 28:15). See O. Eissfeldt, *Der Maschal im alten Testament*, BZAW 24 (Giessen: Töpelmann, 1913) 20, 28, 30, 45–71.

[28] *maqqēl*, Num 22:27 (MT, Sam); OG, *hrabdos;* Vulg, *fustis;* Syr., Onk, *ḥwṭr';* (cf. *ḥṭr*, DAT I:9); PsJon, *šwṭ*, "rod, scourge."

[29] Philo states overtly what the biblical text will not; viz. that Balaam is completely unable, not just unwilling to perceive anything through any of the normal (not to mention supranormal) avenues of sensation. For Philo, Balaam is *anaisthētos*, "anesthetized" (VM I:272).

[30] Indirect confirmation of Balaam's oneiromantic role enactment comes from the strong tendency among many tradents to translate MT *pětôrāh* as "interpreter" in Num 22:5. Cf. Vulg, *ariolum*, "soothsayer"; Syr., *pšwr'*, "the interpreter"; Neo, *ptwrh*, "the interpreter"; FTNum (Ginsburger), *ptwr ḥwlmy'*, "the interpreter of dreams"; LAB 18:2, *interpretem somniorum*, "interpreter of dreams"; VM I:268, *oneirata diēgoumenos*, "describer of dreams."

Nevertheless, the vocable *ptr* has been ascertained as the proper name of a village on the Sagur tributary of the Euphrates, attested in the annals of Shalmaneser III (ANET 278). The mention of Balaam as *mippětôr 'ăram nahărayim* in Deut 23:5 further witnesses to this possibility. Among others, Wayne T. Pitard accepts this geographical identification for *pětôrāh* in the biblical tradition ("The Identity of the Bir-Hadad of the Melqart Stela and Northern Syria," paper read before the Northwest Semitic Epigraphy Group, Annual Meeting of the Society of Biblical Literature, Boston, MA, Dec 7, 1987).

Demonstrating that this ambiguity over *pětôrāh* was a problem very early, PsJon attempts a detailed harmonization of the two views: "And he sent messengers to Laban the Aramean, who was Balaam, the one who sought to swallow up the children of Israel, the son of Beor, who was insane from the magnitude of his wisdom (*d'yṭpš mswg'y ḥkmty*). . . . His residence was in Padan, which is Petor (*ptwr*), a name signifying an interpreter of dreams (*ptyr ḥlmy'*)." Other attempts to make sense of *pětôrāh* are discussed by Mowinckel ("Der Ursprung der Bil'amsage," 235–238).

While the versional evidence can neither be used to justify the translation of MT *pětôrāh* as "the interpreter," nor at all as indisputable evidence for positing an Aramaic source underneath the biblical Balaam tradition, it does at least indicate that at a very early stage in the history of the tradition a sizeable number of tradents interpreted

"diviner/seer" role-set, a role-set which has much in common with the "diviner/seer" role-set in DAT and other ancient Near Eastern texts.

BALAAM AS "EXORCIST"

When Balaam finally arrives, Balak slaughters an ox and a sheep, sending portions to Balaam and his travelling companions (Num 22:40). Some scholars are inclined to view this "sacrifice" as contiguous to[31] or a doublet of[32] the one which follows the next morning at Bamoth Baal (22:41–23:2), but since (1) the narrative indicates a clear change of locale and time, and (2) this "ox/sheep" sacrifice is not repeated before either of the latter two sacrifices in the story (at Sade Ṣopim[33] and Baal Peor[34]), arguments for a phenomenological connection

---

Balaam's nocturnal activity in Num 22 within a context of known oneiromantic behavior in Syria-Palestine. Perhaps some awareness of the DAT tradition, however limited, helped to facilitate this tendency.

[31] See the comments of Hengstenberg, Dillmann, and Strack, cited in G. B. Gray, *Numbers*, ICC (Edinburgh: T. & T. Clark, 1903) 339. P. J. Budd simply theorizes that the sacrifice in 22:40 prepared for that in 22:41–23:5, *Numbers*, WBC 5 (Waco, TX: Word, 1984) 266.

[32] See B. Baentsch, *Numeri*, HKAT I/2 (Göttingen: Vandenhoeck und Ruprecht, 1903) 602; Noth, *Numbers*, 181; L. Schmidt, "Bileamüberlieferung," 239.

[33] *śĕdēh ṣōpîm*, Num 23:14. See above, n. 19.

[34] *rôš happĕʿôr*, "the top of Peor" (Num 23:28, MT, Sam); Neo, *ryš ṭʿwwth pʿwr*, "the top of the idols of Peor" (the root *ṭʿy* means "to lead astray" and can mean "to prostitute" or "to deify"). In Eusebius' time a mountain shrine called *oros phogor* existed between Shittim and Heshbon (cited in Gray, *Numbers*, 358) and is probably to be identified with *bêt pĕʿôr* (the sanctuary, Deut 3:29) and *baʿal pĕʿôr* (the deity, Num 25:3). In Num 25:18; 31:16: & Josh 22:17 *baʿal pĕʿôr* is probably abbreviated to *pĕʿôr* (cf. Baentsch, *Numeri*, 624).

Baʿal pĕʿôr is associated with (a) communal meals for the dead (Psa 106:28; note also that Sheol "opens wide its mouth" [*pāʿărāh pîhā*] to swallow up Jerusalem's nobility, Isa 5:14); (b) licentious cultic activity (Num 25:3; probably related to some kind of homeopathic fertility ritual—cf. Hos 9:10); and (c) sacramental defecation: "He who uncovers himself to Baal Peor" (*hpwʿr ʿṣmw lbʿl pʿwr*, lit., "he who opens himself up to Baal Peor," a play on the root *pʿr*) is to be condemned, because "this is his mode of worship" (*ʿbwdth*, Sanh 7:6; cf. b. Sanh 64a; b. Abod Zar 44b).

On the basis of the parallel between Phoen. *pʿr* and its Luwian equivalent *pa-ḫa-r(a)* in the Phoenician/Luwian bilingual found at Karatepe (Phoen. text in KAI 26A:6), G. E. Mendenhall argues for a North Syrian or Anatolian origin for the Baal Peor cult, translating *baʿal pĕʿôr* as "Lord of Fire" (cf. Hit. *paḫḫuwar*, "fire"); see *The Tenth Generation* (Baltimore: Johns Hopkins, 1973) 109. Such a view would dovetail nicely with that of A. Wolters, who argues that the DAT tradition also originated in North Syria ("The Balaamites of Deir ʿAllā as Aramaean Deportees," paper read before the Northwest Semitic Epigraphy Group, Annual Meeting of the Society of Biblical Literature, Boston, MA, Dec 7, 1987). M. Pope interprets *baʿal pĕʿôr* as a Transjordanian example of *marzēaḥ*, however it may have been planted there (*Song of Songs*, 217).

between it and the one at Bamoth Baal are probably unwarranted.[35]

After what we might therefore style an "initial greeting," Balak and Balaam rise up the next day, ascend to a high place called "Bamoth Baal,"[36] and go to work. As with any apotropaic ritual in the ancient Near East, the first order of business is preparation: Balaam instructs Balak to build seven altars.[37] In the ritual which follows, there appears to be a measurable degree of overlap between the role-sets of "diviner/seer" and "exorcist,"[38] and, should such be the case, we will have to ask what might have caused this overlap. To our knowledge, however, nowhere in the ancient Near East does a magico-religious specialist

[35] See Rudolph, *Der "Elohist,"* 111–112; Gray, *Numbers,* 339; de Vaulx, *Nombres,* 273.

[36] *bāmôt ba'al,* Num 22:41 (MT, Sam); OG, *epi tēn stēlēn tou Baal,* "upon the pillar/ monument of Baal"; Onk, *lrmt dḥlt' dp'wr.* R. le Déaut (*Targum du pentateuque,* 218–219) translates Onk "sur la hauteur de sa divinité" and PsJon "sur la hauteur de l'idole de Peor," reading from the root *dḥl,* "to fear." Another possibility is to compare the Phoen. *ḥlt* ("monument/tomb"), well-attested in KAI 14:3 (*//qbr,* "grave"), 5 (*//mškb,* "resting place"), + the prefixed genitive particle *d.* Such a reading would explain *stēlē* in OG (which normally translates Heb. *bmt* with *hupsēla* or the transliteration *bomoi/ bamoth*), and instead of the problematic "his divinity" in Onk (whose divinity?), makes possible the translation "his (deity's) tomb/monument." Note that Philo also supports OG, stating that Balak took Balaam to a *stēlē . . . hidrusthai daimoniou tinos,* "a monument dedicated to some daimon," VM I:276.

[37] The sacrificing of *šib'āh pārîm wĕšib'āh 'êlîm* ("seven bulls and seven rams," Num 23:1) is found only in purification ritual in the OT; see Ezek. 45:23; 1 Chron 15:26; and esp. Job 42:7–9. Note further the following parallels between Job and the Balaam cycle: (1) emphasis on proper vs. improper facilitation of *dābār;* (2) wrath of *yhwh;* (3) presence of *śāṭān;* (4) employment of *šib'āh pārîm wĕšib'āh 'êlîm;* (5) both describe this ritual as *'ōlâ;* (6) tandem activity (Balaam & Balak // Job & Eliphaz/Bildad/Zophar).

Mesopotamian parallels have been repeatedly noted. See Gray, *Numbers,* 342 (the Sibitti); Mowinckel, "Der Ursprung der Bil'amsage," 260 (only late Assyrian influence on the Elohistic narrative); Largement, "Les oracles de Bile'am," 46; de Vaulx, *Nombres,* 274–275. See also Vergil, *Aeneid* 6, 38–39: "As Aeneas questioned the sibyls, he offered 7 steers and 7 sheep," cited in A. Dillmann, *Die Bücher Numeri, Deuteronomium und Josua* (Leipzig: Hirzel, 1886) 149.

[38] For example, Balaam "calls (the gods) via omens (*liqra't nĕḥāšîm,* Num 24:1). Both diviners and exorcists "summon the gods" in the ancient Near East, but for quite different reasons. In Mesopotamia, *bārû*-diviners "summon the gods" into their sacrifices in order to read a divine *tamītu*-answer in response to prayer (cf. HSM 7494:5, *i-na za-i-im qí-ri i-li ra-bu-tim,* "Invite the great gods by means of [cedar] resin," cited in Starr, *Rituals of the Diviner,* 30, 37). *Āšipu*-exorcists, on the other hand, "summon the gods" in order to manipulate and/or neutralize them by means of homeopathic magic (see, e.g., AGH 14:20–21, *ina muḫḫi akli ù mê ša paliḫi-kunu gu-šá-a-ni,* "come (*// qerû*?, cf. CAD *Q,* 243) to the bread and the water of him who worships you," CAD *G,* 58).

To use anthropological categories, the *bārû's* praxis tends to be more "supplicative," while the *āšipu*'s is "manipulative" (cf. de Waal Malefijt, *Religion and Culture,* 13). The Balaam cycle appears to represent a subtle blend of both categories.

ever conduct a ritual involving seven altars *except* in exorcistic ritual.[39]

It is, of course, quite frustrating that with this altar-building procedure, repeated three times, nothing else is said about the remainder of the preparations or the structure and content of the ritual-incantation itself.[40] That the narrative at this point shows no interest in these matters, however, is not at all surprising, given the Hebrew tradition's customary reticence when dealing with the occult.[41] On the contrary, it would have been *very* surprising if a Hebrew narrator had chosen to elaborate a non-Yahwistic ritual in any detail. In other words, the phenomenological details of Balaam's ritual praxis can be guessed at from exorcistic parallels elsewhere, but from the text alone they are no longer recoverable.

At any rate, Balaam and Balak together "offer up" a bull and a ram on each of these seven altars,[42] and, as the smoke from the charring flesh begins to rise, Balaam tells Balak to "take a stand"[43] by his "whole burnt offering."[44] Balak

[39] A prime example is the *bît rimki* ritual.

[40] For likely Anatolian parallels, cf. Haas & Wilhelm, *Hurritische und luwische Riten;* for Mesopotamia, cf. W. Mayer, *Untersuchungen zur Formensprache des babylonischen "Gebetsbeschwörungen."* Note esp. the careful, extensive preparations for the *bît rimki.*

[41] "There is no mention of any other sacrificial rite in this connection, although magical means were also employed by the non-Israelite prophet, as would be expected" (Levine, *In the Presence of the Lord,* 23). Note Daiches' original suspicion: "It is probable that Balaam's magical work was intentionally referred to in the Bible in a veiled way" ("Balaam: a Babylonian *bārû,*" 69).

[42] Of minor note is the comparable use of male animals from different species in the *bît rimki* ritual: the "he-goat" and the "male sheep" (BBR 26 II:25). J. de Vaulx argues a minority view that there was only one altar for each species. For de Vaulx, the Elohist later multiplied this one altar to seven as a way of exaggerating Balaam's ineffectiveness (*Nombres,* 275).

[43] *hityaṣṣēb,* Num 23:3.

[44] *'ōlātekā,* Num 23:3 (MT); Vulg, LAB 18:7, *holocaustum.* Even though there is some disagreement over the function of the *'ōlâ,* commentators generally agree on the function of the *'ōlâ* here: "um sich die Gunst der Gottheit für dieselben zu sichern" (Dillmann, *Numeri,* 149); "pour disposer le Dieu à réaliser la bénédiction ou la malédiction contenue dans l'incantation" (Largement, "Les oracles de Bile'am," 46); "the *'ōlâ* functions as a complete rite in the ritual activities of Balaam connected with his attempt to pronounce effective execrations over the Israelites" (Levine, *In the Presence of the Lord,* 23).

Against Levine's thesis of an invocatory function for the *'ōlâ* generally, J. Milgrom argues that it functioned instead as a gift for the deity after pacifying him by means of *ḥaṭṭa'āt* ("sin-offering"); Milgrom, "Review of Levine, *In the Presence of the Lord,*" *JBL* 95 (1976) 292. L. Rost hypothesized that the *'ōlâ* may not have been indigenously Semitic, but perhaps of Egyptian or South Arabian origin; *Studien zum Opfer im alten Israel,* BWANT 113 (Stuttgart: Kohlhammer, 1981) 92.

In an earlier study ("Fragen um Bileam," 377–380) Rost apparently assumed (a) that S. Daiches had argued for a *paššûru*-type "Gotterspeisung," linking the sacrifice in 22:40 with that in 23:2, and (b) that the use of *'ōlâ* in the Balaam cycle precludes this type of sacrifice completely, with the result that (c) *any* attempt to discuss Mesopotamian parallels is misguided.

complies with this command.[45]

Now we enter the most dangerous part of any exorcistic ritual in the ancient Near East, or anywhere else for that matter. Although a culturally acceptable and necessary mechanism for "summoning the gods" has now been put into place, the thought of actually facing them when they arrive is always a mysterious, even terrifying prospect, no matter how carefully the procedure for their summons is wrapped in the folds of traditionalized ritual.[46] Unfortunately (but not unexpectedly), the biblical narrative again becomes quite ambiguous at this point. Apparently Balaam "walks"[47] away from (or around?) these seven

---

In response, (a) Daiches made no attempt to link the sacrifice in Num 22:40 with that of 23:2 and (b) Rost does not examine the purificatory function of the *abru* in Mesopotamian ritual, upon which entire animals are burnt whole (see AGH 18:4, a *lamb;* Racc 40:4–5, a *sheep;* 120:6, 13, 16, 22, 25, a *bull*). While one should not argue that these *abru* sacrifices are functionally equivalent to the Israelite *'ōlâ* (and no one has), it is difficult to think of another word the Hebrew writer might have had at his disposal to describe the purificatory sacrifice of Balaam in Num 23:3.

[45] When Balaam returns from his encounter with the deity, Balak is "standing beside his burnt offering" (*niṣṣāb 'al 'ōlātô*, Num 23:6).

[46] Cf. the cry of the *āšipu* in BBR 26 II:28–29 ("Accept it, O Sibitti . . . Accept it!") and note the simple fact that one of the most developed portrayals of the Sibitti's unbridled malevolence—the Epic of Erra—enjoyed a wider circulation in Mesopotamia than even Gilgameš. Copies of it have been found in Nineveh, Assur, Babylon, Ur, and as far northwest as Sultantepe; see L. Cagni, *The Poem of Erra,* SANE I/3 (Malibu, CA: Undena, 1977) 5.

[47] *wayyēlek šepî,* Num 23:3 (MT, Sam); OG, *kai Balaam eporeuthe eperōtēsai ton theon kai eporeuthe eutheian,* "and Balaam walked, inquiring of God, and he walked straight/forthwith (i.e., *eutheian* may modify either "space" or "time"); Vulg, *cumque abiiset velociter occurrit illi Deus,* "as he quickly went away, God encountered him"; Neo, *w'zl bl'm blb yḥydy špy lmylwṭ yt yśr'l,* "and Balaam went out with a singular, tranquil heart to curse Israel"; PsJon, *w'zl gḥyn kṭwy',* "and he went, bending like a snake" (cf. *šûp* in Gen 3:15); Onk, *w'zl yḥydy,* "and he went out singlemindedly/alone." *Šepî* has been a problem for a long time. Reflecting perhaps the majority of modern commentators, Gray rejects the suggestion that *špy* is a corruption of *wylk (lk)špy(m)* ("and he went to seek enchantments"), but instead reads *šepî* as the sg. of *šěpāyîm* (Isa 41:18; 49:9; Jer 3:2, 21; 4:11; 7:29; 12:12; 14:6), translating, "he walked to a bare height" (*Numbers,* 343).

Daiches suggests the equation Heb. *šepî* = Akk. *šēpu,* as in the phrase *kī šēpu parsat,* "after the step had ceased," found in a description of a *bārû*'s ritualistic "walk" ("Balaam: a Babylonian *bārû,*" 66–67, citing BBR 100:10). What Daiches does not mention, however, is that BBR 100 is a description of a ritual for purifying a *bārû* who is having difficulty "getting through" to the gods. Part of this purification ritual involves him in the "mouthwashing" ceremony, a known homeopathic ritual normally conducted by the *āšipu* to purify or bring back to life divine images (see, e.g., TuL 106:46). In other words, even if we were to take Daiches' suggestion seriously, the "step" to which Heb. *šepî* might conceivably refer would more likely have to do with *āšipūtu* than with *bārûtu* ritual.

burning altars, but it is quite impossible to ascertain what he is doing. Still, the ultimate *purpose* for this "walking" *is* clearly specified. Balaam "walks" in order to "meet"[48] the *'lhym*. Balaam may have conducted this part of the ritual alone because he did not want to endanger his client. He might even be taking precautions here not to expose his client to the (possibly) malevolent power of the *'lhym* his occult sacrifice was designed to attract.[49]

Although "purification-priest"[50] and client have thus carefully prepared for this encounter the best way they know how, the *'lhym*, as they (and we) have witnessed, are completely unpredictable. In light especially of the conflicting oneiromantic oracles already received from them, neither Balaam nor Balak could have had any real idea what their response would now be to their *'ōlâ*-offering. Divine unpredictability is a major theme in this tradition, helping to bind the whole narrative together. It should not be relegated to a peripheral status. Instead, this unpredictability helps to pose the questions which the narrative seeks to answer: Will the *'lhym* aid the invading foreigner? or curse him/drive him out? Will they strike Moab with a plague? or the Israelite enemy? Will they bring Moab release from his "great dread?" or plunge him even deeper into the depths of his very real terror? Will they bring war or peace, death or life?

At this point in the narrative, one may be tempted to read ahead and discover "the" outcome to this fascinating story. This would presuppose, however, that (1) there is only one outcome, and (2) that this single outcome is indeed recoverable.[51] The really frustrating part about the biblical Balaam

[48] A. Rofé argues that *qrh* in Num 23:3 should be sharply separated from *qr'*. Citing Exod 3:18 and 5:3 as parallels, Rofé argues that *qrh* refers to an accidental, chance meeting between Balaam and the deity, that *in spite of* Balaam's ritual, Yahweh (not the *'lhym*) encountered him anyway (Rofé, *Spr Bl'm*, 32). Note, however, (a) the term in MT Exod 5:3 is *nqr'*, not *nqrh;* (b) Exod 3:18 (Sam) also has *nqr';* and (c) Sam consistently uses *qr'* to describe Balaam's praxis in the Balaam cycle. Consequently, any sharp separation between *qr'* and *qrh* seems arbitrary. Furthermore, the narrative itself makes a clear distinction between Balaam's "former" praxis and his newly-discovered "prophetic" understanding of Israel's deity (Yahweh), but *not* until Num 24:2.

[49] In the *bît rimki* ritual, this is accomplished by housing the Sibitti in *urigallu*-huts while the king proceeds through the seven chambers of the "wash-house" (see Laessøe, *bît rimki,* pp. 29–31). By this technique the possibility for defilement is thus minimized, if not eliminated entirely. One should keep in mind, however, that the *bît rimki,* at least in its neo-Assyrian guise, represents a rather well-developed purification ritual. Thus there are limitations on its suitability for comparative analysis with the Balaam tradition.

[50] Affixing this role-title to Balaam does not eliminate the possibility that some may have viewed him as a "sacrificial priest" very early within the parameters of a "diviner/seer" role-set, but this is a matter which will be treated in the next chapter.

[51] "Bemerkenswert ist, dass das ganze Zusammentreffen zwischen Israel und Balak gar keine Folgen hat . . . kein Krieg zwischen ihnen; kein resultat" (Mowinckel, "Der Ursprung," 238). Gressmann argued that this lack of resolution was only a cover-up for the fact that Reuben and Gad had in fact conquered Moab (*Mose und seine Zeit,* 322). Against this, Mowinckel argued that the only thing lying at the core of the tradition was

tradition, however, is that it has not one, but several puzzling outcomes. For some tradents, Balaam is from this point on perceived only as a "sorcerer,"[52] his only desire being to "curse" Israel (even if the text is quite clear that he never actually did it!). For others, he is the quintessential "blesser" of Israel.[53] Whatever he may have chanted in his *měšālîm* originally, what we now find in the narrative is a series of beautifully constructed "poems"[54] lauding Israel and her very powerful God. For still others, perhaps troubled by the oversimplicity of these first two solutions, Balaam is transformed from a "curser" into a "blesser." For this latter group, Yahweh alone becomes the real focal point of the tradition. Yahweh, not the *'lhym,* "changes the curse into a blessing" (Deut 23:6).[55] In this scenario, Balaam and Balak are summarily demoted to mere supporting characters.

From a role theory perspective, we simply want to ask at this point in our study what *roles* Balaam enacts in the recoverable biblical tradition about him. To some extent, the pluralistic portrayal of Balaam in the biblical tradition would appear to testify to a significant degree of role overlap and preemption between the same two role-sets we observed in the DAT tradition. In the Bible, Balaam enacts roles as "seer," "oneiromantic," and "oracle-reciter" within an overall "diviner-seer" role-set. But he also enacts roles as "purification-priest," and (*potential*) "sorcerer" within a (now severely restricted) "exorcist" role-set. Thus the Balaam we see in the biblical texts is not a simple figure, but a complex one enacting a plurality of roles for which there is not a minimal but a considerable degree of role overlap and preemption. Should this be a valid assessment, we must now ask analytical questions about the reasons for this.

a series of disputes between Moab and Israel, "sondern in einen Fluchversuch *umgedichtet* worden" (emphasis Mowinckel's, "Der Ursprung," 239). Holzinger theorized only that the story's present "ending" is not original; see H. Holzinger, *Numeri,* KHAT 4 (Tübingen: Mohr/Siebeck, 1903) 106.

[52] See *qll* in Josh 24:9; Deut 23:5; *'rr* in Num 22:6; *qbb* in 22:11; *z'm* in 23:8. Note also LAB 18:12, *quoniam ego eum* (*v.l.*) *maledixii perii,* "when I cursed him, I perished." Rab Yoḥanan argued that Balaam's blessings were first intended as curses and further, that most of them eventually "reverted to the curse" (*ḥzrw lqllh,* b. Sanh 105b).

[53] *měbārăkekā bārûk wě'ōrěrekā 'ārûr,* "Blessed are those who bless you, and cursed are those who curse you" (Num 24:9). The "blessing" encapsulated in this phrase has led many to assume a foundational antiquity for the tradition here. See esp. C. Westermann (*Blessing in the Bible and the Life of the Church,* 49–53); D. Vetter (*Seherspruch und Segensschilderung*); and A. Rofé (*Spr Bl'm,* 28): *šl n'wmym hyh mwṣ' nprd mšl hs'gh,* "that which composed the oracles was a separate utterance from that which belonged to the saga." Others, noting the parallel with Gen 27:29, see it instead as a gloss (e.g., Coppens, "Les oracles de Bileam," 71).

[54] Rofé even hypothesizes rough-hewn "poetic sources" (*mqwrwt šyryym*) for the first two poems in Num 24 (*Spr Bl'm,* 29).

[55] *wayyahăpōk yhwh 'ĕlōhekā lĕkā 'et haqqĕlālāh librākāh,* "Yahweh your God turned the curse into a blessing for you." Other programmatic uses of divine *hapak* are found in Deut 29:22; 1 Sam 10:9; and 2 Kgs 21:13.

4
The Balaam Traditions: Their Character and Development

The previous two chapters of this study attempt to examine the written evidence presently available about Balaam son of Beor and extrapolate from this evidence his primary roles. Now we must reexamine these roles critically and thoroughly against those known to have been enacted by the magico-religious specialists discussed in chapter 1. To restate our thesis, we propose that any significant divergence in these traditions from the phenomenological *realia* represented in chapter 1 indicates a measurable level of development. It has been necessary to focus on matters of congruence in the preceding pages in order to surface and highlight these roles. To investigate the nature and extent of this development more precisely we must now ask critical questions about divergence as well as congruence.

The present analysis seeks to contribute to the study of the Balaam traditions by approaching them within carefully delimited phenomenological parameters. Critics of the Balaam *literature* will probably want to know the degree to which this specialist's roles are dependent upon (1) oral and/or literary development from a common source, (2) unilateral/mutual oral and/or literary interpenetration between the biblical and DAT traditions, and/or (3) combinations of these two possibilities.[1] The present study, however, prefers to analyze the character and development of the Balaam traditions by focusing on the degree to which the plurality, complexity, and preemptiveness of the roles attributed to Balaam in the Bible and at Deir 'Allā reflect known types.

[1] Similar texts are either (a) dependent upon each other in a literary-historical sense, one primary, the other secondary; or (b) dependent upon a third "Q"-type source, yet independent of each other; or (c) the products of different traditio-historical environments in which the similarities between their respective languages and thought-worlds are their *only* common denominators. For a thoughtful elaboration of the problem of dependence, see P. Hugger, *Jahwe meine Zuflucht. Gestalt und Theologie des 91 Psalms,* cited in Armin Schmitt, *Prophetischer Gottesbescheid in Mari und Israel. Eine Strukturuntersuchung* (Stuttgart: Kohlhammer, 1982) 14.

On the inadequacies inherent in hyper-literary criticism, see R. Smend, "Ein halbes Jahrhundert alttestamentliche Einleitungswissenschaft," *ThR* 49 (1984) 19–20.

Accordingly, we will conclude this study by subjecting these traditions to summational phenomenological scrutiny by means of the three primary role theory variables introduced above: *role enactment, role expectations,* and *intra-role conflict.*

ROLE ENACTMENT

It is a fundamental axiom in role theory that the more roles an actor possesses in his/her repertoire, the more prepared he/she is to meet the exigencies of life.[2] We have repeatedly noted how valid this theoretical axiom is with regard to magico-religious role enactment in the ancient Near East, having examined it in some detail for Anatolian, Mesopotamian, and Syro-Palestinian magico-religious specialists. In Anatolia, the "old woman" (*SAL ŠU.GI*) enacts roles as "diviner" and "oracle-reciter" within a "diviner/seer" role-set as well as "purification-priestess," "exorcist," "incantation-reciter," and "sorceress" within an "exorcist" role-set. The "ornithomantic" (*LÚ MUŠEN.DU*) enacts subdivisions of both the "diviner/seer" and "exorcist" role-sets by means of his "augur" and "purification-priest" roles. In Mesopotamia, the "exorcist" (*āšipu*) enacts roles as "exorcist," "purification-priest," "healer," and "sorcerer" within an "exorcist" role-set, while the "diviner/(seer)" (*bārû*) enacts roles as "diviner," "sacrificial-priest," "oracle-reciter," "dream-interpreter," and "government adviser" within a "diviner/seer" role-set. In Syria-Palestine, "diviners/seers" enact a number of complementary divinatory roles, while evidence for the "exorcist" role-set remains relatively muted and oblique.[3]

The Balaam traditions in both DAT and the Bible, in remarkable congruence with this phenomenological *realia* in Anatolia and Syria-Palestine, reveal to us a character who (1) enacts a variety of complementary roles, and (2) enacts roles which overlap to varying degrees both the "diviner/seer" and "exorcist" role-sets. This is perhaps the most fundamental discovery of our study.

While we might choose to argue over whether enough empirical evidence exists to posit actual rhabdomantic behavior behind the coincidental use of *mṭh // ḥṭr* in DAT I:9 and *maqqēl* in Num 22:27, or whether the night-visions in DAT I:1–6 and Num 22:8–20, 21–30 represent stereotypical oneiromantic inquiries ultimately rooted in cognate divine council judgment scenes, it never-

[2] "The person whose repertory includes a *variety* of well-practiced, realistic social roles is better equipped to meet new and critical situations than the person whose repertory is meager, relatively unpracticed, and socially unrealistic," N. A. Cameron, "Role Concepts in Behavior Pathology," *AJS* 55 (1950) 465.

[3] It is important to emphasize that no analysis of the appropriateness, propriety, or convincingness of a given role enactment can be conducted for every magico-religious specialist who ever lived. We are limited to those for whom there are written legacies and further, to those whose written legacies have been archaeologically recovered. We must therefore couch our conclusions in probabilistic instead of dogmatic terms. Cf. Sarbin & Allen, "Role Theory," 490–491.

theless remains difficult to deny that a relatively broad "diviner/seer" role-set lies behind each of these Balaam traditions. While we might also question whether a "purification-priest" role lies behind the fragmentary plaster of DAT II as well as the seven-altared praxis of Num 22:41–23:30, it again remains difficult to deny the essential "exorcistic" role-set underlying these texts.

When we attempt to be more specific about matters of role-overlap and role-preemption, however, the terrain on our spatio-temporal continuum begins to turn slippery. It is relatively difficult to determine either the degree of this overlap or the degree to which one of these role-sets might be preempting the other in the Balaam traditions. Here the problem of calibrating divergence becomes acute, and role theory can potentially make its greatest contribution.

Simplistic solutions should be resisted. As with the problem of distinguishing between magic and religion when examining the phenomenological *realia* itself,[4] we must refuse to draw neat, static distinctions between the poles of "magic" and "religion" when characterizing these traditions. The Balaam traditions are instead characterized by dynamic overlap between the role-sets of "diviner/seer" and "exorcist." Most importantly, the former clearly tends to preempt the latter, albeit in significantly varying degrees.

If this is a defensible assessment, then what we now need to do is to explore some of the factors which may have led to these significantly varying degrees of role preemption within the Balaam traditions. From the pool of evidence at our disposal, the biblical tradition immediately surfaces to the center of attention because, while role *overlap* is a characteristic of both the DAT and the biblical traditions, role *preemption* cannot readily be traced in DAT, at least not from its recoverable fragments. Consequently, the biblical tradition will receive the lion's share of attention in the following discussion.

How can we characterize this role preemption? First, the "diviner/seer" role-set is more clearly articulated than the "exorcist" role-set in each Balaam tradition. Moreover, the oneiromantic element assumes an elevated importance within both. Each Balaam tradition (1) begins with an oneiromantic oracle, (2) indirectly reflects the ancient Near Eastern technique of counterchecking oracles,[5] (3) is clothed in divination language common to oneiromantic and rhabdomantic oracles,[6] and (4) is repeatedly reaffirmed *a posteriori* in several post-biblical traditions via *double entendre* interpretations of the biblical term *pĕtôrāh* (Num 22:5).[7]

Each tradition also portrays Balaam as an "oracle-reciter," a role repeatedly enacted by "diviners/seers" throughout the ancient Near East, and perhaps

[4] Cf. de Waal Malefijt, *Religion and Culture,* 14–15.

[5] *MUŠEN* oracles countercheck *KIN* and *KUŠ*; dreams countercheck *^{GIŠ}ḪUR* in Anatolia (see Kammenhuber, *Orakelpraxis,* 10, 24).

[6] See McCarter ("Balaam Texts," 57) and especially Müller ("Die aramäische Inschrift," 238–242).

[7] See Vulg, *ariolum;* Syr., *pšwr';* Neo, *ptwrh;* FTNum (Ginsburger), *ptwr ḥwlmy';* LAB 18:2, *interpretem somniorum;* VM I:268, *oneirata diēgoumenos.*

especially congruent to a Syro-Palestinian "seer" role-set here. In DAT I:1–2, the "man who sees the gods" "sees a vision like an oracle of El," then "reveals" it to "his people," while in Mic 6:5 Balaam "answers" his client with a divine word. Both traditions draw from a deep traditional font of ancient Near Eastern oracle-recitation when describing Balaam, and this is the same font from which later "prophetic" images eventually coalesce into towering prominence within portions of the Israelite tradition (cf. Sifrê Deut 34:10). Further, while Balaam's "augur" role has been reduced to a vestigial linguistic remnant in the OG biblical tradition,[8] DAT's vigorous, detailed "augur" portrayal is as undeniable as Philo's is persistent.[9]

Second, the "exorcist" role-set, though laconic in the Bible and fragmentary in DAT, is still recoverable from both traditions. Granted, DAT's portrayal of Balaam as a "craftsman of homeopathic images" and as a "reciter of incantations"[10] is carefully and discriminately veiled in the Bible, especially in the Balaam cycle. Yet the continuous, protracted associations of Balaam with (1) the roles of "purification-priest" and "sorcerer," and (2) the ever-mysterious cult of Baal Peor preserve an occult, hidden side of this biblical character which cannot be ignored or denied. This association is further reinforced by (a) the broader ancient Near Eastern parallels to his praxis cited above from the comparative incantation literature, (b) the numerous parallels in DAT, and (c) the vestigial portrayals still retained by several post-biblical Jewish tradents.[11]

Precise exegesis of these exorcistic allusions is impossible, and may remain so indefinitely, yet even a cursory phenomenological analysis has to reckon with an "exorcist" role-set of some substance beneath the surface of these texts. The problem surfaces again and again whenever honest attempts are made to interpret accurately the ubiquitous "sorcerer" role. *Sui generis* interpretations of Balaam as "curser," apart from a clear conception of this role's proper sociohistorical matrix, have not and cannot work. Bereft of the necessary delimitations provided by carefully defined methodological controls, *sui generis* interpretations tend to ignore questions of a sociohistorical nature and thus, tend to position the "cursing" side of Balaam within the parameters of a "diviner/seer" rather than an "exorcist" role-set. This is another major discovery of our study.[12]

ROLE EXPECTATIONS

Role preemption is directly influenced by the expectations of the audiences

[8] Cf. OG *oiōnismos // manteia* for MT *nḥš // qsm* in Num 23:23.

[9] DAT I:7–9; VM I:264.

[10] These roles are hypothesized from our comparative phenomenological reading of DAT II:5–17.

[11] See b Sanh 105a and esp. LAB 18:7, where Balaam's whole burnt-offerings (*holocaustomata*) are cited for their reconciliatory rather than apotropaic value.

[12] *Contra* I. Goldziher, *Abhandlungen zur arabischen Philologie,* 41–44 and M. Noth, *A History of Pentateuchal Traditions,* 74–79.

before whom actors perform.[13] Applied to this study, this means that the many different audiences who respond to this magico-religious specialist perceive him in different ways at different times. These responses accumulated over time and eventually themselves began to influence the overall development of the Balaam stories as they grew from artistic reconstructions into sacred traditions.

Analysis of these layered responses from a sociohistorical perspective should not be used as a pretext to invalidate discussion about the historical Balaam,[14] nor should we simply dismiss all concern about the problem of later literary influences.[15] Sociohistorical questions simply better enable us to ask what may have happened to the tradition as the often drastically different audiences before whom it was told and retold helped to mold and shape it.

Oppenheim is undoubtedly correct when he emphasizes that magico-religious specialists working in urban centers in the ancient Near East were far more specialized than were their non-urban counterparts.[16] More importantly for our discussion, the urban audiences before whom these specialists performed probably held a much more informed understanding of their functions and limitations than did their less-specialized non-urban audiences. Careful application of this generality-specificity continuum[17] to the Balaam traditions may therefore help us to formulate some tangible questions.

Why, for example, does the "sorcerer" role attributed to Balaam in biblical and Jewish tradition eventually preempt all others in certain portions of the tradition, at least when compared alongside the enactment of Balaam's other roles?[18] Although, as our study has shown, the "sorcerer" role functions in the ancient Near East as a secondary role within an overall "exorcist" role-set, the biblical tradition indicates clearly that the Moabite chieftain Balak did not view it secondarily at all. After all, Balak insists that Balaam "curse," not "exorcize" or "divine."[19] Is Balak's behavior here to be viewed as exceptional?

Role theory can help us to formulate a response to this problem. The variable of audience expectations speaks directly to it. Seen in its most likely sociohistorical matrix, the preoccupation within Balaam's initial audience (the king) for a particular role in his larger role-set (the "sorcerer" role) is neither surprising nor unexplainable. What we appear to have at the root of this tradition is a classic conflict in role expectations.

[13] Sarbin and Allen, "Role Theory," 497–506.

[14] Cf. Largement, "Les oracles de Bile'am," 48.

[15] On this approach, see Delcor, "Le texte de Deir 'Allā," 65; Müller, "Einige alttestamentliche Probleme," 58–60; Rofé, *Spr Bl'm*, 69–70.

[16] A. Leo Oppenheim, *Ancient Mesopotamia*, 208. See also Largement, "Les oracles de Bile'am," 48.

[17] Sarbin and Allen, "Role Theory," 499, 503–506.

[18] This trajectory directly includes the portrayals in Josh 24:9–10; Deut 23:4–5; Neh 13:1–2; b Sanh 105–106, and indirectly the material in Josh 13:21–22 and Num 31:8, 16.

[19] Num 22:6, 11, 12, 17; 23:7, 8, 11, 13, 25, 27; 24:10.

Political leaders were not expected to become intimately familiar with the labyrinthine world of the occult. Could they have found the time to study the tablets for themselves and master the thousands of incantations and homeopathic rituals necessary to keep the gods appropriately placated, there would have been no need to hire erudite specialists.[20] Most (perhaps particularly non-urban) politicians were not nearly as informed about the intricacies involved in dealing with the occult as were the highly-qualified professional specialists upon whom they were forced to rely.[21]

Consequently, it is not surprising that Balak the Transjordanian chieftain and Balaam the professional magico-religious specialist brought fundamentally different role expectations to their encounters at Bamoth Baal, Sade Ṣophim, and Baal Peor. In fact, as the narrative itself faithfully records, Balak's view of Balaam's role and Balaam's view of Balaam's role clash repeatedly. The electric discharge generated by these clashes is so strong that the entire apotropaic enterprise, dependent upon their ability to work together, eventually short-circuits altogether.

Balaam repeatedly insists that he will never surrender his "oracle-reciter" role to that of "sorcerer," but Balak continues to insist that he prioritize the latter.[22] Balaam cautiously and dispassionately engages in careful, systematic oneiromantic inquiry, but Balak's naive response to this activity shows how little appreciation he has of the need for caution before the unpredictable *mysterium tremendum et fascinans:*

> Did I not send to you to call you?
> Why did you not come to me?[23]

Three times Balaam engages in a rather dangerous purification ritual on this chieftain's behalf, but Balak remains stubbornly fixated on what for him sums up Balaam's entire *raison d'être:*

> I summoned you to curse my enemies![24]

This tension is never resolved. Eventually, this thoroughly disgruntled employer peremptorily dismisses his equally-thoroughly disgruntled employee—without even paying him! It seems highly unlikely that the written narrative, for all its style and beauty, could have created such a fundamental conflict in expectations *ex nihilo.*

[20] E. Reiner, "La magie babylonienne," 71.

[21] Even from the urban archives which compose the bulk of our documentation, only a few political figures, like Hattušili III, seemed to take more than a nominal interest in things occult (see Kammenhuber, *Orakelpraxis,* 25–32).

[22] Note particularly the responses immediately following the first three *mĕšālîm;* Num 23:11-12, 25–26, and 24:10–13.

[23] Num 22:37.

[24] Num 24:10.

As the Hebrew narrator skillfully manipulates this conflict in order to build the story to a climax,[25] a significant "moment of truth" finally arrives for Balaam. On his third attempt to "summon the gods," Balaam reacts to the petty provincial strictures placed on him by his uninformed patron with what looks to be a mixture of resignation and disgust. He refuses to look for omens any longer, but instead raises his eyes to the heavens and waits passively for divine assistance. Even though the narrator seizes on this behavior and adroitly manipulates it for his own ends,[26] we suspect that this critical moment in the story reflects much more than an enterprising storyteller's fertile imagination. It seems rather to reflect a well-known phenomenological *realia*. Any "specialist" who has ever struggled to communicate with a "lay" audience will readily understand it.

Later "sorcerer" distortions, as they are eventually embroidered into a baroque tapestry of character assassination by some post-biblical tradents, are woven out of the threads of this fundamental conflict. To change the metaphor, Balaam's role as "sorcerer" is probably the result of a progressively crystallizing institutionalization of a conflict in audience expectations. Different audiences standing at different points on the magic-religion spatio-temporal continuum continued, like Balak, to react to Balaam within the parameters of very limited—in some cases increasingly limited—role expectations. Thus Balaam is remembered in some circles only as a "sorcerer," while other audiences choose, by means of phenomenologically similar processes, to remember him instead as "blesser" or "diviner" or "answerer."

INTRAROLE CONFLICT

Few traditions in the Hebrew Bible manifest so great a degree of internal conflict as do the Balaam traditions. The simple task of designating who Balaam was and what he did in Israelite history appears to have been one of the most delicate and complex issues Israelite tradents ever had to face. From a socio-historical perspective, the volatile manner in which the biblical traditions oscillate from one portrayal to another seems a clear indication of enormous *role strain*. Moreover, since the rift separating these Israelite audiences was deep and wide, resolution of this role strain must have been anything but simple. One might even ask whether Israel, or at least segments of Israel, successfully resolved it at all.

Role strain occurs when contradictory expectations are (1) held by different audiences or (2) held within the same audience for the same role.[27] The first of

[25] See van Hoonacker, "Quelques observations critiques sur les récits concernant Bileam," 61–76; Coppens, "Les oracles de Bileam," 71.

[26] Viz., to portray Balaam as a Yahwistic "prophet."

[27] Sarbin and Allen, "Role Theory," 540. Analyzing conflicting expectations by socio-historical means is not the only way to approach the problem of "contradiction" within or between biblical traditions. Cf. J. Goldingay's use of the categories *formal, contextual,*

these subvariables can be illustrated by a cursory comparison of the DAT tradition over against its biblical counterpart. The DAT tradition is straightforward and direct while the biblical tradition is convoluted and indirect. The DAT tradition is characterized by minimal conflict while the biblical tradition is characterized by maximum conflict. The DAT tradition is preserved on an 8th–7th century sanctuary wall, while the biblical tradition is scattered over an extended history of thoroughly edited material. The DAT tradition portrays Balaam in relatively clear, direct language while the biblical tradition sometimes leaves the impression that it really does not know what to do with him.

The second subvariable of intrarole conflict—that which governs conflict between differing segments within the same general audience—is well known to students familiar with Israel's distinctively geminated historiography, even though we are not accustomed to talking about this historiography in "role theory" terms.[28] Caution is always needed when examining this historiography. Facile attempts to oversimplify Israel's "northern"-vs.-"southern" and "tribal"-vs.-"dynastic" perspectives will always tend to harden the fluid, multivalent distinctions between these perspectives into static categories; thus, they should be firmly resisted.[29] Yet the fact remains that Israelite tradents quite often do view important characters and events in their history from profoundly different, often virtually polarized perspectives. Further, these pointed differences often do significantly adhere to the categorical distinctions just mentioned. No tradition, particularly one as controversial as the Balaam tradition, could have passed through such parochial hands unaffected. The evidence indicates, in fact, that "opposing" Israelite audiences tried valiantly to resolve, or at least to ameliorate their role strain over Balaam by both "internal" and "external" means.[30]

---

substantial, and *fundamental* to describe progressively deepening layers of contradiction between and within Old Testament traditions in *Theological Diversity and the Authority of the Old Testament* (Grand Rapids: Eerdmans, 1987) 15–25.

[28] A classic starting-point for this discussion is that of A. Alt, "The Monarchy in the Kingdoms of Israel and Judah," trans. by R. A. Wilson in *Essays on Old Testament History and Religion* (Oxford: Blackwell, 1966; ET of 1951 German essay) 313–335.

[29] Major responses to Alt include G. Buccellati, *Cities and Nations of Ancient Syria. An Essay on Political Institutions with Special Reference to the Israelite Kingdoms,* SS 26 (Rome: Instituto di Studi del Vicino Oriente, 1967); F. M. Cross, *Canaanite Myth and Hebrew Epic,* 222, nt. 10; B. Halpern, *The Constitution of the Monarchy in Israel,* HSM 25 (Chico, CA: Scholars, 1981); and N. Gottwald, *The Hebrew Bible: A Socio-Literary Introduction,* pp. 136–147, 346–348.

[30] "Internal" techniques for resolving role strain do not modify "the external occurrences themselves; that is, the conflicting events are not modified or eliminated. But through the process of belief change, a different meaning or interpretation is placed on the ecological events, making them compatible" (Sarbin and Allen, "Role Theory," 543). "External" techniques, on the other hand, "are behaviors aimed at the external ecology in an attempt to modify the world of occurrences in which the ultimate source of cognitive strain is located" (ibid., 541). Both of these techniques are illustrated above in the introduction to this study.

If the phenomenological analysis of the DAT tradition offered above is correct, then what we most likely see at Deir ʿAllā is a typical magico-religious specialist successively enacting complementary role-sets at a moment of crisis in order to protect a client from demonic attack.[31] Neither set of roles preempts the other because the audience responsible for preserving this tradition evidently felt little or no conflict between them. Like several other magico-religious specialists in the ancient Near East, Balaam first ascertains the nature of his client's problem, then sets about to remedy it. The "diviner/seer" and "exorcist" role-sets do not *conflict* in the eyes of this audience, they *complement*. Were this not the case, one would expect to find at least minimal evidence for conflict resolution in DAT.[32]

As the biblical tradition gradually passed through the hands of Israelite tradents, however, any pluralistic view of Balaam which may have lain at its core began to creak and groan under the increasing strain. Without arguing for a rigid evolutionary view of Israelite religious history, there seems little doubt that Israel's view of "appropriate" magico-religious behavior experienced a shift away from the "magic" pole toward the "religion" pole on the "magic-religion" continuum.[33] Accordingly, this shift must have led to different pressures among different audiences to reinterpret the Balaam tradition. The interpretation offered in Deut 23:4–5 is probably less a major turning point in the history of the tradition[34] than an "official" ratification of one particular audience's attempt to resolve this role strain. The "Balaam problem" was serious enough, however, to provoke several attempts at conflict resolution in Israel.

Some Israelite audiences apparently sought to resolve their role strain over Balaam by *segregating* what they perceived to be "conflicting" role-sets. *Role segregation*[35] is a very primitive external way to resolve an audience's role strain, but not an uncommon one. A clear understanding of this variable may greatly help us, in fact, to understand why the two most antithetical roles attributed to Balaam in the Bible are found preserved in the same book: Balaam the participant in the Baal Peor cult (Num 31:16) stands in stark contrast to Balaam the "obedient prophet" (Num 22:8, 18, 20, 35, 38; 23:12, 26; 24:2, 13). The Israelite

[31] Role theorists sometimes distinguish between "successive" and "simultaneous" role enactment. "Successive" might be illustrated by the wide spectrum of age-roles which all persons enact over time, while "simultaneous" might be illustrated by the surgeon who performs the roles of clown or comedian while he/she continues to act as surgeon (ibid., 536–538).

[32] At the risk of sounding redundant, we want to emphasize again that the lack of empirical evidence forces us to speak only in probabilistic, not deterministic terms.

[33] R. R. Wilson points out how one of these audiences dealt with Balaam: "It is thus clear that the sort of intermediary represented by the traditional figure of Balaam was not acceptable in Ephraimite circles, where, as we will see, only the prophet (*nābîʾ*) was considered a legitimate intermediary," *Prophecy and Society in Ancient Israel,* 150.

[34] Cf. Rofé, *Spr Blʿm,* 48.

[35] Sarbin and Allen, "Role Theory," 541.

tradents responsible for preserving the Balaam tradition in *Numbers* may have tried, in other words, to resolve their problems with Balaam by geographically and literarily segregating, without comment, one role-set (enacted in Moab) from its complement (enacted in Midian).[36]

Role segregation offers a neat and tidy "solution" to the problem of intrarole conflict, but it certainly lacks sophistication and style. Another segment of the Israelite audience, troubled by the "inappropriate" elements of Balaam's "exorcistic" role-set left nakedly unresolved in the tradition, appears to have tried a different tack, one much more subtle. Instead of *segregation,* this audience tried to resolve its problems with Balaam by merging his "conflicting" role-sets into one hybrid *compromise* role.[37]

For this audience, the "Balaam problem" could be ameliorated by moving him ever so slightly away from a role as "purification-priest" within an "exorcist" role-set toward that of "sacrificial-priest" within a "diviner/seer" role-set. What might therefore have been perceived as a major dissimilarity to other audiences in Israel, ultrasensitive to the distinction between magic and religion, was apparently perceived only as minor overlap by this audience. Direct empirical evidence for such a continuum shift is admittedly lacking, but some explanation is required in order that we might somehow explain two significant developments in the biblical tradition: (1) the careful specification that Balaam conducts his sacrificial activity on "high places" (cf. 1 Sam 9:13 and Num 22:41); and (2) the portrayal of Balaam as a "blesser" nowhere else except in segments of the Balaam cycle (cf. 1 Sam 9:13 and Num 24:9).[38]

In other words, the behavioral complexities of certain strands of the biblical Balaam tradition force us to reckon with the possibility that somewhere in the tradition's development a fairly progressive Israelite audience tried to resolve its problems with Balaam by emphasizing Balaam's "diviner/seer" role-set to the exclusion of his (hitherto recognized) "exorcist" role-set. This is *role preemption.* Such preemption assumes that the audience responsible for implementing it must have felt some need, however embryonic, to move Balaam away from the "magic" toward the "religion" pole on the shifting magic-religion spatio-temporal continuum in Israel.

It is not hard to see the tantalizing side benefit which such a solution to the

[36] Noth was particularly attentive to the Moabite/Midianite distinction in his earlier work; see his *History of Pentateuchal Traditions,* 77–78. Perhaps the disjunction of Jacob's complementary roles in Gen 30:37–42 (classically "J") and 31:10–13 (classically "E") may also be due to *role segregation.*

[37] Cf. R. H. Turner, "Role-taking: Process versus Conformity," in A. M. Rose, ed., *Human Behavior and Social Processes* (Boston: Houghton Mifflin, 1962) 20–40.

[38] C. W. Mitchell argues for a type of blessing called "divination blessing pronouncements," basing this "category" solely on the biblical Balaam tradition. This type of approach, however, essentially ignores the profound sociohistorical questions raised by the Balaam traditions as a whole. Cf. Mitchell, *The Meaning of BRK, "To Bless" in the Old Testament,* SBLDS 95 (Atlanta: Scholars, 1987) 90–94.

"Balaam problem" would have helped to provide. By subtly transforming Balaam from a "purification-priest" into a "sacrificial-priest," this audience could conveniently address two needs at the same time: (1) the need to reduce role strain over a controversial character in Israel's history, and (2) the need to enhance one of the most important items on their sociotheological agenda, viz. the conviction that Israel was created to "bless" and "be blessed" by the international community of nations.[39]

Not all were satisfied, however, with so accommodational an "internal" approach to the Balaam problem[40] Radically concerned as many Israelites were to redefine entirely the nature and limitations of oracular revelation within purely "prophetic" parameters (as they defined "prophetic"),[41] critics of this approach chafed against it because, for them, it did not attack the Balaam problem at its roots. For them, religious dogma impelled the declaration that there could be "no *nḥš* against Jacob, no *qsm* against Israel."[42] For this audience, the "normative" parameters of oracular revelation painstakingly hammered out over centuries of polemic reaction to Syro-Palestinian magico-religious praxis were far too precious to be threatened by a troublesome tradition about a foreign "oracle-reciter."

This audience was not at all interested in compromise. Therefore, even the "divination" element within Balaam's "diviner/seer" role-set had to be sanitized and expunged, not to mention his increasingly occultic ("hidden") "exorcist" role-set. That the Balaam tradition was actually "externally" altered in order to satisfy their agenda only demonstrates the degree to which they had become thoroughly dissatisfied with "internal" solutions.[43]

The *coup de grâce* of their carefully engineered attempt at conflict resolution occurred when they rather boldly placed a legislative decree against *nḥš* and

[39] H. W. Wolff, "The Kerygma of the Yahwist," in H. W. Wolff & W. Brueggemann, eds., *The Vitality of Old Testament Traditions* (Atlanta: John Knox, 1975) 41–66, 132–138, ET of "Das Kerygma des Jahwisten," *EvT* 24 (1964) 73–98. Whether one argues for an early or late date for the zenith of this audience's influence, "es ist eine bekannte Tatsache, dass das alte Israel bei der Übernahme der Institution des Königtums zugleich Anleihen an seine Umwelt hinsichtlich der Mittel gemacht, die es ermöglichten, den aufkommenden Bedürfnissen der Repräsentanz und Darstellung der neuen monarchischen Ordnung zu genügen," K. Seybold, "Das Herrscherbild des Bileamorakels Num 24:15-19," *TZ* 29 (1973) 1.

[40] Cf. the discussion in D. L. Petersen, *The Roles of Israel's Prophets*, 51–63.

[41] J. Blenkinsopp speaks of the "major emphasis (within Israel) on prophecy as a native Israelite phenomenon, contrasted with the different forms of divination and mediation practiced among the nations," an emphasis which eventually led to attempts to "bring prophecy within an institutional grid, and thus to define and limit the scope of prophetic authority," *A History of Prophecy in Israel*, 189–190.

[42] Num 23:23. Wellhausen's suspicions about this verse have found many adherents (*Die Composition der Hexateuch*, 111).

[43] Sarbin and Allen, "Role Theory," 540–543.

qsm in Balaam's own mouth! (Num 23:23). Yahwistic abhorrence of divination and exorcism prevailed over the wholistic, traditional view of Balaam. To the carefully nuanced internal attempt to accommodate and modulate Balaam's "exorcist" role-set offered by one segment of the Israelite populace, this audience offered an external legislative solution which attempted to deny not only that he had ever been an "exorcist," but also that he could never have been a "diviner" either.

Neither solution, of course, adequately solved the Balaam problem forever, else there would not have arisen further attempts to resolve it. Instead, it continued to fester in Israel's memory like a wound that simply would not heal. Somehow a way had to be found to reduce the role strain felt by all of Israel's tradents without abandoning what must soon have become clear to every informed observer of the Balaam traditions living in Syria-Palestine. The Balaam tradition at Deir ʿAllā, along with perhaps other traditions now forgotten, must have made it uncomfortably clear, at least to those aware of their existence, that Balaam son of Beor was capable of being both a "diviner" as well as an "exorcist," *regardless* of what the "official" Israelite portrayals were saying about him.

Contributing significantly to this nagging problem was the growing reality that many Israelites no longer really cared where Balaam may have stood on a "magic-religion" continuum, since, for many, *nḥš* or *qsm* was increasingly becoming a dead issue. Instead, many Israelites seemed to be growing profoundly dissatisfied with all previous solutions to the Balaam problem, in part, because each "solution" lacked what was rapidly becoming *the* vital prerequisite for admitting *any* tradition into Israel's sacred history: viz., an "appropriate" emphasis on Yahweh's transcendent power. For this audience, Yahweh simply could not be relegated to an incidental role on the stage of Israelite history, regardless of a given tradition's sociohistorical character or development.[44]

For these tradents, the tradition about Balaam son of Beor could therefore best be "solved" by removing it from the confines of a *magic-religion* continuum altogether, and transplanting it toward the "transcendent" pole of an "immanent-transcendent" *theological* continuum. Within such explicitly *theological* parameters, the Balaam tradition was therefore completely transformed, never again to look quite the same. Here Balak, the Moabite king, is not even mentioned by name, while Balaam himself, the very focal point of the story in Num 22–24, is summarily expelled from the tradition's starring role. Another character now assumes center stage:

> Yahweh your God would not listen to Balaam.
> Yahweh your God turned the curse into a blessing for you.[45]

[44] H. W. Wolff, "The Kerygma of the Deuteronomistic Historical Work," in H. W. Wolff & W. Brueggemann, *The Vitality of Old Testament Traditions,* 83–100, ET of "Das Kerygma des deuteronomistischen Geschichtswerk," *ZAW* 73 (1961) 171–185.

[45] Deut 23:6.

The ultimate rationale behind this final biblical attempt to solve the "Balaam problem" seems to be as profound as it was simple:

> Yahweh your God loves you.[46]

This adamant theocentric posture, independently emerging alongside the persistent problem of unresolved role strain over the Balaam problem, ultimately led to a reformulation of the tradition which reset its parameters along an entirely different spatio-temporal continuum. The advantages of this "solution" were simple and several: (1) both role-sets ("diviner/seer" and "exorcist") could be recognized and preserved, thus demonstrating a genuine concern for some measure of sociohistorical accuracy; (2) both "official" versions of Israel's common history could be maintained with a minimum of role conflict, thus demonstrating a reverence for the totality of Israel's epic tradition; and most importantly, (3) Yahweh could be restored to his "rightful" place, demonstrating above all an intense concern for restoring a theocentric perspective to the telling of Israelite history.

[46] Ibid.

Conclusion

In many ways the Balaam traditions still puzzle us. We would like to know much more about the phenomenological *realia* surrounding ancient Near Eastern divination and exorcism, especially the precise contours of the roles customarily enacted by Syro-Palestinian "seers." We would like to know better how to contrast and compare these "seers" against this *realia.* We would like to know better how to compare the *ḥzh* Balaam against this *realia.* We would like to explore further the continuities between the Balaam traditions and later Jewish apocalyptic, both of which are structured upon the visions of "seers." We would like to know more about the dynamics which led each Israelite audience to preempt Balaam's "exorcist" role-set by his "diviner/seer" role-set. The frustrating lack of data in all these areas probably means that progress will be slow.

Yet the questions need not lay dormant. As is common when dealing with ancient Near Eastern texts, fragmentary remains of texts and artifacts mean that we often have to couch our work in terms of theory. This is true of many traditions, but with the Balaam traditions, it is unavoidable. The only truly relevant question is, "Which theory will prove to be the most useful?"

Role theory has been chosen to guide this study because it so thoroughly and fruitfully opens up for us the dynamically complex interactions which take place between a given actor and a given audience. The hope is that it has also helped us to understand better the dynamics which may have flowed between *this* actor and *these* audiences, and thus the traditions which preserve his memory.

This study is therefore more suggestive than determinative. While we would defend it as an integrated, coherent attempt to describe the character and development of the Balaam traditions, the present lack of hard evidence means that we must keep an open mind to what new discoveries, like the discovery of DAT itself, might tell us about Balaam in the future.

Bibliography

Abusch, I. Tzvi. *Babylonian Witchcraft Literature.* Brown Judaic Studies 132. Atlanta: Scholars, 1987.

Albright, William F. "The Oracles of Balaam." *JBL* 63 (1944) 207–233.

———. "A Prince of Taanach in the Fifteenth Century B.C." *BASOR* 94 (1944) 12–27.

———. *Yahweh and the Gods of Canaan.* London: Athlone, 1968.

Anderson, Gary A. *Sacrifices and Offerings in Ancient Israel: Studies in their Social and Political Importance.* Atlanta: Scholars, 1987.

Astour, M. C. "Two Ugaritic Serpent Charms." *JNES* 27 (1968) 13–36.

Avishur, Y. "The Ghost-Expelling Incantation from Ugarit (Ras Ibn Hani 78/20)." *UF* 13 (1981) 13–25.

Baentsch, Bruno. *Exodus—Leviticus—Numeri.* HKAT I/2. Göttingen: Vandenhoeck und Ruprecht, 1903.

Banton, M., Ed. *The Relevance of Models for Social Anthropology.* London: Tavistock, 1965.

———. *Roles: An Introduction to the Study of Social Relations.* New York: Basic, 1965.

Bascom, W. *Sixteen Cowries: Yoruba Divination from Africa to the New World.* Bloomington, IN: Indiana University Press, 1980.

Baskin, J. R. "Origen on Balaam: The Dilemma of the Unworthy Prophet." *VC* 37 (1983) 22–35.

———. *Pharaoh's Counselors: Job, Jethro, and Balaam in Rabbinic and Patristic Tradition.* Brown Judaic Studies 47. Chico, CA: Scholars, 1983.

Beckman, G. M. *Hittite Birth Rituals,* 2nd ed. SBT 29. Wiesbaden: Harrassowitz, 1983.

Benedict, R. F. *Patterns of Culture.* New York: Mentor, 1946. First pub. in 1934.

Bewer, Julius A. "The Literary Problems of the Balaam Story in Numbers, Chapters 22–24." *AJT* 9 (1905) 238–62.

Birnbaum, S. A. "The Kephar Bebhayu Marriage Deed." *JAOS* 78 (1958) 12–18.

Blenkinsopp, J. *A History of Prophecy in Israel.* Philadelphia: Westminster, 1983.

Böhl, F. M. T. de L. "Das Zeitalter der Sargoniden." In *Opera Minora.* Gröningen: J. B. Wolters, 1953, pp. 384–422.

Bowman, Charles H. & Robert B. Coote. "A Narrative Incantation for Snake Bite." *UF* 12 (1980) 135–139.

Buber, Martin. *Kingship of God,* 3rd ed. Trans. by Richard Scheimann. London: George Allen and Unwin, 1967. First published in 1936.

Budd, P. J. *Numbers.* WBC 5. Waco, TX: Word, 1984.

Buss, M. J. "The Social Psychology of Prophecy." In J. Emerton, Ed. *Prophecy: FS G. Fohrer.* Berlin: de Gruyter, 1980, pp. 1–11.

Cagni, L. *L'epopea di Erra.* SS 34. Roma: Istituto di Studi del Vicino Oriente, Universita di Roma, 1969.

———. *The Poem of Erra.* SANE I/3. Malibu, CA: Undena, 1977.

Cameron, N. A. "Role Concepts in Behavior Pathology." *AJS* 55 (1950) 464–467.

Cantineau, J. "Tadmorea." *Syria* 19 (1938) 153–71.

Caplice, R. I. *The Akkadian Namburbi Texts.* SANE I/1. Los Angeles: Undena, 1974.

Caquot, A. "Nouvelles inscriptions araméennes de Hatra (4)." *Syria* 32 (1955) 261–72.

———, and M. Leibovici, Eds. *La Divination.* Paris: Presses universitaires de France, 1968.

———, and A. Lemaire., "Les textes araméennes de Deir 'Allā." *Syria* 54 (1977) 189–208.

Carroll, R. P. *When Prophecy Failed: Cognitive Dissonance and the Prophetic Traditions of the Old Testament.* London: SCM, 1979.

Cheyne, T. K. "Some Critical Difficulties in the Chapters on Balaam." *ExpT* 10 (1898–99) 399–402.

Clark, Ira. "Balaam's Ass: Suture or Structure?" In Kenneth R. R. Gros Louis and James S. Ackerman, Eds. *Literary Interpretations of Biblical Narrative, II.* Nashville: Abingdon, 1982, 137–44.

Clarke, E. G., Ed. *Targum Pseudo-Jonathan of the Pentateuch: Text and Concordance.* Hoboken, NJ: KTAV, 1984.

Coats, George W. "Balaam: Sinner or Saint?" *BR* 18 (1973) 21–29.

———. "The Way of Obedience: Traditio-historical and Hermeneutical Reflections on the Balaam Story." *Sem* 24 (1982) 53–79.

Colby, B. N. *The Daykeeper: The Life and Discourse of an Ixil Diviner.* Cambridge: Harvard, 1981.

Coppens, Joseph. "Les oracles de Bileam: leur origine littéraire et leur portée prophétique." In *Mélanges E. Tisserant, Vol. I: Ecriture sainte-ancien orient.* SeT 231. Citta del Vaticano: Biblioteca Apostolica Vaticana, 1964, pp. 67–80.

Cowley, A. *Aramaic Papyri of the 5th Century B.C.* Oxford: Clarendon, 1923.

Cross, F. M. "Epigraphic Notes on the Amman Citadel Inscription." *BASOR* 193 (1969) 13–19.

———. "Notes on the Ammonite Inscription from Tell Siran." *BASOR* 212 (1973) 12–15.

———. *Canaanite Myth and Hebrew Epic.* Cambridge: Harvard University, 1973.

———, and Richard J. Saley. "Phoenician Incantations on a Plaque of the Seventh Century B.C. from Arslan Tash in Upper Syria." *BASOR* 197 (1970) 42–49.

Cutler, B. & J. MacDonald. "On the Origin of the Ugaritic Text KTU 1.23." *UF* 14 (1982) 33–50.

Dahood, Mitchell. "Hebrew-Ugaritic Lexicography IV." *Bib* 47 (1966) 415–17.

———. "Review of *Aramaic Texts from Deir 'Allā*, by J. Hoftijzer and G. van der Kooij." *Bib* 62 (1981) 124–27.

Daiches, Samuel. "Balaam, a Babylonian *bārû:* The Episode of Num 22.2–24.24 and Some Babylonian Parallels." *Assyriologische und archaeologische Studien Hermann von Hilprecht gewidmet.* Leipzig: J. C. Hinrichs'sche, 1909, pp. 60–70.

Day, Peggy L. *An Adversary in Heaven: śāṭān in the Hebrew Bible.* HSM 43. Atlanta: Scholars, 1988.

Degen, Rainer. *Altaramäische Grammatik.* Wiesbaden: Steiner, 1969.

Delcor, M. "Le texte de Deir 'Allā et les oracles bibliques de Bala'am." *VTSup* 32 (1981) *Congress Volume, Vienna 1980,* 52–73.

———. "Bala'am Patorah, interprete des songes au pays d'Ammon d'apres Nombres 22:5. Les temoignages épigraphiques paralleles." *Semitica* 32 (1982) 89–91.

Dietrich, M., O. Loretz, and J. Sanmartin. *Die keilalphabetischen Texte aus Ugarit.* AOAT 24. Kevelaer: Butzon and Bercker, 1976.

Diez Macho, A. *Neophyti 1: Targum Palestinense. Tomo IV Numeros.* Madrid: Consejo Superior de Investigaciones Cientificas, 1974.

Dillmann, August. *Die Bücher Numeri, Deuteronomium und Josua.* 2nd ed. KHAT XIII. Leipzig: S. Hirzel, 1886.

Donner, Herbert. "Balaam Pseudopropheta." In H. Donner, R. Hanhart, R. Smend, Eds. *Beiträge zur alttestamentlichen Theologie: FS W. Zimmerli.* Göttingen: Vandenhoeck und Ruprecht, 1977, 112–123.

———, and W. Röllig. *Kanaanäische und aramäische Inschriften.* 3 vols. Wiesbaden: Harrassowitz, 1962–64.

Ebeling, E. *Tod und Leben nach den Vorstellungen der Babylonier.* Berlin: de Gruyter, 1931.

———. *Die akkadische Gebetsserie "Handerhebung."* Berlin: Akademie-Verlag, 1953.

Eissfeldt, Otto. *Der Maschal im alten Testament.* BZAW 24. Giessen: Töpelmann, 1913.

———. "Die Komposition der Bileam-Erzählung: Eine Nachprüfung von Rudolphs Beitrag zur Hexateuchkritik." *ZAW* 57 (1939) 212–41.

———. "Sinai-Erzählung und Bileam-Sprüche." *HUCA* 32 (1961) 179–90.

Eliade, Mircea. *Shamanism: Archaic Techniques of Ecstasy.* New York: Pantheon, 1964.

Ellermeier, F. *Prophetie in Mari und Israel.* ThOrAr 1. Herzberg am Harz: Jungfer, 1968.

Fahd, Toufic. *La divination arabe.* Leiden: Brill, 1966.

Festinger, L., H. W. Riecken, and S. Schlachter. *When Prophecy Fails.* Minneapolis, MN: University of Minnesota, 1956.

Fishbane, Michael. *Biblical Interpretation in Ancient Israel.* Oxford: Clarendon, 1985.

Fitzmyer, Joseph A. *The Aramaic Inscriptions of Sefire.* BibOr 19. Rome: Pontifical Biblical Institute, 1967.

———. "Review of *Aramaic Texts from Deir 'Allā,* by J. Hoftijzer and G. van der Kooy." *CBQ* 40 (1978) 93–95.

Frazer, James G. *The Golden Bough: A Study in Magic and Religion.* Abridged ed. New York: Macmillan, 1922.

von Gall, August Freiherrn. "Zusammensetzung und Herkunft der Bileam-Perikope in Num. 22–24." In *Festgruss Bernhard Stade.* Giessen: J. Ricker'sche, 1900, pp. 1–47.

———. *Der hebräische Pentateuch der Samaritaner.* Giessen: Töpelmann, 1918.

Galling, K. "Das Gemeindegesetz in Deuteronomium 23." W. Baumgartner, O. Eissfeldt, K. Elliger, L. Rost, Eds. *FS Alfred Bertholet.* Tübingen: Mohr/Siebeck, 1950, pp. 176–91.

Garbini, G. "L'iscrizione di Balaam Bar-Beor." *Henoch* 1 (1979) 166–88.

Garr, W. R. *Dialect Geography of Syria-Palestine, 1000–586 BCE.* Philadelphia: University of Pennsylvania, 1985.

Gaster, T. *Myth, Legend, and Custom in the Old Testament.* New York: Harper and Row, 1969.

Geller, S. "Die Rezension von 'Ištars Höllenfahrt' aus Assur." *OLZ* 20 (1917) 41–48.

Gerth, H. and C. W. Mills. *Character and Social Structure.* New York: Harcourt, Brace, and World, 1953.

Gibson, J. C. L. *Textbook of Syrian Semitic Inscriptions.* 3 vols. Oxford: Clarendon, 1971, 1975, 1982.

———, Ed. *Canaanite Myths and Legends,* 2nd ed. Edinburgh: T. and T. Clark, 1977. Originally edited by G. R. Driver, 1956.

Ginsburger, Moses, Ed. *Das Fragmententhargum (Thargum Jeruschalmi zum Pentateuch).* Berlin: Calvary, 1899.

Goetze, A. *Old Babylonian Omen Texts.* YOS X. New Haven: Yale, 1947.

———. *Kulturgeschichte Kleinasiens,* 2nd ed. HAW III/2. München: C. H. Beck'sche, 1957.

———. "An Old Babylonian Prayer of the the Divination Priest." *JCS* 22 (1968) 25–27.

Goldziher, I. *Abhandlungen zur arabischen Philologie.* Erster Teil. Leiden: Brill, 1896.

Goode, W. J. "A Theory of Role Strain." *ASR* 25 (1960) 483–496. Reprinted in *Explorations in Social Theory.* New York: Oxford, 1973, 97–120.

Gottwald, N. *The Hebrew Bible: A Socio-Literary Introduction.* Philadelphia: Fortress, 1985.

Gray, George B. *A Critical and Exegetical Commentary on the Book of Numbers.* ICC. Edinburgh: T. and T. Clark, 1903.

Greenfield, J. C. "The Zakir Inscription and the Danklied." *Proceedings of the Fifth World Congress of Jewish Studies*. Jerusalem: World Union of Jewish Studies, 1969, vol. I, pp. 178–91.

———. Review of *Aramaic Texts from Deir 'Allā*, by J. Hoftijzer and G. van der Kooij." *JSS* 25 (1980) 248–52.

Gressmann, Hugo. *Die älteste Geschichtsschreibung und Prophetie Israels*. Göttingen: Vandenhoeck und Ruprecht, 1910.

———. *Mose und seine Zeit*. FRLANT 1. Göttingen: Vandenhoeck und Ruprecht, 1913.

———. "*Hē koinōnia tōn daimoniōn*." *ZNW* 20 (1921) 224–230.

Gross, Walther. *Bileam: Literar- und formkritische Untersuchung der Prosa in Num 22–24*. StANT 38. München: Kösel, 1974.

Guillaume, A. *Prophecy and Divination Among the Hebrews and Other Semites*. London: Hodder and Stoughton, 1938.

Gunneweg, A. H. J. "Anmerkungen und Anfragen zur neueren Pentateuchforschung." *ThR* 48 (1983) 227–53; 50 (1985) 107–31.

Gurney, O. R. *The Hittites*. Baltimore: Penguin, 1952.

———. *Some Aspects of Hittite Religion*. Oxford: University Press, 1977.

———. "The Babylonians and Hittites." M. Loewe and C. Blacker, Eds. *Oracles and Divination*. Boulder, CO: Shambhala, 1981, pp. 142–173.

Haag, H. "Gad und Nathan." A. Kuschke and E. Kutsch, Eds. *Archäologie und altes Testament. FS K. Galling*. Tübingen: Mohr/Siebeck, 1970, pp. 135–43.

Haas, V. and G. Wilhelm. *Hurritische und luwische Riten aus Kizzuwatna*. AOATS 3. Kevelaer: Butzon und Bercker, 1974.

Haas, V. and H. J. Thiel. *Die Beschwörungsrituale der Allaituraḫ(ḫ)i und verwandte Texte*. AOAT 31. Kevelaer: Butzon und Bercker, 1978.

Hackett, Jo Ann. *The Balaam Text from Deir 'Allā*. HSM 31. Chico, CA: Scholars, 1984.

———. "Some Observations on the Balaam Tradition at Deir 'Allā." *BA* 49 (1986) 216–222.

Halpern, Baruch. "Dialect Distribution in Canaan and the Deir 'Allā Inscriptions." David M. Golomb and Susan T. Hollis, Eds. *Working with No Data: Semitic and Egyptian Studies Presented to Thomas O. Lambdin*. Winona Lake, IN: Eisenbrauns, 1987, pp. 119–139.

Harrington, D. J. "Pseudo-Philo: A New Translation and Introduction." J. H. Charlesworth, Ed. *The Old Testament Pseudepigrapha*. Vol. 2. Garden City, NY: Doubleday, 1985, pp. 297–377.

Harris, Z. *The Development of Canaanite Dialects*. New Haven: American Oriental Society, 1939.

Heintz, J.-G. "Review of *Aramaic Texts from Deir 'Allā*, by J. Hoftijzer and G. van der Kooij." *RHPR* 60 (1980) 210–12.

Hempel, Johannes. "Die israelitischen Anschauungen von Segen und Fluch im Lichte altorientalischer Parallelen." *Apoxysmata*. BZAW 81. Berlin: Töpelmann, 1961, 30–113. Originally published in 1925.

Hoftijzer, J. "Die Ontcijfering van Deir 'Allā teksten." *Oosters Genootschap in Nederland* 5 (1973) 111–34. ET by W. L. Holladay, *BA* 39 (1976) 11–17.

———. "Aramäische Prophetien: Die Inschrift von Deir 'Allā." O. Kaiser, Ed. *Texte aus der Umwelt des alten Testaments II/1: Religiöse Texte.* Gütersloher: Gerd Mohn, 1986, pp. 138–148.

———, and G. van der Kooij. *Aramaic Texts from Deir 'Allā.* Leiden: Brill, 1976.

Holzinger, H. *Numeri.* KHAT IV. Tübingen: Mohr/Siebeck, 1903.

van Hoonacker, Albin. "Quelques observations critiques sur les récits concernant Bileam (Nombres XXII–XXIV et XXXI)." *Le Museon* 7 (1888) 61–76.

Huffmon, H. B. "Prophecy in the Mari Letters." *BA* 31 (1968) 101–124.

———. "The Origins of Prophecy." F. M. Cross, W. Lemke, and P. D. Miller, Eds. *Magnalia Dei. FS G. E. Wright.* Garden City, NY: Doubleday, 1976, pp. 171–86.

———. "Prophecy in the Ancient Near East." *IDBSup* (1976) 697–700.

Hutter, Manfred. *Behexung, Entsühnung und Heilung. Das Ritual der Tunnawiya für ein Königspaar aus Mittelhethitischer Zeit (KBo XXI 1–KUB IX 34–KBo XXI 6).* OBO 82. Göttingen: Vandenhoeck und Ruprecht, 1988.

———. *Altorientalische Vorstellungen von der Unterwelt. Literar- und religionsgeschichtliche Überlegungen zu "Nergal und Ereškigal."* OBO 63. Göttingen: Vandenhoeck und Ruprecht, 1985.

Isbell, Charles D. *Corpus of the Aramaic Incantation Bowls.* SBLDS 17. Missoula: Scholars, 1975.

Jackson, Kent P. *The Ammonite Language of the Iron Age.* HSM 27. Chico, CA: Scholars, 1983.

Jacobsen, T. *The Treasures of Darkness: A History of Mesopotamian Religion.* New Haven: Yale, 1976.

James, M. R. *The Biblical Antiquities of Philo.* Prolegomenon by Louis H. Feldman. New York: KTAV, 1971.

Jenks, Alan W. *The Elohist and North Israelite Traditions.* SBLMS 22. Missoula: Scholars, 1977.

Josephus, Flavius. *Jewish Antiquities.* LCL. Trans. by H. Thackeray. Cambridge: Harvard, 1930.

Kalisch, M. M. *Bible Studies. Part I: The Prophecies of Balaam.* London: Longmans, Green, and Co., 1877.

Kammenhuber, Annelies. *Orakelpraxis, Träume und Vorzeichenschau bei den Hethitern.* TdH 7. Heidelberg: Carl Winter, 1976.

Kaufman, S. "Review of *Aramaic Texts from Deir 'Allā,* by J. Hoftijzer and G. van der Kooij." *BASOR* 239 (1980) 71–74.

Kisch, G. *Pseudo-Philo's Liber Antiquitatum Biblicarum.* South Bend, IN: University of Notre Dame, 1949.

Klein, Michael L. *The Fragment-Targums of the Pentateuch.* AnBib 76. Rome: Biblical Institute Press, 1980.

Knauf, E. A. "Review of *The Balaam Text from Deir 'Allā,* by Jo Ann Hackett." *ZDPV* 101 (1985) 187–91.

Knudtzon, J. A. *Assyrische Gebete an den Sonnengott.* Leipzig: E. Pfeiffer, 1893.

———. *Die El Amarna Tafeln.* Aalen: Zeller, 1964. Reprint of 1915 ed.

Köcher, F. *Die babylonisch-assyrische Medizin in Texten und Untersuchungen.* Berlin: de Gruyter, 1963.

———, and A. L. Oppenheim. "The Old Omen Text VAT 7525." *AfO* 18 (1957–58) 62–77.

Koenig, Jean. "La declaration des dieux dans l'inscription de Deir 'Allā (I, 2)." *Semitica* 33 (1983) 77–88.

Kuenen, A. "Bijdragen tot de Critiek van Pentateuch en Josua. X. Bileam." *Theologisch Tijdschrift* 18 (1884) 497–540.

Labat, R. *Traité akkadien de diagnostics et pronostics médicaux.* Leiden: Brill, 1951.

Laessøe, J. *Studies on the Assyrian Ritual and Series bît rimki.* Copenhagen: Munksgaard, 1955.

La divination in mésopotamie ancienne et dans les régions voisines. XIVe rencontre assyriologique internationale. Paris: Presses universitaires de France, 1966.

Lambert, W. G. *Babylonian Wisdom Literature.* Oxford: Clarendon, 1960.

Lane, E. W. *An Arabic-English Lexicon.* 8 vols. Beirut: Librairie du Liban, 1968.

Largement, René. "Les oracles de Bileam et la mantique suméro-akkadienne." *Memorial du cinquantenaire 1914–1964.* Paris: Travaux de l'Institut de Paris, 1964, 37–50.

Le Déaut, R. *Targum du pentateuque. Tome III, Nombres.* Paris: Les editions du Cerf, 1979.

Leichty, E. *The Omen Series šumma izbu.* Locust Valley, NY: J. J. Augustin, 1970.

Lemaire, A. "La disposition originelle des inscriptions sur plâtre de Deir 'Allā." *Studi Epigrafici e Linguistici* 3 (1986) 79–93.

———. "Fragments from the Book of Balaam Found at Deir 'Allā." *BAR* 11, 5 (1985) 26–39.

———. "L'inscription de Balaam trouvée à Deir 'Allā: épigraphie." In *Biblical Archaeology Today: Proceedings of the International Congress of Biblical Archaeology, April 1984.* Jerusalem: Israel Exploration Society, 1985, pp. 313–25.

Le monde du sorcier. SO 7. Paris: Editions du Seuil, 1966.

Les songes et leur interpretation. SO 2. Paris: Editions du Seuil, 1959.

Levine, Baruch A. *In the Presence of the Lord: A Study of Cult and Some Cultic Terms in Ancient Israel.* SJLA 5. Leiden: Brill, 1974.

———. "The Deir 'Allā Plaster Inscriptions." *JAOS* 101 (1981) 195–205.

———. "The Balaam Inscription from Deir 'Allā: Historical Aspects." In *Biblical Archaeology Today: Proceedings of the International Congress of Biblical Archaeology, April 1984.* Jerusalem: Israel Exploration Society, 1985, pp. 326–39.

Lewis, I. M. *Ecstatic Religion: An Anthropological Study of Spirit Possession and Shamanism.* Baltimore: Penguin, 1971; London: Routledge, 1989.

L'Heureux, C. E. *Rank Among the Canaanite Gods: El, Ba'al and the Repha'im.* HSM 21. Missoula, MT: Scholars, 1979.

Lindblom, J. *Prophecy in Ancient Israel.* Oxford: Blackwell, 1962.

Linton, R. *The Study of Man.* New York: Appleton-Century-Crofts, 1936.

———. *The Cultural Background of Personality.* New York: Appleton-Century-Crofts, 1945.

Liver, Ya'akov. "The Figure of Balaam in Biblical Tradition." *EI* 3 (1954) 97–100.

Loewe, M. and C. Blacker, Eds. *Oracles and Divination.* Boulder, CO: Shambhala, 1981.

Löhr, M. "Bileam. Num 22,2–24,25." *AfO* 4 (1927) 85–89.

Long, B. O. "The Social Settings for Prophetic Miracle Stories." *Sem* 3 (1975) 46–63.

Loretz, O. and Werner R. Mayer. *Šu-ila Gebete. Supplement to L. W. King, Babylonian Magic and Sorcery.* AOAT 34. Neukirchen-Vluyn: Neukirchener, 1978.

Lust, J. "Balaam, An Ammonite." *EThL* 54 (1978) 60–61.

Matthiae, Paolo. "Princely Cemetery and Ancestors Cult at Ebla during Middle Bronze II." *UF* 11 (1979) 563–569.

Mauchline, J. "The Balaam-Balak Songs and Saga." *SSO* 2 (1945) 73–94.

Mayer, Werner. *Untersuchungen zur Formensprache der babylonischen "Gebetsbeschwörungen."* SPSM 5. Rome: Biblical Institute Press, 1976.

McCarter, P. Kyle. "The Balaam Texts from Deir 'Allá: The First Combination." *BASOR* 239 (1980) 49–60.

Meier, G. *Die assyrische Beschwörungssammlung Maqlû.* AfO Beiheft 2. Osnabruck: Biblio-Verlag, 1967. First published in 1937.

Mendenhall, G. *The Tenth Generation.* Baltimore: Johns Hopkins, 1973.

Merton, R. K. "The Role-set: Problems in Sociological Theory." *BJS* 8 (1957) 106–120.

du Mesnil du Buisson, R. "Une tablette magique de la région du Moyen Euphrates." *Mélanges syriens offerts à M. René Dussaud.* Paris: Bibliotheque archeologique et historique, 1939, pp. 421–434.

Mitchell, C. W. *The Meaning of BRK "To Bless" in the Old Testament.* SBLDS 95. Atlanta: Scholars, 1987.

de Moor, Johannes C. & Klaus Spronk. "More on Demons in Ugarit (KTU 1.82)." *UF* 16 (1984) 237–250.

Morris, Brian. *Anthropological Studies of Religion: An Introductory Text.* Cambridge: University Press, 1987.

Moscati, S., Ed. *An Introduction to the Comparative Grammar of the Semitic Languages.* Wiesbaden: Harrassowitz, 1980.

Mowinckel, Sigmund. *Psalmenstudien V. Segen und Fluch in Israels Kult und Psalmendichtung.* Oslo: Videnskapsselskapets Skrifter II. Hist.-Filos. Kl. no. 3, 1923.

———. "Der Ursprung der Bil'amsage." *ZAW* 48 (1930) 233–71.

Mullen, E. T. *The Assembly of the Gods: The Divine Council in Canaanite and Early Hebrew Literature.* HSM 24. Chico, CA: Scholars, 1980.

Müller, Hans-Peter. "Einige alttestamentliche Probleme zur aramäischen Inschrift von Dēr 'Allā." *ZDPV* 94 (1978) 56–67.

———. "Die aramäische Inschrift von Deir 'Allā und die älteren Bileamsprüche." *ZAW* 94 (1982) 214–44.

Myhrman, D. W. "Die Labartu-Texte. Babylonische Beschwörungsformeln nebst Zauberverfahren gegen die Dämonin Labartu." *ZA* 16 (1902) 141–95.

Naroll, R. and R. Cohen, Eds. *A Handbook of Method in Cultural Anthropology.* New York: Natural History Press, 1971.

Naveh, Joseph. "The Date of the Deir 'Allā Inscription in Aramaic Script." *IEJ* 17 (1967) 256–58.

———. "Review of *Aramaic Texts from Deir* 'Allā, by J. Hoftijzer and G. van der Kooy." *IEJ* 29 (1979) 133–35.

Nöldeke, T. "Phönicische Inschrift." *ZA* 9 (1894) 400–405.

Noort, Edward. *Untersuchungen zum Gottesbescheid in Mari.* AOAT 202. Neukirchen: Neukirchener-Vluyn, 1977.

Noth, Martin. *A History of Pentateuchal Traditions.* Englewood Cliffs, NJ: Prentice-Hall, 1972. German edition published in 1948.

———. *Numbers.* OTL. Philadelphia: Westminster, 1968. German edition published in 1966.

Nötscher, F. "*Šumma ālu.*" *Or* (old series) 51–54 (1930) 150–190.

Nougayrol, J. "'Oiseau' ou Oiseau?" *RA* 61 (1967) 23–38.

———. "La divination babylonienne." A. Caquot and M. Leibovici, Eds. *La Divination.* Paris: Presses universitaires de France, 1968, pp. 25–81.

del Olmo Lete, Gregorio. *Mitos y Leyendas de Canaan.* Madrid: Ediciones Cristiandad, 1981.

Oppenheim, A. L. *The Interpretation of Dreams in the Ancient Near East, with a Translation of an Assyrian Dreambook.* TAPS 46/3. Philadelphia: American Philosophical Society, 1956.

———. *Ancient Mesopotamia.* 2nd ed. Chicago: University of Chicago, 1977. First published in 1964.

Otten, H. *Hethitische Totenrituale.* Deutsche Akademie der Wissenschaften zu Berlin, Institut für Orientforschung Veroffentlichung Nr. 37. Berlin: Akademie-Verlag, 1958.

von Pákozdy, L. M. "Theologische Redaktionsarbeit in der Bileam-Perikope (Num 22–24)." J. Hempel, Ed. *Von Ugarit nach Qumran: FS O. Eissfeldt.* BZAW 77. Berlin: de Gruyter, 1958, 161–76.

Payne Smith, R. and J. Payne Smith, Eds. *A Compendious Syriac Dictionary.* Oxford: Clarendon, 1903.

Petersen, D. L. *Late Israelite Prophecy: Studies in Deutero-Prophetic Literature and in Chronicles.* SBLMS 23. Missoula, MT: Scholars, 1977.

———. *The Roles of Israel's Prophets.* JSOTSup 17. Sheffield: JSOT Press, 1981.

Popitz, H. *Der Begriff der sozialen Rollen als Element der sociologischen Theorie.* Tübingen: Mohr, 1967.

Powell, T. M. "The Oracles of Balaam: A Metrical Analysis and Exegesis." Unpublished Ph.D. Dissertation. Pasadena, CA: Fuller Theological Seminary, 1982.

Puech, Emile. "Review of *Aramaic Texts from Deir 'Allā,* by J. Hoftijzer and G. van der Kooy." *RB* 85 (1978) 114–117.

———. "Response." In *Biblical Archaeology Today: Proceedings of the International Congress of Biblical Archaeology, April 1984.* Jerusalem: Israel Exploration Society, 1985, pp. 354–65.

———. "Les texte 'ammonite' de Deir 'Allā: les admonitions de Balaam (première partie)." In *La vie de la Parole: Mélanges offerts à P. Grelot.* Paris: Gabalda, 1986.

Philo. *Vita Mosis.* LCL. Trans. by F. H. Colson. Cambridge: Harvard, 1935.

Reiner, E. *Šurpu: A Collection of Sumerian and Akkadian Incantations.* AfO Beiheft 11. Osnabruck: Biblio-Verlag, 1970. First published in 1958.

Rendtorff, R. "Bileam und Bileamsprüche." *RGG,* 3rd ed. Tübingen: Mohr/Siebeck, 1957, I, 1290–91.

———. *Das überlieferungsgeschichtliche Problem des Pentateuch.* BZAW 147. Berlin: de Gruyter, 1977.

Renger, J. "Untersuchungen zum Priestertum in der altbabylonischen Zeit." ZA 58 (1967) 110–188; 59 (1969) 104–230.

Richter, W. *Exegese als Literaturwissenschaft.* Göttingen: Vandenhoeck und Ruprecht, 1971.

Ringgren, H. "Balaam and the Deir 'Allā Inscription." A. Rofé and Y. Zakovitch, Eds. *Isac Leo Seeligmann. Essays on the Bible and the Ancient World.* Jerusalem: Rubenstein, 1983 (1985), vol. III, pp. 93–98.

Ritter, E. K. "Magical Expert (=*āšipu*) and Physician (=*asû*): Notes on Two Complementary Professions in Babylonian Medicine." *Studies Presented to Benno Landsberger on His 65th Birthday.* AS 16. Chicago: University of Chicago, 1965, pp. 299–321.

Rofé, Alexander. *Spr Bl'm. The Book of Balaam (Numbers 22:2–24:25): A Study in Methods of Criticism and the History of Biblical Literature and Religion with an Appendix: Balaam in the Deir 'Allā Inscription.* JBS 1. Jerusalem: Simor, 1979.

Ross, J. F. "Prophecy in Hamath, Israel, and Mari." *HTR* 63 (1970) 1–28.

Rost, Leonhard. "Fragen um Bileam." H. Donner, R. Hanhart, and R. Smend, Eds. *Beiträge zur alttestamentlichen Theologie: FS W. Zimmerli.* Göttingen: Vandenhoeck und Ruprecht, 1977, pp. 377–87.

———. *Studien zum Opfer im alten Testament.* BWANT 6/13. Stuttgart: Kohlhammer, 1981.

Rouillard, H. "L'anesse de Balaam: Analyse littéraire de Nomb. 22.21–35." *RB* 87 (1980) 5–37, 211–41.

———. *La pericope de Balaam (Nombres 22–24).* EBib 4. Paris: Gabalda, 1987.

Rudolph, Wilhelm. *Der "Elohist" von Exodus bis Josua.* BZAW 68. Berlin: Töpelmann, 1938.

Saebø, M. *Sacharja 9–14.* WMANT 34. Neukirchen-Vluyn: Neukirchener, 1969.

Sarbin, T. R. and V. L. Allen. "Role Theory." G. Lindzey and E. Aronson, Eds. *The Handbook of Social Psychology,* 2nd ed. Reading, MA: Addison-Wesley, 1968, pp. 488–567.

Sasson, V. "Two Unrecognized Terms in the Plaster Texts from Deir 'Allā." *PEQ* 117 (1985) 102–03.

———. "The Language of Rebellion in Psalm 2 and in the Plaster Texts from Deir 'Allā." *AUSS* 24 (1986) 147–154.

———. "The Book of Oracular Visions of Bal'aam from Deir 'Allā." *UF* 17 (1986) 283–309.

Savignac, R. and J. Starcky. "Une inscription nabatéene provenant du Djôf." *RB* 64 (1957) 196–215.

Scharbert, J. *Solidarität in Segen und Fluch im AT und in seiner Umwelt, I: Väterfluch und Vätersegen.* BBB 14. Bonn: Hanstein, 1958.

Schmid, Hans Heinrich. *Der sogenannte Jahwist.* Zurich: Theologischer, 1976.

Schmidt, L. "Die alttestamentliche Bileamüberlieferung." *BZ* 23 (1979) 234–61.

Schmitt, A. *Prophetischer Gottesbescheid in Mari und Israel. Eine Strukturuntersuchung.* Stuttgart: Kohlhammer, 1982.

Schottroff, W. *Der altisraelitische Fluchspruch.* WMANT 30. Neukirchen-Vluyn: Neukirchener, 1969.

Schutzinger, H. "Die arabische Bileam-Erzählung." *Der Islam* 59 (1982) 195–221.

Segert, S. *Altaramäische Grammatik.* Leipzig: VEB Verlag Enzyklopädie, 1975.

———. *A Grammar of Phoenician and Punic.* München: C. H. Beck, 1976.

Seybold, Klaus. "Das Herrscherbild des Bileamorakels: Num 24.15–19." *TZ* 29 (1973) 1–19.

Smith, Sidney. *The Statue of Idri-mi.* London: British Institute of Archaeology at Ankara, 1949.

Sperber, A. *The Bible in Aramaic: Vol. 1: The Pentateuch according to Targum Onkelos.* Leiden: Brill, 1959.

Spiegel, J. P. "Interpersonal Influences within the Family." W. Bennis *et al.,* Eds. *Interpersonal Dynamics.* Homewood, IL: Dorsey Press, 1964.

Stachowiak, L. "Die Prophetie als religiöses Phänomenon des alten Orients." J. Reindl, Ed. *Dein Wort beachten. Alttestamentliche Aufsätze.* Leipzig: St. Benno-Verlag, 1981, pp. 58–75.

Starr, I. "The Bārû Rituals." Unpublished Ph.D. Dissertation. New Haven, CT: Yale University, 1974.

———. *The Rituals of the Diviner.* Bibliotheca Mesopotamica 12. Malibu, CA: Undena, 1983.

Stefanek, S. "Les oracles de Balaam et leur relecture dans les traditions prophétiques." Unpublished Dissertation. Warsaw, 1980.

Szabo, G. *Ein hethitisches Entsühnungsritual für das Königspaar Tutḫaliya und Nikalmati.* TdH 1. Heidelberg: Carl Winter, 1971.

Tal, Abraham. *The Samaritan Targum of the Pentateuch.* Tel Aviv: Tel Aviv University, 1981.
Thureau-Dangin, F. *Rituels accadiens.* Osnabruck: Otto Zeller, 1975. First published in 1921.
Turner, R. H. "Role-taking: Process versus Conformity." A. M. Rose, Ed. *Human Behavior and Social Processes.* Boston: Houghton-Mifflin, 1962, pp. 20–40.
Ugaritica V. Mission de Ras Shamra, Tome XVI. Paris: Geuthner, 1968.
Ugaritica VI. Mission de Ras Shamra, Tome XVII. Paris: Geuthner, 1969.
Ünal, A. "Zum Status der 'Augures' bei den Hethitern." *RHA* 31 (1973) 27–56.
de Vaulx, J. *Les Nombres.* SB. Paris: Gabalda, 1972.
de Vaux, R. *Studies in Old Testament Sacrifice.* Cardiff: University of Wales, 1964.
Vermes, G. *Scripture and Tradition in Judaism. Haggadic Studies.* SPB 6. Leiden: Brill, 1961.
Vetter, Dieter. "Untersuchungen zum Seherspruch." Unpublished Dissertation. Heidelberg: University of Heidelberg, 1962.
———. *Seherspruch und Segensschilderung* CTM 4. Stuttgart: Calwer, 1974.
de Waal Malefijt, A. *Religion and Culture: An Introduction to Anthropology of Religion.* New York: Macmillan, 1968.
Weber, Max. *Ancient Judaism.* Glencoe, IL: Free Press, 1952. First published in 1921.
———. *The Sociology of Religion.* Boston: Beacon, 1963.
Wegner, Ilse. *Gestalt und Kult der Ištar-Šawuška in Kleinasien.* AOAT Hurritologische Studien 3. Kevelaer: Butzon und Bercker, 1981.
Wehr, Hans. *A Dictionary of Modern Written Arabic.* J. Milton Cowan, Ed. Ithaca, NY: Cornell, 1966.
Weinfeld, M. "Balaam's Prophecy in the Text from Deir 'Allā (Sukkoth)." *Shnaton* 5/6 (1978/79) 141–47.
Weippert, Helga und Manfred. "Die 'Bileam'-Inschrift von Tell Dēr 'Allā." *ZDPV* 98 (1982) 77–103.
Weisberg, David B. "An Old Babylonian Forerunner to *šumma ālu.*" *HUCA* 40 (1969) 86–104.
Wellhausen, Julius. *Die Composition des Hexateuchs und der historischen Bücher des Alten Testaments,* 3rd ed. Berlin: G. J. Goschen'sche, 1899.
Westermann, C. "Arten der Erzählung in der Genesis." *Forschung am alten Testament.* München: Chr. Kaiser, 1964.
———. *Blessing in the Bible and the Life of the Church.* Philadelphia: Fortress, 1978. First published in 1968.
Wevers, John W. *Numeri.* Göttinger Septuaginta III/1. Göttingen: Vandenhoeck und Ruprecht, 1982.
Wilson, R. R. *Prophecy and Society in Ancient Israel.* Philadelphia: Fortress, 1980.
Wiseman, D. J. *The Alalakh Tablets.* London: British Institute of Archaeology at Ankara, 1953.

Wolff, H. W. "The Kerygma of the Yahwist." H. W. Wolff and W. Brueggemann, Eds. *The Vitality of Old Testament Traditions.* Atlanta: John Knox, 1975, 41–66, 132–138. ET of "Das Kerygma des Jahwisten." *EvT* 24 (1964) 73–98.

———. "The Kerygma of the Deuteronomistic Historical Work." H. W. Wolff and W. Brueggemann, Eds. *The Vitality of Old Testament Traditions.* Atlanta, John Knox, 1975, 83–100. ET of "Das Kerygma des deuteronomistischen Geschichtswerk." *ZAW* 73 (1961) 171–185.

Wolters, A. "Review of *The Balaam Text from Deir 'Allā,* by J. Hackett." *WTJ* 49 (1987) 424–427.

———. "The Balaamites of Deir 'Allā as Aramean Deportees." *SBLASP,* 1987 Annual Meeting of the Society of Biblical Literature. Forthcoming in *HUCA.*

Wright, David P. *The Disposal of Impurity: Elimination Rites in the Bible and in Hittite and Mesopotamian Literature.* SBLDS 101. Atlanta: Scholars, 1987.

Zimmern, H. *Beiträge zur Kenntnis des babylonischen Religion. Die Beschwörungstafeln Šurpu. Ritualtafeln für den Wahrsager, Beschwörer, und Sanger.* Assyriologische Bibliothek 12. Leipzig: J. C. Hinrichs'sche, 1896–1901.

Modern Author Index

Reference Index

AKKADIAN SOURCES

AT 126:17-25 31
281 48

bît rimki 36, 106
28-83 38
29-31 108
39-40:32-47 41
39:35 35
83-89 38

BBR 1-20:5-6 42
1-20:8 30
1-20:18 94, 100
1-20:27 94, 100
1-20:52 37, 56
1-20:83 37
1-20:86 37
1-20:119 94, 100
1-20:120 51
1-20:124 82
24:9 53, 72
24:23 51
26 36, 38, 97
26 I:11 36, 90
26 I:19 37
26 I:20-32 90
26 I:20 40, 53
26 II 37
26 II:10-17 37
26 II:17 90
26 II:18 37
26 II:22 37
26 II:25 37, 89, 106
26 II:28-29 38, 107
26 III:20-21 64
26 III:24 38
26 III:25 64
26 III:35-IV:12 68
26 IV:18 35
26 IV:34 38
26 IV:39-40 56
26 IV:43 33, 38
26 IV:50 38
26 VI:64 38
27 II:12 37
31-37 II:8 38
49 VI:4-5 6
52:2 90
53 36
53:7 36
53:12 36
53:14 38, 91
53:16 36, 87, 91
54:12 87, 91
54:15 63
54:38 63
54rev:10 36
60-70 60
60:30-31 43
75-78:21 67
79-82:21-22 43
79-82 III:16-25 67
83 III:22 91
100 107
100:10 107

BWL 42:69 38
126-138 84
135:177 84
135:180 84
136:182 84

Dreambook (Oppenheim)
187-189 82
245-246 78
248 82
249 93
254-55 30
339:19 50

EA 35:26 31, 48, 70
226:11 52

Erra 107

HITTITE SOURCES

ARAMAIC SOURCES

22:27	103	*Targums, Fragment (FTNum)*	
22:28	102	Num 22:5	66, 103, 112
22:41	105	22:7	98
23:3	101	22:30	1
23:7	102		
23:14	101		

SYRIAC SOURCES (PESHITTA)

Num 22:3	97	22:25	102
22:5	103, 112	22:27	102, 103
22:6	98	22:31	101
22:7	98	23:3	101
22:18	99, 100	23:7	102
22:19	100, 101	23:14	101
22:22	101	24:4	101
22:23	102	24:16	101

UGARITIC SOURCES

CTA 4 III 10	59	1.15 III 3	53
		1.15 III 46-51	50
KTU 1.2 IV 11	75	1.16 II 25-26	91, 92
1.4 I 16	63	1.16 II 27	38, 92
1.4 III 10-11	86	1.16 V 26	52
1.4 III 10	98	1.16 VI 8	40, 52, 71
1.4 III 11	59		
1.4 VII 45-48	59	1.19 I 32-35	48
1.4 VIII 8-9	53	1.19 II 56-III 45	48, 69
1.5 III 16-17	74	1.19 III 3-4	57
1.5 III 17	74	1.19 III 10	57
1.5 III 24	74	1.19 III 24	57
1.5 V	84	1.19 III 32-33	57
1.6 I 8-15	84	1.19 III 38	57
1.6 I 17-18	38	1.20 I 2	54
1.6 III 1-24	77	1.20 II 3	54, 66
1.6 VI 22-35	84	1.21 II 1	54
1.6 VI 45-53	84	1.21 II 5	54
1.14 II 17-18	69	1.23	72, 88
1.14 III 59	69	1.23 33-35	72

1.23 37	72, 75, 91	Ugaritica V 1:11	92
1.23 38-39	69	V 7:4	75
1.23 39-46	71	V 7:5	61
1.23 48	75	V 7:61-76	72
1.23 49-51	82	V 7:64-67	62
1.82 5-6	54	V 9:9′	74
1.82 20-30	63	UT 19:1505	75
1.114 15	54	19:2313	54
1.161	84	23:5	63
		51 III 10	59
Ras Ibn Hani 78/20 9	93	73rev:6	63
10	93	89:14-15	86
14-19	93		

CANAANITE SOURCES

Arsl. Tash I:1	61, 62	14:5	105
I:2	63	26A:6	104
I:4	62	27:11-12	85
I:5-6	46	27:21	63
I:16	62	35:1	63
I:20	34, 62	40:3	63
I:21	63, 85	43:11	9
I:27	63	49:11	63
II:1	61, 63	60:1	54
II:2	63	69:11-16	54
II:3	63	69:11	54
II:4	63	69:16	54
II:5-6	63	162	9
II:8	63	163	9
II:9-10	63	181:17	74
II:11	63	181:19	98
II:12-13	64	277:8-9	38
II:12	63		
II:13	75	SSI III:6	48
KAI 14:3	105	III:78-92	62

HEBREW SOURCES

GREEK SOURCES

LATIN SOURCES

DEIR 'ALLĀ TEXTS

www.ingramcontent.com/pod-product-compliance
Lightning Source LLC
Chambersburg PA
CBHW022132080426
42734CB00006B/324
* 9 7 8 1 5 5 5 4 0 3 2 8 7 *